The
ULTIMATE
Book of
MASTIFF
Breeds

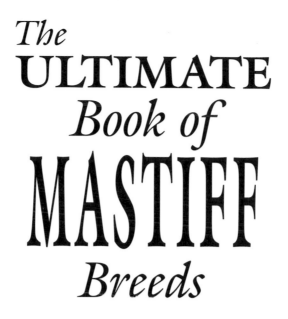

Edited by Douglas Oliff

Howell Book House

HOWELL
BOOK
HOUSE

New York

HOWELL BOOK HOUSE
A Macmillan Company
1633 Broadway
New York, NY 10019

MACMILLAN is a registered trademark of Macmillan, Inc.

ISBN 1-58245-080-3

Library of Congress Cataloging-in-Publication Data
available on request

Printed in Hong Kong

10 9 8 7 6 5 4 3 2 1

Contents

CONTRIBUTORS

THE EDITOR: Douglas Oliff is internationally accepted as an expert on Mastiffs of all types. He has carried out considerable research into the origins of many of these breeds, and has an expert knowledge of their temperament. Although specialising in Bullmastiffs, and in Mastiffs to a lesser extent, he was among the first to own a Neapolitan Mastiff in the UK – a breed which he still owns and greatly admires.

He is the senior judge of Bullmastiffs in Britain, having awarded Challenge Certificates since 1962. He has judged Bullmastiffs and Mastiffs at Crufts, and was elected to officiate as judge at the American Bullmastiff Association Golden Jubilee Show in 1983, which brought a world entry for that time. Douglas has judged Mastiffs at the World Show, and has judged Mastiffs and Bullmastiffs at specialist club events in Europe and Scandinavia. He writes extensively on canine matters, and is author of a book on the Mastiff and Bullmastiff.
See Chapter One: Dogs of the Mastiff Type; Chapter Two: The Mastiff Character; Chapter Six: The Bullmastiff; Chapter Seven: The Neapolitan Mastiff; Chapter Sixteen: Breeding a Litter.

RAFAEL MALO ALCRUDO was brought up with Pyrenean Mastiffs at his family home near the Pyrenees. In 1975 he established his kennel – La Tajadera del Tio Roy – and has bred more than 60 Pyrenean Mastiff Champions. This is a world record among all kennels dedicated to Spanish dog breeds. In 1977 he was instrumental in founding the Spanish Pyrenean Mastiff Club (CMPE); he was general secretary until 1986 and since that time he has served as president.

Rafael, a well-known writer on the breed, has been an international judge since 1982 and has judged Molosser Shows throughout Europe, Scandinavia, Asia and in the USA. He is president of the Aragon Kennel Club, and manages one of the top CACIB shows in Spain.
See Chapter Nine: The Pyrenean Mastiff.

ANNE-MARIE CLASS is well-known in the dog world, contributing regularly to the canine press. She became a judge in 1981 and is qualified to judge Dogues de Bordeaux, Mastiffs, Bullmastiffs, Bulldogs, Rottweilers and German Wirehaired Pointers. She is co-author with Gilbert Colas of *Mastiff Bullmastiff ...Un Peu De Cynotechnine En Prime*, and she is president of the French Mastiff and Bullmastiff Club.
See Chapter Twelve: The Dogue de Bordeaux.

Photo: Anne-Marie Class.

PAMELA JEANS-BROWN has owned Bullmastiffs since 1979 and is well-known in the show ring. She judges Bullmastiffs at Championship level, but is also very interested in all the Molosser breeds in the UK and abroad. She travels to European all-breed and club shows whenever her job, as head of Modern Languages in a large London comprehensive school, allows her time.

Pamela is on various Molosser breed committees, including the Tibetan Mastiff Club of Great Britain, and was formerly deputy editor of *Molosser Magazin*, an international publication devoted to all Molosser and allied breeds. She judges most breeds in the working and Pastoral Group at Open Show level, but the highlight of her career was handling the Crufts Best of Breed Tibetan Mastiff in 1997.
See Chapter Ten: The Tibetan Mastiff.

ALISON JONES BVetMed MRCVS qualified as a veterinary surgeon from the Royal Veterinary College, University of London, in 1987. After a short period in research she joined a mixed practice in Gloucestershire where she worked for seven years. During this time Alison developed a keen interest in the use of diet for the management of clinical conditions in both dogs and cats. In 1987 Alison joined Hill's Pet Nutrition where she is now Veterinary Affairs Manager. Alison has had several articles published on various aspects of canine nutrition and is a regular contributor to *Your Dog* magazine where she answers readers questions on canine nutrition.
See Chapter Three: Diet And Nutrition.

DICK LANE BSC FRAgS FRCVS has worked as a veterinary surgeon in practice for the last thirty-five years, and is a consultant to the Guide Dogs for the Blind Association. He was awarded the Fellowship of the Royal College of Veterinary Surgeons in 1968, and the Fellowship of the Royal Agricultural Societies in 1993. Other successes include the BSAVA's Dunkin Award in 1977 and the BSAVA's Melton Award in 1987. Dick's literary work includes joint authorship of the *A-Z of Dog Diseases and Health Problems* (published by Ringpress Books in the UK and Howell Book House in the USA), editing *Animal Nursing*, now in its fifth edition, and joint editor of *Veterinary Nursing*. He is an occasional contributor to the *New Scientist, Veterinary Times* and *Veterinary Practice*.
See Chapter Fourteen: Health Care; Chapter Fifteen: Breed Associated Diseases.

JAIME PÉREZ MARHUENDA is well-known as an expert on the Fila Brasileiro. He has travelled all over the world studying the breed, and has written many articles on its history and development . He has bred Fila Brasileiro since 1993 under his Acaboclado affix, and judges at Open Show level.

Jaime has been vice president of the Alicante Kennel Club since 1992, and has been editor of the Spanish Molosser Club magazine since 1993.
See Chapter Eleven: The Fila Brasileiro.

CARLOS SALAS MELERO has dedicated the whole of his life to dogs. His interest started inthe Working and Obedience side, and by the 1970s Carlos was a top guard dog trainer as well as a top professional show handler. In 1983 he had achieved one of his greatest successes, winning BIS at the World Dog Show with a Spanish Mastiff.

His kennel prefix – La Villa y Corte – is well-known for its success with Yorkshire Terriers and Miniature Schnauzers, as well as for producing many top winning Spanish Mastiffs. Carlos is an international judge of all the Schnauzers breeds, the Bullmastiff, the Mastiff, the Pointer, and the West Highland White Terrier as well as all the Spanish breeds. He is an international specialist judge of the Spanish Mastiff, the Yorkshire Terrier, the Podenco Ibicence and the Spanish Galgo.
See Chapter Eight: The Spanish Mastiff.

MAGARET MELLOR met her first Anatolian Shepherd Dog in 1976 and has been a devotee of the breed ever since. She has travelled widely in Turkey to research the background and work of the country's livestock protection dogs, with the help of government officials from the state kennels and Ankara Zoo, and veterinary staff from Ankara University. In the 1980s she imported working Kangal stock into the UK, which she bred under her Masallah affix. Progeny from these lines has since been introduced into well-known British show kennels.

Margaret is breed correspondent and a regular contributor to the British weekly *Our Dogs*. For many years she was the editor of *Karabas*, newsletter of the Anatolian Karabash Dog Club – the first officially recognised breed society for Anatolians outside Turkey.
See Chapter Thirteen: The Anatolian Shepherd Dog.

LYN SAY and her husband kept Mastiffs for nearly thirty years, and their Bulliff kennel enjoys a reputation for producing top-quality dogs. On three occasions, Bulliff Mastiffs have won the dog CC at Crufts, twice with the same dog, and going BOB on two occasions. They have made up a number of Champions, both in the UK and overseas.

A Championship judge of the breed, Lyn is also very active in breed club administration. She has served on the committee of the Old English Mastiff Club for three terms, and is now vice president. She is the editor of the club magazine, and is breed note correspondent for Dog World.
See Chapter Five: The Mastiff.

NICK WATERS has been involved with dogs since the mid-1950s. He has bred Challenge Certificate winners in Mastiffs, Standard Poodles and Irish Water Spaniels, and, with Liz Waters, he shares the Zanfi kennel, one of the most successful connected with the Irish Water Spaniel.

By profession, Nick is a canine art historian and freelance writer, and he contributes regularly on the dog in art to magazines and weekly dog papers in both the UK and the USA. For many years, his trade stand featuring canine antiques and collectables was a familiar sight on the British show scene.
See Chapter Four: Celebrating the Mastiff.

REFACE

When this book was being planned some basic principles about its contents were agreed. The first was that only contributors with practical experience and a deep knowledge of the individual breeds would be invited to participate. I do not consider that the necessary expertise can be acquired without owning a dog from one of the Mastiff breeds and thereby being given the opportunity of studying it in all its stages of development.

It was also agreed to dispense with lengthy histories of each breed, many of which are supposition tinged with fable. It seemed to be of greater importance to concentrate on proven and more recent history. There is an understandable degree of pride in ownership of a breed whose presumed association with man is alleged to cover thousands of years. From a purely practical point of view the space which would be required to give each breed an in-depth history would have created a book of unwieldy proportions. We cannot ignore breed history when it gives us a better understanding of a breed, but to repeat old suppositions and flights of fancy was not part of our concept. There are already many books which speculate on canine history and manage to incorporate old-time theories with newly-found imagination. At the same time we should not ignore artistic evidence of the existence of animals of Mastiff type, some of which can be seen in various museums throughout the world.

Our aim has been to update breed knowledge and explore how – or probably which – Mastiff breeds can fit into conditions imposed by an ever-changing modern society. My thanks go to the authors for their unique contributions and to those who have kindly loaned the photographs used in the book, which come from many parts of the world and so give readers a broader view of the breeds described.

Douglas Oliff, Editor.

Bullmastiff and Mastiff: Loumio de Molossie and Ice Cream de Molossie.

Photo courtesy: Anne-Marie Class.

1 DOGS OF THE MASTIFF TYPE

By Douglas Oliff

The symbiotic association of man and dog has probably existed since the era of our cave-dwelling ancestors. It has been suggested that the dog is descended from the wolf, and there is evidence that the wolf existed in the earliest of times, but the dog/wolf theory has never been conclusively proven. Others have postulated that an extinct animal, which was canine in appearance but neither wolf nor dog, was the basic progenitor of the dog as we know it today.

Did the primitive dog discover that our cave-dwelling ancestors habitually discarded the bones and entrails of the animals which they had caught, killed and eaten? To live in the proximity of a cave with such a food source would have been advantageous to the existence of the dog. Having taken that initial step, perhaps the dog began to lose his instinctive fear of man and established his lair even closer to the cave dwelling. Having thus entrenched himself, his natural reaction would be to defend his territory against predators and intruders. If a strange animal approached the lair, the dog would growl and bark as a warning of possible danger to his canine family. Human cave-dwellers would soon associate those growls and barks with warnings of possible dangers to themselves, and so the first link between man and guard dog would have been formed, albeit in a primitive and somewhat haphazard form.

If we accept that possibility of how the link was established thousands of years ago, it can be appreciated that the basic requirement of any guard dog bred today is the ability to bark and thus give due warning. Having given that warning, the dog's subsequent actions and reactions will, to a major extent, be the result of training.

EVOLUTION AND DEVELOPMENT
The breeds featured in this book are all guarding breeds, though their specific functions may differ. Some have been developed as guards of humans and property. Others as guards of sheep or goats. Those breeds have a strong sense of association with flocks, but are devoid of any instinct to herd. All are large breeds. They may differ in coat, weight, height and activity, but there are common characteristics such as natural guarding ability, unflinching courage and an exceptional devotion to their owners.

Probably every dog breed of today has been produced by cross breeding. The fact that the word 'Mastiff' has been used over the centuries should not be taken as proof that any dog within the group today is similar to the dogs alleged to have fought in the Roman arena or in pre-Christian times. In the Middle Ages the word 'Mastiff' was used as a generic term for any large dog with

In the Middle Ages, the name Mastiff was used for a large dog with guarding ability.

Photo courtesy: Betty Baxter.

distinct guarding abilities. There were Mastiffs used to draw carts, "butchers' Mastiffs' whose function was to pin down the animals in the slaughter house, and fighting and baiting Mastiffs, but the term was usually applied to large dogs used as guards of houses and other property. The 'Bandog' was another name for the Mastiff. It derived from the Saxon word 'banda', meaning a chain, as the dog was chained by day and allowed to roam on the property at night.

While much Mastiff lore is fable, there are facts which suggest that the type, in recognisable form, was known in the pre-Christian era. In the British Museum are the Nineveh bas reliefs of 850 BC; when studying them we cannot deny that here is a powerfully built dog with tremendous bone, a big head, a short muzzle and all the loose skin and dewlap which are the hallmarks of today's Neapolitan Mastiff. There are convincing theories that 'Indian' dogs of large size originated in Tibet and travelled with migrating tribes through India, Persia, Mesopotamia and Syria, and then to Greece and Europe. Quite apart from the migrating people, further spread of the 'Indian dogs' would have been feasible due to the warring factions of the nations. Dogs would be likely to accompany invading armies. The Greek and, later, the Roman Empire, would have further enhanced the transportation of the dogs into Western Europe.

There were certainly various types of Mastiff – lighter built, hound-like dogs used for hunting and the heavier, low-slung type, used as a guard and watchdog.

Aristotle, the great Greek writer, recommended that a suitable cross for the famous 'hounds of Sparta' would be the 'Molossus'. Such a cross was considered to produce "an animal with unsurpassed courage, fidelity and endurance". The alternative name for the Molossus was the Epirote, presumably from the area known as Epirus, opposite Corfu. The Molossus is described as a "large strong dog with a heavy muzzle" and "the size, appearance and temperament of the breed is such that it is widely believed to be descended from Cerberus, the dog that Hercules brought from Hell."

The history of dog breeds has intrigued many writers over the centuries and the authors of the breed chapters in this book will be writing on the history of their particular breeds. Although differing physically and in some aspects of temperament, I have found among the Bullmastiffs, Neapolitan Mastiffs and Mastiffs which I have owned that there are several mental aptitudes which are common to all.

There is the need for human companionship and contact if the high intelligence is to be developed. Then, once a relationship has been established, the dog has a genuine desire to please and protect the owner and his property. Lastly, they share a fidelity which is second to none.

What more can we ask of any breed?

GROUP CHARACTER

Even with (or perhaps because of) the highly organised distribution of news and information, there are still members of the public to whom the words 'guard dogs' are synonymous with characters such as Bill Sykes and Bullseye, so expertly portrayed by Charles Dickens. It has to be admitted that, through the ages, the Mastiff and Bulldog types have been owned and used by what can only be described as the dregs of society. Had unadulterated viciousness been the only constituent of such breeds, it is doubtful if they would be in existence today.

In my experience of ownership of some of the breeds of the group, there may be a tough exterior shown to the outside world, but this is balanced by an amazing and unique loyalty and affection to their owner, provided that such an owner cultivates this side of the dog's nature and does not attempt to stimulate aggression. Indifference to anyone outside the immediate family is a common trait of the Mastiff group but, to those who are within the family, the dogs have an inherent desire to please, and they show genuine contrition if they realise that they have caused offence.

We receive from a dog only as much as we

The Mastiff: A tough exterior is balanced with a unique sense of loyalty.

Photo: Anne-Marie Class.

are prepared to put into the building of a relationship. If the dog is shut away from human companionship, the true liaison between dog and owner will never be fully developed. Obviously when numbers of dogs are kept, it is necessary for them to be kennelled, but they should always be allowed time with their owner, such as walking, or be given some other suitable exercise and companionship. It is the latter which is so vital in the development of the animal's potential, and preparation for its future as a companion and guard – and the order in which those words are written is intentional.

There are differences of temperament among the breeds described in this book. Each contributor will comment on the capabilities and suitability of their particular breed, but all breeds described here have the ability and the natural instinct to guard.

THE GUARDING INSTINCT

In recent years it has never failed to puzzle me why, in an age in which it can be statistically proven that petty crime has increased, the words 'guard dog', which are such a deterrent to crime, bring such abuse and adverse publicity. The public has been fed with lurid descriptions of unprovoked attacks by what irresponsible journalism describes as "devil dogs" or "irresponsible killers". Such sensationalism has not as yet been applied to the group in Britain and North America, but in some of the European countries, dogs of well-known guarding ability are not being encouraged. Legislation on their control steadily increases and, in some of the countries, the cost of a licence to own such dogs is far higher than in other canine groups.

Is such a bias justified? In my opinion it is not. Where mistakes and incidents have happened, the fault invariably lies with the owner's failure to anticipate the dog's action and to control it. The breeds in the group are

spirited dogs. They have been developed from dogs which, over the centuries, have acted as guards or fighting dogs and, all too often, encouraged to react violently. Spirit is expected and needed, but it can and must be controlled. What is not wanted in a dog of this size is nervousness. Nervous dogs, through abject fear, can often react violently and are more potentially dangerous than a dog of a calm, yet determined, temperament.

Beneath the surface of any dog of any breed is the desire to dominate, and the pack instinct to hunt and kill. The Mastiff group is no exception to these traits but their overall size, strength and determination calls for a higher degree of experience in ownership and overall control. Perhaps I should admit that, while I was carrying out official inspections of boarding and breeding establishments under current legislation, the kennels of guard breeds such as German Shepherd Dogs, Dobermanns and Rottweilers proved no problem. The only occasion on which I got bitten was by a Chihuahua!

All too often the concept of a guard dog is a teeth-baring, barking brute throwing itself against the gate or fence and giving every indication that, if given the opportunity, it would attack and seriously maul anyone within range. Such an animal is not a guard dog. It is a vicious brute, quite out of control and a sad reflection on its owner's ability to understand it and train it.

DOGS OF SPIRIT

I am often asked by people who are thinking of having one of these breeds whether aggression is necessary in a guard dog and at what age one of these dogs starts to show the instinct to guard. Again, I write on this aspect of the group as a whole, and readers should refer to the specialist chapters on specific breeds.

Breed characteristics are, to a major extent, inborn and usually follow a pattern. The

The Bullmastiff: Ch. Lepsco Lady Elise of Flinstock JW. Bred by Mr W. Scott. Before recognition as a pure breed, crosses between Mastiff and Bulldog were often referred to as "strong Bulldogs"

Photo courtesy: Janet and Alex Gunn.

pattern often reflects the nature of the work which humans have given the breeds to perform over many generations. Most dogs are happiest in doing the job which their forefathers were mentally and physically bred to do. Whippets and Greyhounds like to run and to chase. Sheepdogs instinctively herd sheep, terriers go to ground. Not only are they physically adapted to be specialists in such work, but generations of breeding have given them a natural aptitude and enjoyment of their specialist task. Conrad Heresbatch wrote a descriptive account of the Mastiff and the account was "newly Englished by Barnaby Googe, London 1586".

"In choosing a mastie that keepeth the house, you must provide such a one as hath a large, mightie body, a great shrill voice, that both with his barking – yea being not seen, with the horror of his voice, put him to flight. His stature must neither be long nor short, but well set. His head great, his eyes sharp and fierce, either brown or grey. His lips blackish, neither turning up, nor hanging too much down. His mouth blacke and wide, his neather jaw fat, and coming out of it on either side a fang appearing more outward than his other teeth, his upper teeth even with his neather, not hanging too much over, sharpe and hidden with his lips. His countenance like a lion's, his breast great and shag haired, his shoulders broad, his legs big, his tail short, his feet very great. His disposition must neither be too gentle, nor too curst, that he neither fawn upon a thief, nor fly upon his friends. Very waking, no gadder abroad, nor lavish of his mouth, barking without cause. It maketh no matter that he be not swift, for he is but to fight at home and give

Neapolitan Mastiff:
Dolli de Néropolis.
Courage and alertness
is combined with a
watchful mentality.

Photo: Sauchez.
Courtesy: Vos Chiens.

warning of the enemy. A black dog is best,
because of the hurt he may do to the thief by
reason of not being seen".

To give warning is the basic requirement of
every guard dog and excessive aggression is
not condoned in today's dog laws. What is
needed is courage, alertness and a watchful
mentality, which will enable the dog to act in
a very decisive manner should an emergency
occur and his assistance be required. The fact
that he is a housedog and companion will in
no way detract from his abilities; in fact it
can increase them. If the dog is to guard, he
must feel that the person to be guarded is
worth guarding. We should never
underestimate the hypersensitivity of a dog's
senses. They quickly discern in a person
tensions which may not be obvious to a
human. Unless a wrong-doer is an
accomplished perpetrator of crime, before
taking the risk of being caught he must be
under some form of nervous tension. The
dog, especially one of the guard breeds, will
quickly sense this tension and react
accordingly.

In most of the breeds, guarding instincts
usually begin to show themselves at
approximately 18 months of age or slightly
later. I would be a little perturbed if a young
puppy showed determined guarding instincts
at a very early age. This could be indicative of

a high level of guarding instinct which may
be troublesome when the animal matures.
What often happens is that if a quite
demonstrative adult, especially if it is a bitch,
shares the premises with the puppy, the
youngster soon begins to imitate the adult. If
she runs to the front gate barking it will not
be too long before the puppy is doing
likewise. The reverse can also happen. If the
puppy's adult companion is nervy and highly-
strung these character faults can also get
imitated, which is, to say the least, very
counterproductive.

SENSIBLE PURCHASING
Not all guard dogs have the benefit of living
as a member of a household and some may
be destined to be a guard dog to such people
as night watchmen on business premises.
Such animals need professional handling and
training and, I feel, are outside the scope of
this book. What must never be done to this
or any other breed of dog is perpetually to
chain it or closely confine it with no contact
with the outside world. Long periods of
chained existence will ruin the character of
any dog, making it bad-tempered and
unreliable.

Having studied the text and photographs
within the book I hope that you are inspired
to decide to make one of the Mastiff breeds
your enviable companion. Unless you are

Spanish Mastiff, Trabuco: Legendary defender of herd and master. Photo: Carlos Salas.

very experienced you should only consider purchasing a puppy. The puppy can then grow up with you, and the necessary relationship between the two of you can develop, so that each has a respect and understanding of the other. My recommendation is that, however touched you may be with stories and pictures of one of the Mastiff types in need of rescue, you harden your heart. Your compassion is to be admired but, for the very inexperienced, rescues could end in a disaster.

WHICH BREED TO CHOOSE
It is not easy to select a breed from those which are described in the book. Much is dependent upon cost, circumstances, personal tastes and the type and location of your house. All the breeds mentioned in this book

are exhibited and bred in Europe. Many have spread to the USA and to countries such as Australia and New Zealand, and are proving to be popular working dogs in a variety of environments. At the moment British laws do not allow the importation of the Fila Brasiliero as some anti-dog lobbyists, who at one time wished to prevent the importation of the Dogue de Bordeaux, have now decided that the Fila Brasiliero is a dangerous dog. Without doubt the existing UK quarantine regulations will either be abolished or drastically modified over the next few years. This will open the doors to many interesting breeds which are inaccessible at the moment.

We humans have an infinite variety of taste in most things but, if you admire large, companionable dogs, there should be a breed described in this book to suit you.

Remember that, even with a large breed which, generally, does not enjoy the longevity of the toy and terrier breeds, you must make a well-thought-out decision before you buy your puppy. You can expect to own it for about eight years. You should, therefore, consider your immediate personal circumstances before plunging into ownership of a large breed.

THE RIGHT ENVIRONMENT

You have to consider whether, for instance, there is a strong likelihood of a change of home in the foreseeable future and would the new house accommodate a large dog? What of its location? It must have, at a very minimum, a garden area in which the growing puppy can play and exercise itself. At the same time I have known instances of Mastiffs being kept in a first floor apartment, but exercised several times a day in a local park. This is not, in my opinion, an ideal environment for a dog of Mastiff proportions, but it can be done, even if it is not generally recommended. Much depends upon the owner's ability and willingness to reduce the effects of the under-exercise and boredom which is likely to result from such an environment.

On the other extreme, a house which has a high degree of isolation has some disadvantages from a dog-rearing point of view. The dog in such an environment grows up without experiencing the hurly-burly of a more urban location. In some circumstances this can affect the temperament by either making the dog apprehensive of urban sights and noises, or making it over-aggressive due to its lack of common experience.

Whatever the house and wherever it is situated, it is essential that, before you take possession of your puppy, the curtilage of your property is securely fenced. This is to ensure that not only can your dog not stray and get blamed for all sorts of crimes, chiefly

Pyrenean Mastiff, Sp. Ch. Ulises Del Castillo De Al: This breed has been saved from near extinction and is now thriving once again.
Photo: Rafael Malo Alcrudo.

by virtue of his size, but that the secure fence will prevent stray dogs getting into your property, which will soon be considered to be your dog's territory which must be guarded. Whether the intruder is human or canine, it makes no difference; it is, to your dog, an intrusion and must call for a reaction, even if it is only a warning bark.

You should also consider whether your vehicle is big enough to accommodate a large breed, if you intend exhibiting it, or even if the animal has to be taken to a veterinary surgeon.

COAT-TYPE AND COLOUR

There are other considerations which are so often overlooked. Do you prefer a short-haired breed such as a Bullmastiff or Dogue

The Tibetan Mastiff: A thick coat and a cast-iron constitution were needed to withstand the harsh conditions of the Tibetan plateau.

Photo courtesy: Pamela Jeans-Brown.

de Bordeaux or a longer-coated breed such as a Tibetan Mastiff with its fairly thick coat, which also has a woolly undercoat in winter. This may seem trivial to you, but dog hairs on the carpet and the need for regular grooming in the case of a longer-haired breed, may become a chore and should be considered.

Colour is not as unimportant as some would have us believe, a fact borne out by choices of colours for your cars, house decor or clothing. Black, to some, is too funereal, but I personally consider it to be a wonderful colour for a night-patrol guard dog. Rich red is very attractive and I easily recall the wonderful red Bullmastiffs which Doris Mullen owned pre-war and in the early post-war period. These dogs were the exact colour of the wild red deer and, although there are some red Bullmastiffs in Britain today, there are none of this colour. When I last judged in America there were a few who were very close to this almost extinct red. Brindle,

especially good brindling over a red background, is a wonderful combination of colours and very practical as it is a natural camouflage. I remember years ago Mrs Warren of Harbex had a deep red brindle bitch aptly named Harbex Dancing Flame. Should I ever own a Mastín Espanol of such a colour I would call it Fuego, the Spanish word for fire.

DOG OR BITCH?
A very important issue is whether to choose to have a dog or a bitch puppy. In the breeds which are under consideration there is a good deal of difference between the male and female, both physically and, often, in temperament. Physically the bitch is smaller, though needless to say, still a large dog. She is therefore easier to accommodate, slightly cheaper to feed and does not normally have the wanderlust of the male dog of every breed. This is a distinct advantage.

Anyone owning one of these breeds is, or

should be, proud of the privilege of ownership. Having mentioned the advantages of owning a bitch, I freely admit that there is something even more impressive about a good, hefty male. The physical differences between the two sexes is approximately that which exists between a lion and a lioness, so you have an option, but it is an important decision. The advantage of owning a bitch is that, by and large, they are more tolerant of other dogs. A male can be very disinclined to allow another male on his property; hence my advice earlier in this section about secure fencing.

The bitch will, or should, come on heat every six months after approximately a year old, although some may start earlier than this. I have owned bitches which only came on heat once a year, which is a great boon to anyone not wishing to breed them. To ensure that the bitch never comes on heat, she can be surgically spayed by a vet, but such an operation should not be carried out until she has had a minimum of one heat. While on heat she is going to be sexually attractive to any male dog.

There are occasions when a bitch is due in season but there may be some problem which means that the owner would be unable to have the necessary care and control over an in-season bitch. By arrangement, a veterinary surgeon can give an injection which will delay the heat. My advice would be to use this only as a last resort, or as an emergency, as there have been instances where bitches which have had the treatment become non-breeders, and develop ovarian problems in later life. Should the bitch get accidentally mated, conception can be terminated, provided that she is taken to the veterinary surgeon promptly. Such accidents should not happen in a well-organised establishment, but you must take prompt action if they do.

Compared with most breeds the Mastiff types are not great wanderers, probably because for centuries they have been used to guard specific areas. In every breed, from a Chihuahua to a Great Dane, the male is always the more liable to stray, as compared to the bitch.

RESPONSIBLE OWNERSHIP
In many parts of the world today there is a tendency towards anti-dog legislation. I

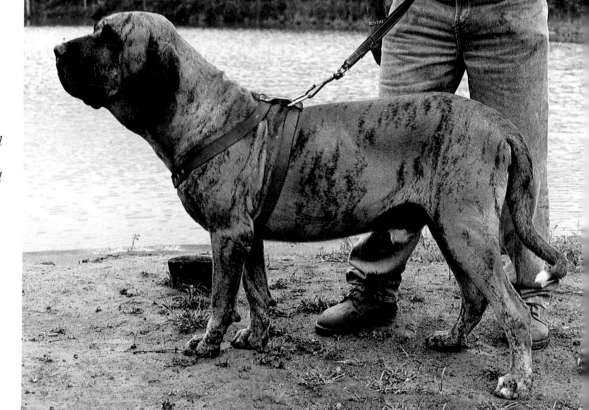

Fila Brasileiro, Neon Do Engenho Velho: A breed designed to guard and attack, combined with exceptional tracking ability.

Photo courtesy: Jaime Pérez Marhuenda.

regret to admit that the irresponsibility of some owners is partly to blame for this. In Britain, for example, it is an offence to allow any dog, male or female, to be in a public place unless on a lead and wearing a collar with its owner's name and address inscribed thereon. There are parks in some cities and towns which have dog exercise areas with free exercise permitted if accompanied by the owner, but even in rural areas where there are named public footpaths or bridle ways open to the public, the dog must be on a lead.

In periodicals and in many dog books road exercise is advocated for all types of foot defects, weak pasterns etc. but, again, the dog must be on a lead. Emergencies can and do happen. If the dog is on a lead the chances of a problem occurring are minimal. Country roads are probably more dangerous due to their narrowness, which is a hazard for traffic, and also to the fact that there are many instances where farm livestock are in fields alongside such roads. If the hedges are not in good repair the temptation to chase livestock is a very real one. Any dog suddenly confronted with a flock of sheep, especially if they start to run, will be tempted to chase. Farmers are very unappreciative of any dog, and more especially a large dog, wishing to investigate livestock, even if it is just curiosity

The Dogue de Bordeaux: An ancient French breed used for hunting, fighting, guarding and pulling loads. Photo: Anne-Marie Class.

The Anatolian Shepherd Dog or Kangal: A treasured part of Turkey's national heritage.

Photo: Margaret Mellor.

on the part of the dog. If you adopt the basic principle "When off the property always be on collar and lead" you may avoid much heartache and expense.

A few final points for your consideration before taking the plunge and buying your puppy. Do not be persuaded to buy two puppies of the same sex in these breeds in the mistaken belief that they will be "company for one another". As puppies they will be good company but, by about two years of age when the need to dominate rears its head, there is every chance that the two sweet companions will become determined combatants. If you must have two, get one of each sex, but realise that the bitch will one day come on heat and ensure that you can cope with this situation.

Study the Breed Standard, attend a few Championship shows and get familiarised with your chosen breed. Critics will probably accuse me of being over-cautious in my assessment of Mastiff group character. To some extent I would accept such criticism but, as a breed-note correspondent of a weekly dog periodical for many years, I have heard numerous somewhat tragic stories from owners, where problems and heartache have occurred simply because people have been unaware of the correct management of animals within the group. There have been occasions where so-called 'breeders' have deliberately sold puppies without any reference to the snags which every new owner should be made aware of even though they may never occur. This is complicated by the fact that many people are breeding dogs today who have scant experience of the breeds themselves and would, therefore, be unable to advise, even if they wished to do so.

Mastiff-type breeds are handsome, often ridiculously affectionate to their owners and immediate family, reliable, highly companionable but, by virtue of their size and strength, they must always be under control. With guard dogs, as with humans, there are always a few rogues. It is this small minority which hit the headlines, and not those calm, determined, guard companions which, for twenty-four hours a day, give reassurance to their owners that as long as they are on watch all will be well.

2 THE MASTIFF CHARACTER

By Douglas Oliff

All the breeds within the group have been developed as working dogs. Their duties may have differed in some respects but the common factor lies in their instinct to guard, whether it be humans, animals or property. To some extent the specific duties for which they were evolved find little demand in a modern society. We have few estates requiring a night dog to accompany the gamekeeper and assist him in apprehending poachers. Mobile phones and shortwave radio have, to a major extent, superseded that need, but any breed which has been specifically bred for a particular duty is mentally and physically fulfilled when performing such a duty in a contemporary setting. Every owner of any breed of dog should be aware that, just beneath the veneer of domestication, is the primeval pack instinct to dominate and to suppress any opposition to that dominance. When something like a Chihuahua develops this quite natural urge it can be a nuisance, but little or no damage will result, unless it is to the equally small residents of the kennel. If and when an animal of Mastiff-group proportions develops such traits, the results could be serious.

BREED AGGRESSION

If it is true that the ancient forebears of today's breeds were exactly what we have now both mentally and physically, then we would have a group of dogs which would be difficult to own in the present-day environment.

Shakespeare, in his play *Troilus and Cressida* wrote:
"Two curs shall tame each other, pride alone Must tarre the Mastiffs on as 'twere their bone." (Act 1 scene 3 line 391)

This well-documented excessive aggression has been reduced, chiefly because the dogs have taken on a more domestic role than in previous centuries, but it is still there and it is still something which must never be lost sight of. Anything which reduced these dogs into a subservient lap-dog mentality would be sacrilege in my opinion. Any of the Mastiff group which lacks the true Mastiff spirit, either by being vicious or, on the other extreme, nervous, is untypical of the breed. As a judge I would be more inclined to penalise an exhibit which, by virtue of its nervous temperament, is mentally unsound, than to penalise an exhibit for slight physical unsoundness. A nervous dog is often a dangerous dog, as it will attack out of fear and react unpredictably.

The males in the breeds are probably the more difficult to control, not only because of their greater size but because of the masculine desire for dominance over any other male. Bitches, by and large, are easier

Spanish Mastiff, Tigre: Loyal, powerful and intrepid, this noble-looking dog sums up all that is best in the Mastiff character.
Photo: Carlos Salas.

to control as they lack the size and weight of the males, but some bitches tend to change their mental attitudes when the oestrus cycle approaches. When in full heat they can get very belligerent with other bitches with whom they normally live peacefully. I have never been able to house two males together but have found them quite amenable to one another when being exercised on a leash. To attempt to house two males together when a bitch is on heat is courting disaster. There are exceptions, but generally, caution and commonsense should be observed.

DEALING WITH AGGRESSION

I am often asked how to break up a fight when it occurs. The answer is to prevent its occurrence by good management. Once animals have had a fight, all too often they develop a taste for such pugilism, and this is not confined to fights between the males. When two bitches fight they do so with far more ferocity and determination than two males. They never forget and must never be housed or exercised together again. The hoary old story that a dog will never fight a bitch is not true. If a belligerent bitch chooses to test her strength against a male she will do so with all the ferocity of which she is capable, with the result that the male has to retaliate and will normally win.

Aggression is something about which you should always be aware and be ready to nip in the bud. If, on seeing signs of aggression such as the pricking up of the ears, the defiant stiff back leg gait, and the fur on the back rising, a sharp jerk on the choke chain and a stern "No" will often divert the dog from his belligerent intentions. It is for this reason that I always advocated that, when off the owner's premises, the animal must be on a leash and therefore more likely to be under control. Despite their size and weight, large dogs can move at amazing speeds once off the lead.

During puppyhood any sign of aggression, such as when a toy or the feeding bowl is taken away, should be immediately checked.

A small puppy should be picked up by the scruff of the neck and shaken. This may sound drastic but it is the punishment which the bitch gives to a recalcitrant puppy. The owner must always be able to assert his position as the head of the pack to which all others must be subservient. I am not an advocate of corporal punishment for any dog but have, on more than one occasion, given a sharp hand-slap across the thigh of a dog actually caught in the act of breaking one of the rules of the house such as "thou shall not steal". My bitch has the habit of stealing anything from the kitchen work-top which is edible, but makes no attempt to do so if someone is present in the room.

Quite often a youngster, usually a male between the age of eighteen months and two years, will go through an adolescent rebellious stage, probably due to the

Am. Can. Ch. Statrugo's Jonathan O' Higgins.   *Bred and owned by Mr and Mrs McIntock.*

hormone changes of puberty. Any rule-breaking must be promptly dealt with, even if this is only a passing phase, as many intelligent dogs are quite capable of taking a liberty just to see how much they can get away with. You must demonstrate your displeasure not by corporal punishment but by tone of voice and by banning him from the house for half an hour. To be separated from the owner is a punishment to a sensitive dog, and these dogs are particularly sensitive to those whom they hold in respect.

I have no wish to give the impression that specimens of these breeds are uncontrollable gladiators. They are certainly not, but so much future heartache and so many problems can be avoided if new owners are aware of all sides of the character of these breeds, and the functions for which they were bred in past generations. As with humans, we cannot generalise on breed reactions, but we should be aware of what those reactions could be.

THE OBEDIENT MASTIFF

One side of their character is the natural desire to act as a watch dog, giving voice only when necessary, and a calm watchfulness at all other times. They have great fidelity to the owner and all members of the household but invariably attach themselves to one of the family for whom they develop a deep affection. They also respond to affection and thrive on human contact, especially from the object of their deep affection.

Mastiff-group responses are not the somewhat servile but instantaneous reactions of a German Shepherd Dog, for instance. They are calculating thinkers and quite willing to respond once having thought the command out. We should never get the impression that show obedience is beyond possibility. Many of the early Bull-Mastiffs (as the name was then spelt) were highly trainable, and this aspect is being encouraged by some owners today. For example, the

Xuxa de los Tres Naranjos, bred and owned by Pedro and Ines Van Damme. The Fila Brasileiro has such strong inherited character traits that it can only be kept in a controlled environment.
Photo courtesy: Jaime Perez Marhuenda.

Bullmastiff Eckweek Diemos of Wraxallvale, owned by Carolyn Jenkins, is doing not only Obedience demonstrations but performs in agility and man-work.

The breeder, Mr V.J. Smith, who became a household name in Bullmastiffs both pre- and post-war, first became attracted to the breed shortly after his marriage. A new owner moved into the house opposite and owned a Bullmastiff bitch who rarely barked, but who loved to sit outside the house and just watch, which is often the favourite occupation of an alert Bullmastiff. One afternoon Mr Smith noticed a hawker go through the front gate of the house opposite and walk round to the back door. The bitch was sitting behind an open bay window near the front door. She lifted her head and obviously noted the man but remained at her window, just watching and listening. Obviously his proposed sale did not materialise and voices between him and the lady of the house became raised. As

quick as lightning the bitch jumped through the window, ran to the rear door and rough-handled the man until called off by the householder. It was this spontaneous defensive action that decided Mr Smith's choice of a dog. He owned, exhibited, bred and judged Bullmastiffs for the rest of his life.

Matuszak, owned by Mary Montgomery and Michael Rogers – the first Dogue de Bordeaux in the USA to win an Obedience title and to go BIS at a Rare Breed Show.
Photo: Holloway. Courtesy: Montgomery/Rogers.

THE GUARDIAN MASTIFF

The average owner of any of these breeds is looking for a guard dog who will act as a deterrent to a wrongdoer, protect the family in an emergency, be tolerant of other animals, give warning if anything strange is seen, heard or smelled, yet it is expected to also be a show dog and endure the indignity of having the judge, who is a complete stranger, pressing, pulling and poking its body and opening its mouth. The animal is expected to stand and in no way react. Many do, but is it logical to expect all these capabilities and responses? The guard dog, if he is to become efficient at guarding, must be suspicious. Unless suspicion is aroused, strange noises and occurrences will not be noted. A degree of socialisation is essential but, if from early puppyhood every visitor to the house is allowed to handle and pet the dog, the necessary element of suspicion will be minimised. On the other hand, a puppy which is not brought up to experience the normal noises and activities of life stands the risk of becoming withdrawn and nervous due to lack of experience.

My suggestion is not for complete isolation but that strangers should not be allowed to treat the dog as if he were their personal possession. When adult, a good guard will observe and sniff the stranger and, from these fundamentals, will gauge what next step to take. If he decides that the stranger is acceptable, the reaction will be friendly but should always have a degree of reserve. If the visitor is seated in a room the dog will

Above & below: Surprisingly agile for their size, the Mastiff thrives on having a job of work to do.
Photos: Beretti.

Beleno de Los Lirones and Reina del Espinillo – two Spanish Mastiff Champions, with Ana Mesto. A good upbringing will result in the desired qualities of vigilance and loyalty.

Photo: Carlos Salas.

probably come alongside, wag his tail and give the overall signs of acceptance. This means that he can be petted, in a dignified way, and spoken to and will not react adversely. No guard dog can be, or should be, rushed into automatic acceptance of everyone. He will accept them if he thinks fit, but you should be careful of those which are unacceptable to him. His senses are more highly tuned than yours and he has probably detected something of which you are unaware.

All too often owners have told me that their dog, although an integral part of the household, is "a hopeless guard and would quite willingly show a burglar over the house". In a few instances this could be true. If everyone visiting the house is allowed to treat the dog as if he was their own, how do we expect him to differentiate between friend or foe if his sixth sense is undeveloped or

ignored? Never overlook the dog's ability to pick up conditions of tension and stress in humans. Anyone visiting the house with ill-intent is bound to be somewhat tense and stressed and these factors will be picked up by the dog. The resultant reactions of the animal can be quite out of keeping with his normal behaviour.

My first Neapolitan, who was an integral part of my life for nearly nine years, although fiery and extremely formidable, would very begrudgingly accept visitors in the house, with one proviso – if I left the room in which visitors were sitting they had to remain in their chair and not walk around the room.

Many found it unnerving as, for the whole time, she would lie there and watch every movement. Looking at a watch which necessitated moving the arm, or even taking a handkerchief from the pocket, would produce a quick movement of the head and a hard

The well-socialised Mastiff will learn to live in harmony with all members of his 'family'.

Photos: Anne-Marie Class.

expression in her eyes. Had someone decided to move when I was not present she would have reacted violently. Needless to say, they had previously been warned to remain seated. Once I was present she relaxed and, provided that everyone appreciated her dislike of familiarity, she would grudgingly accept that visitors should be allowed to go home unmolested. During her reign as chatelaine

she certainly managed to almost eliminate the incidence of casual callers.

SOCIALISATION AND TRAINING

The dividing lines between spirit, guarding and aggression are arbitrary. Spirit is necessary in any guard dog if it is required to act as a guard and not just as an ornament on a property. The sight of one of these dogs

Children and dogs should always be supervised, but good, basic training will ensure that the Mastiff poses no threat.   Photo: Nash.

Mastiffs of various types can sometimes live alongside each other, but it is difficult to keep two males.   Photo: Anne-Marie Class.

will usually be a sufficient deterrent, but would soon lose its credibility should the dog run off with its tail between its legs. In the show ring a spirited animal, if its handler has the exhibit under control, is bound to catch the eye of the judge. High spirits can be controlled and channelled into acceptable and impressive behaviour, but spirit can never be instilled into an obvious coward. Guarding comes naturally to animals within the group and, although some of the breeds are more volatile than others, there are also temperament variations within the same breed. Guarding is the result of instinctive suspicion and subsequent trained reaction. Training the guard dog is a very complex subject and the techniques applied must be tailor-made to suit each dog. To train a dog to man-work is, in my opinion, beyond the scope of the average owner.

Socialisation and training go hand in hand. From quite an early age a puppy must have basic training to enable it to be socialised and accustomed to situations such as visits to the veterinary surgeon for health checks or inoculations. As these visits will normally entail travelling to the surgery, the puppy

must have early acquaintance with car travel. The secret of all successful training is to make it fun for the puppy, and for the owner or trainer to show patience and never to lose their temper, even when severely provoked.

ACCEPTING THE COLLAR AND LEAD
The first stage is to get the puppy accustomed to wearing a collar. A light leather collar is the most suitable, worn so that it does not cause discomfort, but not so loose that the puppy can get its back foot caught in it when trying to scratch it off. I have known some puppies which will accept the collar without flinching; others will be distressed by it and make every attempt to remove it. Make the acclimatisation training gradual and remove the collar after it has been worn for a couple of hours. Put the collar on daily and gradually extend the time that it is worn until the puppy accepts it.

Once this stage has been reached, attach a light leather lead and let it drag along behind the puppy. This, too, is usually resented but just leave it for an hour or so, then unfasten the lead but leave the collar in position. Repeat the lead attachment later in the day, all the time making a great fuss of the youngster, then quietly pick up the lead. One of two things will happen; either he will make half-hearted attempts to chew the lead, or he will start to panic and go backwards, bucking and obviously resenting it. If this happens just drop the lead and return to the 'free trailing' as in the first lesson. If repeated daily, within a week or so most of the lead panic will have disappeared. Always remember that a food reward to a puppy being trained can work wonders. Once he is walking easily on the collar and lead, a major part of training is then easier as, on a leash, the animal is under control and its education can progress from step to step.

LEARNING COMMANDS

The next important lesson is the appreciation of the word "No". It is the tone in which the word is spoken which is of importance. When the puppies are with the dam, she will growl when a puppy is, in her opinion, misbehaving, so "No" should not necessarily be shouted but be spoken in a harsh tone. You will probably be agreeably surprised at how quickly the word will bring a response.

The other rather fundamental word is "sit". To country-dwelling owners this is not so important but to dogs living in towns or cities it is essential while waiting at kerb sides etc. If you gently press the dog's back just over the hips and says the word "sit", again using the command tone, it is something which most puppies quickly learn. You can do even more practice at home if, when the puppy sits on command, a biscuit or something similar is given.

Never forget the teachings of Pavlov who proved that animals can be trained by pleasurable association. Pavlov rang a bell immediately before feeding his dogs on a favourite food. The bell would ring, a fixed time would elapse, then the food was distributed. Needless to say, during the waiting period the dogs would salivate in preparation and anticipation of feeding. After some weeks the dogs would salivate as soon as the particular bell was rung, yet there was no food given and none was in the vicinity of the room. The sound had been fixed in the dogs' brains as the preliminary to eating. If the word "sit" can be associated with the pleasure of having a biscuit, the lesson will soon be learned.

The other very necessary order that must be obeyed in the breeds which are under consideration is the order "down". It may be

Ippolite de Molossie: It is important to teach a number of basic commands that will bring a swift response.

Photo: Berthou.

fun when a two or three-month old puppy wishes to jump up to greet you but, if the habit becomes fixed, it will not be as much fun when the animal weighing 150 lbs still wishes to do it.

Another word of disapproval which is fully understood by my dogs is "hey", again in the 'growling' tone. By using that word I find that, more often than not, I can prevent the animal from performing the mischief which he obviously had in mind. Reward and praise are two of the strongest inducements of any trainer and should always be given when the dog deserves them.

HOUSE TRAINING

In my experience house training of some of these Mastiff breeds is far easier than with many other breeds. Always allow the puppy out of doors after he has had a meal and stay out with him until he has emptied his bladder or bowels, praise him, then bring him back indoors. In a very short time the puppy will go to the outside door when he feels the necessity for relieving himself. Never refuse to allow him out even if he has only just come back to the house. Dogs tend to adopt toilet areas and return them, so it is preferable for them to adopt your garden rather than the lounge carpet.

TRAINING FOR THE SHOW RING

Those who wish to exhibit their puppy must in due course, train him for the show ring. Needless to say, the puppy will have been lead-trained and inoculated and will be reasonably comfortable with strangers and other dogs. Find out if there are show and obedience training classes available near you. There your youngster will start to become accustomed to the instructor imitating the judge by running his hands over the 'exhibit', moving the puppy up and down in a straight line and generally practising the activities of an indoor show. If shows are your aim you

Italian Champions Paco and Marlotta: Despite their size and strength, these Neapolitan Mastiffs accept the discipline of lead training, and are well-mannered companions on their daily outing.

Photo: Sheila Atter.

should make it quite clear that you do not require Obedience classes, the reason being that at many such classes the youngster is trained to sit whenever the handler comes to a halt. If this becomes habitual it would be a great disadvantage in the show ring, where the dog is required to stand and not to sit.

You may decide to show-train the puppy yourself without recourse to a class and, as you are likely to be handling the exhibit on his first show appearance, the more time you spend on show-ring procedure training both for yourself and the exhibit, the greater the necessary level of rapport between the two of you can be built up.

Ch. Iron Hills Into The Night winning his second national Speciality at the Mastiff Club of America 1998 show. The Mastiff can be trained to be an impressive show dog, but the most successful candidates are those with natural presence and showmanship.

When the puppy is eight weeks old the elementary lessons in a show-ring stance can be given. Pick the puppy up and place him on a table (preferably outside). Stand him with what the old-time dog exhibitors called "a leg at each corner" – head up and slightly forward, level top-line and correctly placed tail. Having placed him, put one hand just under his head, and gently stroke him down the back with the other hand, saying in a soft voice "stay". Do not bore him; as long as he keeps his pose and is happy for three or four minutes, finish the stay section of the training, give him a reward such as a piece of cheese (all dogs love cheese), lift him off the table or, if you are posing him on the ground, give him a pat and let him free, but with his collar on.

The next stage is to train him to walk and then trot round in a circle, keeping always to your left side. After these two exercises have been learned, repeat the "stand" and the trotting circle, but then suddenly stop and, when he stops too, place him in the stand position and give a new order "stay". The next step is to teach him to stay but to watch you, the handler, for the reward which a good stay should always bring. Give him the reward, then repeat your trotting circle.

REWARDS
Rewards are the basis of good training. You

will find that, if the puppy is correctly constructed, when he comes to a stop and realises that the reward is imminent, he will stand four-square and in a natural alert pose. Any judge will always look twice at a well-trained specimen which is happy in the show ring and responsive to the handler. The formula for show success is for each dog and handler to know what is expected of them. A reasonably good dog which is well trained, enjoys shows and is well presented, can frequently score over what may be a better specimen but which lacks that rapport with the handler.

CHOKE CHAINS
As the puppy grows it will be necessary to introduce the wearing of a choke chain both for shows and for exercise off the premises. Many trainers dislike the term 'choke chain' and prefer it to be called a 'check chain', which it is. It consists of a chain at the end of which is a metal ring and at the other end a similar ring to which the lead is attached. The principle is that if the dog pulls, the chain tightens, and he usually realises that pulling results in discomfort, so desists. Before using the choke chain, get a trainer to show you the correct way of putting it on so that the chain quickly slackens once the dog stops pulling.

Unless you are very fortunate you will, at

some stage, be faced with aggression from your own dog, provoked by the snarling or growling of another. It is then that the choke chain will prove its worth.

COMING WHEN CALLED

A lesson which must be established in quite early puppyhood is to come when called by name. If you find difficulty in getting this very necessary response, have a few lessons at an Obedience training class. Practise calling the youngster and, when he returns to you, make a fuss of him and always reward him. My dog bribes have always been a piece of cheese, which my dogs find irresistible, but a biscuit or a piece of cooked liver will do equally well. It is establishing in the dog's mind that to be called means a reward that is so essential. Never punish the dog for either ignoring your call or for doing it too slowly. To return to you should be a pleasure, but if on his return he gets punished for not coming to you immediately, any automatic reaction previously made by reward will be ruined.

COMPANIONSHIP

In most breeds you get from the dog as much, or more, of the care and affection which you put in. All of the Mastiff group thrive on human companionship, they want to be with their owner for twenty-four hours a day, they enjoy physical contact. They quite literally wish to share their life with the person or persons to whom they have become attached. No matter how well a dog is fed or treated, if he is living as a kennel dog his personality and companionship never reaches its true potential. To get the best from him the owner must unstintingly give of his best, and will be well rewarded.

Guard dogs of most breeds are understandably aggressive towards the intrusion of any dog straying on their domain, and the same attitude applies to the

It. Ch. Wilson Tajadera Del Tio Roy, a Pyrenean Mastiff, shows the ideal relationship between dog and owner.
Photo: Rafael Malo Alcrudo.

bitches. This does not imply that a fight will necessarily ensue, as the body language will pass the message to the intruder that it would be in his interest to return quickly the way he came in. Deliberate aggression towards humans can be dangerous and should not be tolerated, especially when it occurs off the owner's premises. This is one of the reasons why the animal should always be on a collar and lead and therefore under control in any public place.

MASTIFF DISLIKES

Before leaving the subject of puppy acclimatisation, there is a little problem which I have experienced with both Mastiff and Bullmastiff puppies and young adults. They have an aversion to walking beneath anything which is projecting a few feet above them, such as the open tailgate on an estate car or a station wagon, or a low garden topiary arch. My present young Bullmastiff, who greatly enjoys car travel, will never jump into the back of the car via the tailgate. This is not because he is incapable, as he jumps into the passenger's seat with great ease, then over the back seat into the luggage section in which he normally travels. On returning home the same thing happens. He stands inside the car looking up at the tailgate and refuses to jump out. A Mastiff which I once owned had the same aversion, except that he basically wished to travel in comfort spread out on the back seat rather than be subjected to third-class travel in the luggage compartment.

At shows I notice that some dogs dislike judges who bend low over them. Perhaps the breeds have claustrophobic feelings, which is why anything which closely overhangs them is resented. Dogs of Mastiff proportions are not easy to lift into any car and so I have never insisted that access and egress must be via the tailgate which they obviously dislike. Although a rarity now, it was not many years ago that some of the elderly lady judges wore hats when judging and an abundance of jangling jewellery. It looked traditional and decorative but a surprising number of dogs were apprehensive of such judges.

MOUTH AND EAR EXAMINATIONS
Even if the owner has no intention of exhibiting, the dog should be accustomed to having his teeth and mouth examined by pulling back the lips. A show judge will require this but, should teething problems occur, so will the veterinary surgeon. It is a lesson which should be taught at an early age. The same applies to routine examination of the ear which must be checked regularly for signs of discharge, inflammation, or other abnormalities. If you do the ear examination as part of the grooming routine, the dog will accept this as normal practice.

Qassaba Ausables Kie Of Rockanoar.
Likes and dislikes of the Mastiff breeds should be understood and appreciated.

Photo: E. Haynes (Riches).

DOG-RELATED LEGISLATION

There is an increasing amount of legislation relating to dog ownership. This varies from country to country, and in some cases the legislation is applicable to the larger guarding breeds. It is essential that all owners of Mastiff-type dogs are aware of any legal requirements and comply with them. This type of responsible ownership will ensure that future restrictive legislation is kept to a minimum.

NON-BARKERS

A problem which has frequently been referred to me is the fear by the owners that their young dog does not appear to have much inclination to bark when someone knocks at the door or rings the door bell. In the large breeds time must be considered necessary, not only for physical development but mental development as well. To own a breed like the Mastiff types, who are not unnecessary barkers, is a great advantage when considering the legislation just referred to, but one does need to have a dog which will signal any departure from the normal for the household. It is essential that the dog barks when the door is knocked or the doorbell sounds.

We are back to the Pavlov idea of associating with the dog's mind the required physical reaction. Most dogs are greedy and tidbits are great stimulators of their mind. If it is felt that the young dog is somewhat slow in developing the requirement of barking when the door is knocked, adopt an easy approach. Hold a piece of cheese or favourite tidbit in the hand and ensure that the dog is aware of what you are holding. Now say "speak" as an order. It is doubtful if there will be a response, so the trainer must alter the order to "woof" and imitate a bark and repeat the order "speak". If and when the dog responds, give him the tidbit and much praise. Practise this regularly during the day but gradually use the order "speak" or "bark"; when the dog responds again give the 'bribe' and much praise.

The next time that the door bell rings give the order to "speak"; when he does, again give the tidbit. It will not be long before he will bark automatically to a knock on the door or the bell ringing.

It is important that, as the animal grows and his mind develops, he responds to the door-knocking stimulus automatically. If, for instance, the lady of the house is alone and anyone hears the deep sound of the guard dog from inside the house, they are unlikely to be tempted to carry out any nefarious business. It is advantageous to train the dog to the "speak" or "bark" order other than when it is sitting down. It is not uncommon to train the dog first to sit and then to bark,

It is advantageous to train Mastiff types to bark to order.

Photo: Anne-Marie Class.

but what is required is for the dog to bark when in any position rather than when just sitting. The most perfect show pose is often seen when a dog is up on his toes, back straight, muscles taut, head uplifted and barking at something which has attracted him. This is mentioned because the command to "speak", quietly spoken at a show when the judge is attempting to make his final selection of winners, could have a decisive effect.

THE EFFECT OF THE DAM

Young dogs are imitative by nature and one of the best tutors is their own dam, provided that she is an active and reliable watchdog. If she hears something which she decides to investigate and barks a few warnings, the youngster, in the first instance, may be unsure of the procedure and hang behind just watching and looking puzzled. After a few weeks of association with the older animal, not only will the young dog pick up the signal to bark but, if he has the correct

temperament, will soon be rushing down to investigate for himself. This should be encouraged, but dogs should also be trained to desist from barking without cause.

Never underestimate the influence which a bitch has on her litter, something which is more fully dealt with in Chapter 16: Breeding a Litter. A nervous, jumpy bitch will often pass her untypical temperament to her puppies while they are in the nest and their eyes have not opened. Often we see such puppies, when a few months old, dash back into their kennel, should their dam panic at the sight or sound of anyone strange. On the other side of the coin, I have owned puppies of several of the Mastiff breeds which, at eight weeks would stand and growl at whatever a bold bitch is barking at. Nature plays an important role, but nurture is of equal importance.

HUMAN ASSOCIATION

Although the characteristics vary from breed to breed there are some which are common

Never underestimate the value of human contact.   *Photo: Anne-Marie Class.*

to all the breeds under consideration. The first, and probably one of the most important, is their need for human contact and companionship and their genuine desire to please the human to whom they have become attached. Charles Hastings, writing in *Harper's New Monthly Magazine* May 1887, wrote (and this is very applicable to all the group today): "There is no dog more fitted for human association than the Mastiff and there is no dog which goes wrong so quickly without it." Marshall was writing of Mastiffs which had been imported from England to the USA. He went on to eulogise about their calm and reliable temperaments and tolerance to animals smaller than themselves.

His article continued: "Not long since, the writer had occasion to visit the stock farm of a gentleman who has been one of the pioneers in American Mastiff breeding. On this farm there were, at the time, ten full grown Mastiffs with whom the little child was accustomed to roam at will. The dogs were loose at the time and it was a strange sight to see the troop of ten following after a playfellow so much smaller than themselves. The owner said that they had always been accustomed to the child and always treated him with the greatest gentleness."

I cannot truthfully say that I would have such complete confidence as Mr. Marshall had late in the last century, but the Mastiff is still the one with the easiest temperament today.

Marshall continues: "With the Mastiff, as with all dogs, the disposition is largely the result of his training. Environment influences the character of the puppy as well as of the child. The man who relegates his Mastiff to the confinement of a stable and the exclusive attention of the man-of-all-work will probably succeed in rearing a dog that will be anything but desirable either in disposition or habits."

I cannot over-emphasise this real need of human contact and devotion as, with all of the group, this is the instinct which makes them the guards and companions par excellence.

DUAL-ROLE MASTIFFS

In the case of the Anatolian Shepherd dog, the Mastín Espanol and the Mastín Pirenos, the ability to guard must obviously be something of a dual role, guarding both the animals and the human minders. These dogs obviously have an affinity for livestock but are in no way herding dogs. Their function is that of a guard and protector, but I know that, in the more primitive parts of Turkey, no Anatolian is reared unless it shows a desire to live with the flocks.

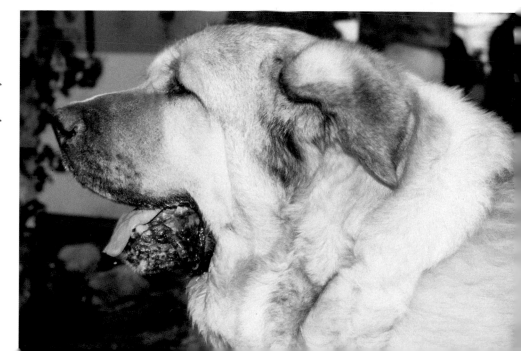

The Spanish Mastiff, along with the Pyrenean Mastiff and the Anatolian Shepherd, has a dual role of guarding both animals and human minders.

Photo: Sheila Atter.

The discerning Mastiff: An ability to perceive situations and draw conclusions is a unique aspect of the group.
Photo courtesy: Betty Baxter.

In the early days of the Anatolian's first introduction to Britain they were referred to as 'Turkish Mastiffs', a name which both suited and described them. I was invited to a private showing of a film taken in the Sivas region of Turkey showing a typical day in the dog's life. The scenery was unforgettable but living conditions hard and matched by the temperament of the watchdogs. The large flock of sheep was moved daily for grazing on the mountains and high plateau; the lambs, after feeding from the ewes, were kept in a compound at the homestead. Four Anatolian dogs, wearing their protective collars made from interlocking nails with the spikes turning outwards as protection against wolves, walked with the flock and were obviously happy in their company. A few cross-bred herding-type dogs of about Collie size were assisting in the actual driving of the sheep.

When on the high plateau the herdsman shouted an order, the herding dogs remained circling around him, rather in the manner of sheepdogs, and the four Anatolians took up their guarding positions at some distance from the grazing sheep. The film crew had followed in a Land Rover, and to reach the plateau over such a terrain was no mean feat. The shepherd, through an interpreter, explained that the dog taking up the position furthest from the sheep was an old dog who had killed many wolves. He explained that the pecking order had long been established, and the others, which were his progeny, were quite subservient to him. He was the pack leader and instructor.

The camera crew unpacked their equipment with the pack leader just watching but making no sign of aggression. Like the good sentinels which these dogs are, all of them just lay down, front paws in front of them, heads moving as they scented the air, watched and listened. The film crew, apart from showing the magnificent views of the region, wanted to obtain a picture of these dogs reacting to the presence of a wolf but, as so often happens, despite some hours of waiting, no wolf appeared. In the meanwhile the flock had moved on and the watchdogs had taken up their same watching pose at the new site.

The interpreter then explained that the camera crew would like to see the dogs' reaction if the shepherd shouted "wolf", which he normally did if, through his rather old-fashioned binoculars, he could see wolves in the distance. The film crew got prepared, climbed back into their vehicle and the word for "wolf" was shouted as the Land Rover began to move steadily forward. The leading dog immediately sprang into action, obviously presuming that it was the vehicle or its occupants which needed to be eliminated. He chased and jumped at the vehicle baring his teeth. The crew took shots of him running alongside, then filming the speedometer reading and back to the dog. He was running and jumping at 30 miles per hour. He suddenly stopped, although in no way looking exhausted, lay down and took up his watching pose. When asked about this, the shepherd explained that where he had stopped was the end of the territory which the flock was allowed to graze and, therefore, anything that happened beyond that line was of no further interest to him. The film was later sold to a television company in the USA.

This demonstrates another group characteristic – the determination to defend owner, home and property, but a degree of disinterest in the defence of anything else.

THE DISCERNING MASTIFF

Discernment in these dogs is almost uncanny. Thirty or more years ago my Bullmastiff, Wyaston Elizabeth Tudor, a determined guard and much-loved house companion, used to always place herself between me and any stranger to whom I was talking. She had never been trained to do this – it was a spontaneous reaction. Occasionally she would lift her top lip and give a low growl if, for instance, I was handed something. I presume that she translated the extending arm as being a possible danger and, therefore, gave due warning.

At that time we had a local man who did part-time help in the garden, whom she knew well and was on good terms with. One of his non-gardening jobs was to bring small sawn logs into the house and place them in a log box. The bitch always checked this. As long as the logs were placed in the box she was quite happy. However, if the log box was too full so that the lid could not be closed and it was necessary to take a log from the box, she would grab his arm in her mouth and firmly hold it until he replaced the log in what she obviously considered to be "her" box. She never bit him as such, but the arm was very securely held. There was no growling but, as the arm was being held, she just looked at him in that old "at you and through you" expression which used to be the hallmark of the Bullmastiff. She had the most amazing discernment and intelligence and was one of those dogs it is impossible to forget. Luckily I have a descendant of hers today, although many years have intervened between the two.

There is no need to train the dogs of the group to guard, provided that they have a home and owner which they consider to be worthy of guarding. Dogs of this size, strength and intelligence, if isolated, restricted in exercise and deprived of being able to give and to receive the companionship and affection which they need, can so easily turn into unpleasant, surly and unreliable animals. This is a theme which runs throughout this book and cannot be over-emphasised, as it is the key to successful ownership. You, as the owner, must "get inside the dog's mind". You must control it, channel its abilities and temperament to your advantage, whether for showing or as a guard and companion. Of course the dog will occasionally transgress and will have to be corrected, but this is part of the partnership which will be accepted as long as it realises that you, the owner, are the pack leader and in overall control. These roles must never be tolerated in reverse.

3 DIET AND NUTRITION

By Alison Jones BVetMed MRCVS

Nutrition has never been the sole domain of the medical practitioner or of the veterinary surgeon. It is relatively recently that the medical profession has developed clinical nutrition to the point where there are professors in the subject, and that vets in companion animal practice have realised that they have an expertise to offer in this area of pet health care. This is curious, because even the earliest medical and veterinary texts refer to the importance of correct diet, and, for many years, vets working with production animals such as cattle, pigs and sheep have been deluged with information about the most appropriate nutrition for these species.

Traditionally, of course, the breeder, neighbours, friends, relatives, the pet shop owner and even the local supermarket have been a main source of advice on feeding for many pet owners. Over the past fifteen years there has been a great increase in public awareness about the relationships between diet and disease, thanks mainly to media interest in the subject (which has at times bordered on hysteria), but also to marketing tactics by major manufacturing companies. Few people will not have heard about the alleged health benefits of 'high fibre', 'low fat', 'low cholesterol', 'high polyunsaturates', 'low saturates' and 'oat bran' diets. While there are usually some data to support the use of these types of diets in certain situations, frequently the benefits are overstated, if they exist at all.

Breeders have always actively debated the 'best way' to feed dogs. Most Mastiff owners are aware of the importance of good bone development and the role of nutrition in achieving optimal skeletal characteristics. However, as a vet in practice, I was constantly amazed and bewildered at the menus given to new puppy owners by breeders. These, all too frequently, consisted of complex home-made recipes, usually based on large amounts of fresh meat, goat's milk, and a vast array of mineral supplements. These diets were often very imbalanced and could easily result in skeletal and other growth abnormalities.

Domestic dogs have little opportunity to select their own diet, so it is important to realise that they are solely dependent upon their owners to provide all the nourishment that they need. In this chapter, I aim to explain what those needs are, to dispel a few myths, and to give some guidance about selecting the most appropriate diet for your dog.

ESSENTIAL NUTRITION

Dogs have a common ancestry with carnivores, and are still often classified as such although, from a nutritional point of

Good bone development is essential in the Mastiff breeds, and nutrition plays a vital part in achieving this.

Photo courtesy: Betty Baxter.

view, they are actually omnivores. This means that dogs can obtain all the essential nutrients that they need from dietary sources consisting of either animal or plant material. As far as we know, dogs can survive on food derived solely from plants – that is, they can be fed a "vegetarian diet". The same is not true for domesticated cats, which are still obligate carnivores, whose nutritional needs cannot be met by an exclusively vegetarian diet.

ENERGY
All living cells require energy, and the more active they are the more energy they burn up. Individual dogs have their own energy needs, which can vary, even between dogs of the same breed, age, sex and activity level. Breeders will recognise the scenario in which some littermates develop differently, one tending towards obesity, another on the lean side, even when they are fed exactly the same amount of food. For adult maintenance a Mastiff will need an energy intake of approximately 30 kcal/lb body weight (or 65 kcal/kg body weight). If you know the energy density of the food that you are giving, you can work out how much your dog needs; but you must remember that this is only an approximation, and you will need to adjust the amount you feed to suit each individual dog. This is best achieved by regular weighing of your dog and then maintaining an "optimum" body weight.

If you are feeding a commercially prepared food, you should be aware that the feeding guide recommended by the manufacturer is also based on average energy needs, and therefore you may need to increase or decrease the amount you give to meet your own individual dog's requirements. In some countries (such as those within the European Union) legislation may not allow the energy content to appear on the label of a prepared pet food; however, reputable manufacturing companies can and will provide this information upon request.

When considering different foods it is important to compare the 'metabolisable energy', which is the amount of energy in the food that is available to a dog. Some companies will provide you with figures for the 'gross energy', which is not as useful, because some of that energy (sometimes a substantial amount) will not be digested, absorbed and utilised.

There are many circumstances in which your dog's energy requirement may change from its basic adult maintenance energy requirement (MER):

WORK	
Light	1.1 - 1.5 x MER
Heavy	2 - 4 x MER
Inactivity	0.8 x MER
PREGNANCY	
First 6 weeks	1 x MER
Last 3 weeks	1.1 - 1.3 x MER
Peak lactation	2 - 4 x MER
Growth	1.2 - 2 x MER
ENVIRONMENT	
Cold	1.25 - 1.75 x MER
Heat	Up to 2.5 x MER

Light to moderate activity (work) barely increases energy needs, and it is only when dogs are doing heavy work, such as pulling sleds, that energy requirements are significantly increased. Note that there is no increased energy requirement during pregnancy, except in the last three weeks, and the main need for high energy intake is during the lactation period. If a bitch is getting sufficient energy, she should not lose weight or condition during pregnancy and lactation. Because the energy requirement is so great during lactation (up to 4 x MER), it can sometimes be impossible to meet this need by feeding conventional adult maintenance diets, because the bitch cannot physically eat enough food. As a result she will lose weight and condition. Switching to a high-energy diet is usually necessary to avoid this.

As dogs get older their energy needs usually decrease. This is due in large part to being less active either caused by getting less exercise, e.g. if their owner is elderly, or enforced by locomotor problems such as arthritis, but there are also changes in the metabolism of older animals that reduce the amount of energy that they need. The aim should be to maintain body weight throughout old age, and regular exercise can play an important part in this. If there is any tendency to decrease or increase weight this should be countered by increasing or decreasing energy intake accordingly. If the body weight changes by more than ten per cent from usual, veterinary attention should be sought, in case there is a medical problem causing the weight change.

Changes in environmental conditions and all forms of stress (including showing), which particularly affects dogs with a nervous temperament, can increase energy needs. Some dogs when kennelled for long periods lose weight due to a stress-related increase in energy requirements which cannot easily be met by a maintenance diet. A high-energy food containing at least 1900 kcal of metabolisable energy/lb dry matter (4.2 kcal/gram) may be needed in order to maintain body weight under these circumstances. Excessive energy intake, on the other hand, results in obesity that can have very serious effects on health.

Orthopaedic problems such as rupture of the cruciate ligaments are more likely to occur in overweight dogs. This condition, which often requires surgical intervention, may present as a sudden-onset complete lameness or a gradually worsening hindleg lameness. Dogs frequently develop heart disease in old age, and obesity puts significant extra demands on the cardiovascular system, with potentially serious consequences. Obesity is also a predisposing cause of non-insulin dependent diabetes mellitus, and has many other detrimental effects on health, including reducing resistance to infection and increasing anaesthetic and surgical risks. Once obesity is present, activity tends to decrease and it becomes even more necessary to decrease energy intake; otherwise more body weight is gained and the situation is made worse.

Energy is only available from the fat, carbohydrate and protein in a dog's diet. A gram of fat provides 2 1/4 times as much energy as a gram of carbohydrate or protein and so high-energy requirements are best met by feeding a relatively high-fat diet. Dogs rarely develop the cardiovascular conditions, such as atherosclerosis and coronary artery disease, that have been associated with high-fat intake in humans.

Owners may think that protein is the source of energy needed for exercise and performance, but this is not true. Protein is a relatively poor source of energy because a large amount of the energy theoretically available from it is lost in 'meal-induced heat'. Meal-induced heat is the metabolic heat 'wasted' in the digestion, absorption and utilisation of the protein. Fat and carbohydrates are better sources of energy for performance.

For obese or obesity-prone dogs a low energy intake is indicated, and there are now specially prepared diets that have a very low energy density; those which are most effective have a high fibre content. Your vet will advise you about the most appropriate type of diet if you have such a problem dog. Incidentally, if you do have an overweight dog it is important to seek veterinary advice in case it is associated with some other medical condition.

CHOOSING A DIET

The first important consideration to make when selecting a maintenance diet is that it should meet the energy requirements of your dog. In some situations, specially formulated high-energy or low-energy diets will be needed to achieve this. Other nutrients that must be provided in the diet include essential amino acids (from dietary protein), essential fatty acids (from dietary fat), minerals and vitamins. Carbohydrates are not an essential dietary component for dogs, because they can synthesise sufficient glucose from other sources.

Do not fall into the trap of thinking that if a diet is good for a human it must be good for a dog. There are many differences between a human's nutritional needs and those of the dog. For example, humans need a daily supply of vitamin C in the diet, but under normal circumstances a dog can synthesise its own vitamin C, and so a dietary source is not essential. The amount of nutrients that a dog needs will vary according to its stage of life, environment and activity level. For the rest of this chapter life-cycle feeding will be discussed.

FEEDING FOR GROWTH

Growing animals have tissues that are actively developing and growing in size, and so it is not surprising that they have a relatively higher requirement for energy, protein, vitamins and minerals than their adult counterparts (based on the daily intake of these nutrients per kg body weight).

Birth weight usually doubles in seven to ten days and puppies should gain 1-2 grams/day/lb (2-4 grams/day/kg) of anticipated adult weight. An important key to the successful rearing of neonates is to reduce the puppies' energy loss by maintaining their environmental temperature, as well as by ensuring sufficient energy intake. Bitch's milk is of particular importance to the puppy

GROWTH AND DEVELOPMENT IN THE TIBETAN MASTIFF

Photos courtesy: Pamela Jeans-Brown.

Three days old (two gold, one grey, and three black and tan).

Six weeks old, showing good bone and overall conformation.

Ten weeks old – note the muzzle and head development.

Twelve weeks old, showing good back and tail-set.

Thirteen weeks old: The puppy appears balanced and in proportion.

Sixteen weeks old: The littermates are showing reasonably uniform development.

Eighteen weeks old: Large, strong bones are evident.

Six months old: The adult shape is apparent, with large bone and good muscle tone. This youngster shows a deep muzzle and a strong neck, good depth of body, a level back with good tail-set and carriage

during the first few hours of life, as this early milk (called colostrum) provides some passive immunity to the puppy because of the maternal antibodies it contains. These will help to protect the puppy until it can produce its own immune response to challenge from infectious agents.

Survival rate is greatly decreased in puppies that do not get colostrum from their mother. Orphaned puppies are best fed a proprietary milk replacer, according to the manufacturer's recommendations, unless a foster mother can be found. Your vet will be able to help if you find yourself in such a situation.

Obesity must be avoided during puppyhood, as so-called "juvenile obesity" will increase the number of fat cells in the body, and so predispose the animal to obesity for the rest of its life. Overeating is most likely to occur when puppies are fed free choice (ad lib) throughout the day, particularly if there is competition between littermates. A better method is to feed a

puppy a daily ration based on its body weight divided into two to four meals per day – the number decreasing as it gets older. Any food remaining after twenty minutes should be removed.

Charts can be used to check that your puppy is gaining weight at the right rate for his age. Remember they are only a guide, but if consulted in conjunction with your veterinary surgeon they can be very beneficial in helping to reduce not only juvenile obesity but also many developmental orthopaedic conditions such as hip dysplasia and Osteochondritis dissecans (OCD).

Hip dysplasia has now been shown to be affected not only by genetics but also by environmental factors in the early weeks of life (such as the condition of the flooring the puppies are reared on) and by food intake. Studies have shown that feeding large-breed puppies, such as the Mastiff, ad lib increases the risk of the dog developing hip dysplasia later in life. Many pet food manufacturers now produce special growth diets indicated for larger-breed puppies. These are beneficial at helping to reduce developmental bone disease, if fed according to the manufacturer's recommendations. They contain a lower level of energy and a reduced calcium content. It may at first seem odd that a breed such as the Mastiff, which has to develop a lot of bone during the period of growth, would actually benefit from a reduced level of calcium. However, many studies have now shown the dangers of excessive calcium intake in the development of optimal skeletal structure. The larger and heavier the dog, the greater the risk.

Proper growth and development is dependent upon a sufficient intake of essential nutrients, and if you consider how rapidly a puppy grows, usually achieving half its adult weight by four months of age, it is not surprising that nutritional deficiencies, excesses or imbalances can have disastrous results, especially in breeds such as the Mastiff. Deficiency diseases are rarely seen in veterinary practice nowadays, mainly because proprietary pet foods contain more than sufficient amounts of the essential nutrients. When a deficiency disease is diagnosed it is usually associated with an unbalanced home-made diet. A classic example of this is dogs fed on an all-meat diet. Meat is very low in calcium but high in phosphorus, and demineralisation of bones occurs on this type

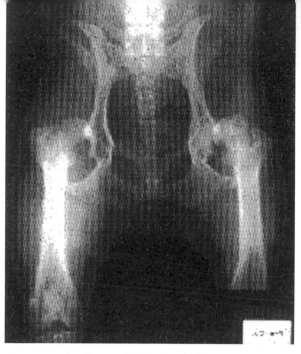

An example of severely dysplastic hips.

of diet. This leads to very thin bones that fracture easily, frequently resulting in folding fractures caused simply by weight-bearing.

Development of a good skeleton results from an interaction of genetic, environmental, and nutritional influences. The genetic component can be influenced by the breeder in a desire to improve the breed. Environmental influences, including housing and activity level, can be controlled by the new puppy owner with good advice from the breeder. However, nutrition is one of the most important factors influencing correct development of the puppy's bones and muscles.

In growing puppies it is particularly important to provide minerals, but in the correct proportions to each other. The calcium: phosphorus ratio should ideally be

Levels of calcium must be monitored when feeding large-breed puppies.
Photo: Nash

This Neapolitan bitch shows good muscle tone, an important factor in a breed of this size and weight.

1.2-1.4:1, and certainly within the wider range of 1-2:1. If there is more phosphorus than calcium in the diet (i.e. an inverse calcium:phosphorus ratio), normal bone development may be affected. Care also has to be taken to avoid feeding too much mineral. A diet for growing large-breed puppies should not contain more than about one per cent calcium (this is about half the maximum amount recommended for smaller-breed puppies). Excessive calcium intake actually causes stunting of growth, and an intake of 3.3 per cent calcium has been shown to result in serious skeletal deformities, including deformities of the carpus, OCD, wobbler syndrome and hip dysplasia. These are common diseases, and while other factors such as genetic inheritance may also be involved, excessive mineral intake should be considered a risk factor in all cases. Bullmastiffs are genetically predisposed to a form of OCD known as ununited anconeal process (also called elbow

dysplasia), in which a small bone within the elbow joint fails to develop correctly. This leads to arthritis at a very young age. If diagnosed early enough the condition can be surgically treated; however, normal joint function may not be possible in all cases.

If a diet already contains sufficient calcium, it is dangerously easy to increase the calcium content to well over three per cent if you give mineral supplements as well. Some commercially available treats and snacks are very high in salt, protein and calories. They can significantly upset a carefully balanced diet, and it is advisable to ask your vet's opinion of the various treats available and to use them only very occasionally.

A growing puppy is best fed a proprietary pet food that has been specifically formulated to meet its nutritional needs. Those that are available as both canned and dry are especially suitable to rear even the youngest of puppies. Home-made diets may theoretically be adequate, but it is difficult to

A bitch's nutritional needs are at their greatest during lactation

Photo courtesy: Lyn Say.

ensure that all the nutrients are provided in an available form. The only way to be sure about the adequacy of a diet is to have it analysed for its nutritional content and to put it through controlled feeding trials.

Supplements should only be used with rations that are known to be deficient, in order to provide whatever is missing from the diet. With a complete balanced diet nothing should be missing. If you use supplements with an already balanced diet, you could create an imbalance, and/or provide excessive amounts of nutrients, particularly minerals.

Nutritional management alone is not sufficient to prevent developmental bone disease. However, we can prevent some skeletal disease by feeding appropriate amounts of a good-quality balanced diet. Dietary deficiencies are of minimal concern with the ever-increasing range of commercial diets specifically prepared for young growing dogs. The potential for harm is in over-nutrition from excess consumption and supplementation.

FEEDING FOR PREGNANCY AND LACTATION

There is no need to increase the amount of food being fed to a bitch during early and mid-pregnancy, but there will be an increased demand for energy (i.e. carbohydrates and fats collectively), protein, minerals and vitamins during the last three weeks. A bitch's nutritional requirements will be maximum during lactation, particularly if she has a large litter to feed. Avoid giving calcium supplementation during pregnancy, as a high intake can frustrate calcium availability during milk production, and can increase the chances of eclampsia (also called milk fever or puerperal tetany) occurring.

During pregnancy a bitch should maintain her body weight and condition. If she loses weight her energy intake needs to be increased. A specifically formulated growth-type diet is recommended to meet her nutritional needs at this time. If a bitch is on a diet formulated for this stage of her life, and she develops eclampsia, or has had previous episodes of the disease, your vet may advise calcium supplementation. If given during pregnancy, this is only advisable during the very last few days of pregnancy when milk let-down is occurring, and preferably is given only during lactation (i.e. after whelping).

It should be noted that due to their reduced calcium and energy content, the special larger-breed growth diets mentioned earlier are contraindicated for pregnancy and lactation, regardless of the size of the dam.

FEEDING FOR MAINTENANCE AND OLD AGE

The objective of good nutrition is to provide all the energy and essential nutrients that a dog needs in sufficient amounts to avoid deficiency, and at the same time to limit their supply so as not to cause over-nutrition or toxicity. Some nutrients are known to play a role in disease processes, and it is prudent to avoid unnecessarily high intakes of these whenever possible. The vets at Hill's Science and Technology Centre in Topeka, Kansas, are specialists in canine clinical nutrition and they are particularly concerned about the potential health risks associated with too high an intake of the following nutrients during a dog's adult life:

• Protein
• Sodium (salt)
• Phosphorus

These nutrients are thought to have an important and serious impact once disease is present, particularly in heart and kidney diseases. Kidney failure and heart failure are very common in older dogs and it is believed to be important to avoid feeding diets high in these nutrients to such an "at risk" group of dogs. Furthermore, these nutrients may be detrimental to dogs even before there is any evidence of disease. It is known that salt, for example, can be retained in dogs with subclinical heart disease, before there is any outward evidence of illness. Salt retention is an important contributing factor in the development of fluid retention (congestion),

swelling of the limbs (oedema) and dropsy (ascites).

A leading veterinary cardiologist in the USA has claimed that 40 per cent of dogs over five years of age, and 80 per cent of dogs over ten years have some change in the heart – either endocardiosis or myocardial fibrosis (or both). Both of these lesions may reduce heart function. Phosphorus retention is an important consequence of advancing kidney disease, which encourages mineral deposition in the soft tissues of the body, including the kidneys themselves, a condition known as "nephrocalcinosis". Such deposits damage the kidneys even more, and hasten the onset of kidney failure.

As a dog ages there are two major factors that determine its nutritional needs:

1. The dog's changing nutritional requirements due to the effects of age on organ function and metabolism;
2. The increased likelihood of the presence of subclinical diseases, many of which have protracted courses during which nutrient intake may influence progression of the condition.

Many Mastiff owners are aware of a condition called gastric dilatation and torsion, commonly known as "bloat". This potentially life-threatening condition was previously thought to be due to the ingestion of a high fat or carbohydrate meal. Current thinking is that bloat is due to aerophagia (the intake of large amounts of air with a meal), common in greedy individuals, and the predisposing factors may be:

• Genetic make-up
• Competitive feeding
• Strenuous exercise around meal times
• Excitement at feeding time.

The last three factors encourage rapid eating.

Special highly digestible diets are available from vets to feed to at-risk individuals.

Energy requirements usually decrease with increasing age, and food intake should be adjusted accordingly. Also the dietary intake of some nutrients needs to be minimised – in particular, protein, phosphorus, sodium and total energy intake. Dietary intake of other nutrients may need to be increased to meet the needs of some older dogs, notably essential fatty acids, some vitamins, some specific amino acids and zinc. Unlike humans, calcium and phosphorus do not need to be supplemented in ageing dogs – indeed to do so may prove detrimental.

INTERPRETATION OF LABELLING ON PET FOODS

Labelling laws differ from one country to the next. For example, pet foods sold in the USA must carry a Guaranteed Analysis, which states a maximum or a minimum amount for the various nutrients in the food. Pet foods sold in Europe must carry a Typical (as fed) Analysis, which is a declaration of the average amount of nutrients found from analysis of the product.

"COMPLETE" VERSUS "COMPLEMENTARY"

In the UK a pet food must declare whether it is "Complete" or "Complementary". A "Complete" pet food must provide all the nutrients required to satisfy the needs of the group of pet animals for which it is recommended. At the time of writing there is no obligation for a manufacturer to submit such a diet to feeding trials to ensure that it is adequate.

In the USA some manufacturers submit their pet foods to the feeding trials approved by the Association of American Feed Control Officials (AAFCO) to ensure that they meet the nutritional requirements of the National Research Council (e.g. the Hill's Pet Nutrition range of Science Plan products). A "Complementary" pet food needs to be fed with some other foodstuff in order to meet the needs of the animal. Anyone feeding a complementary food as a substantial part of a dog's ration is obliged to find out what it should be fed with, in order to balance the ration. Failure to do so could result in serious deficiency or imbalance of nutrients.

DRY MATTER

The water content of pet foods varies greatly,

Recordbreaker: Zorba de la Susa earned a place in the 'Guinness Book of Records' as the heaviest dog in the world, weighing 315 lbs.

particularly in canned products. In the USA there is a legal maximum limit (78 per cent) which cannot be exceeded, but no such limit is in force in Europe and some European canned pet foods contain as much as 86 per cent water. Legislation now makes it compulsory for the water content to be declared on the label and this is important, because to compare one pet food with another, one should consider the percentage of a nutrient in the dry matter of food.

For example, two pet foods may declare the protein content to be 10 per cent in the Typical Analysis printed on the label. If one product contains 75 per cent water it has 25 per cent dry matter, so the protein content is actually $10/25 \times 100 = 40$ per cent. If the other product contains 85 per cent water, the protein content is $10/15 \times 100 = 66.6$ per cent. This type of calculation (called Dry Weight Analysis) becomes even more important when comparing canned with dry products, as the water-content of dry food is usually only 7.5-12 per cent.

You can only effectively compare pet foods if you know:

1. The food's energy density
2. The dry weight analysis of the individual nutrients.

COST

The only valid way to compare the cost of one food against another is to compare the daily feeding costs to meet all the needs of your dog. A high-energy, nutritionally concentrated type of diet might cost more to buy per kilogram of food, but it could be cheaper to feed on a cost per day basis. Conversely, a poor-quality, poorly digestible diet may be cheaper per kilogram to buy, but actually cost more per day to feed, because you need to feed much more food to meet the dog's requirements. The only valid reason for feeding a food is that it meets the

nutritional requirements of your dog. To do that, you need to read between the marketing strategies of the manufacturers and select a diet that you know provides your dog with what it needs.

HOME-MADE DIETS

What about home-made recipes? Well, theoretically it is possible to make a home-made diet that will meet all the nutritional requirements of a dog, and all foodstuffs have some nutritional value, but not all published recipes may actually achieve what they claim. The reason is that there is no strict quality control of ingredients, and the bioavailability of nutrients may vary from one ingredient source to another. If you feed a correctly balanced home-made diet, they are often time-consuming to prepare, usually need the addition of a vitamin/mineral supplement, and if prepared accurately can be expensive. Variations in raw ingredients will cause fluctuations in nutritional value.

The only way to be absolutely sure that a home-made diet has the nutritional profile that you want is to mix all the food ingredients plus supplements, treats, snacks, scraps etc. in a large pot, homogenise them and have a sample analysed chemically (this costs well over £100 (US$160) for a partial analysis). Then compare this analytical content with the published levels for nutrient requirements.

You may feel that feeding an existing home-made recipe passed on to you or developed over a number of years is adequate. But how do you know? What is the phosphorus level of the diet that you are feeding? An undesirably high level of intake may take a long time before it results in obvious problems.

Sometimes the condition of your dog(s) will give you an idea that all is not well with the diet you are feeding. One of the most common questions asked by breeders at dog shows is "Can you recommend a diet that will keep weight on my dogs?" Unless there is a medical problem (and in such cases you should always seek veterinary attention first), the only reason, usually, that dogs have difficulty maintaining their weight is simply that they have an inadequate energy intake. This does not mean that they are not eating well – they could be eating like a horse, but if the food is relatively low in energy content, and if it is poorly digestible, your dog may be unable to eat sufficient food to meet its energy needs. Large bulky faeces are an indicator of low digestibility. A poor-looking, dull, dry or scurfy coat, poor skin and other external signs of unthriftiness may also be an indicator of poor nutrition. How many "poor-doers" and dogs with recurrent infections are on a diet with a marginal nutritional level of adequacy?

SUMMARY

The importance of nutrition has been known for many years and yet, sadly, it is still surrounded by too many old wives' tales, myths and unsubstantiated claims. The emergence of clinical nutrition as a subject in its own right has set the stage for the future. Hopefully, in the future we shall hear about the benefits and dangers of different feeding practices from scientists who can base their statements on fact, not merely opinion. Already we know that a dog that is ill has different nutritional requirements to a healthy dog. In some cases dietary management can even offer an alternative way to manage clinical cases. For example, we currently have the ability to dissolve struvite stones in the urinary bladder simply by manipulating dietary intake instead of having to resort to surgery.

But please note, dietary management is not "alternative medicine". Proper nutrition is key to everything that a living animal has to do, be it work or repairing tissues after an injury. It is not an option; it is a crucial part of looking after an animal properly. If you own a dog, you should at least ensure that the food you give supplies all his/her needs, and avoids the excessive intake of energy or nutrients that may play a role in diseases which your pet could develop.

4 CELEBRATING THE MASTIFF

By Nick Waters

The concept of purity of lineage and the aesthetic qualities which we appreciate in dogs are, in relationship to the history of the dog as a species, a comparatively recent phenomenon. How dogs performed their duty, or did a job of work, was far more important than how they looked. However, if one considers the Mastiff as being a large, powerful, well-boned dog, used for guarding, hunting and to wage war, and the name used in that context, then the 'breed' has changed little over the centuries.

The main properties of the Mastiff breeds which have changed over the last century or so have been head size and shape. For the purpose of this chapter, the word 'Mastiff' will, in the main, be used to describe types of dogs which were known as such throughout the centuries prior to c.1850 and will not necessarily refer to what we today know as the 'English' Mastiff.

EARLY REPRESENTATIONS

Looking firstly at some of the early representations of the Mastiff, of the four dogs shown on the lower portion of the limestone Steel of Antef-AA of XIIth Dynasty Egypt, about 2,000BC, one is a dog of Mastiff proportions when compared to the other three dogs represented. No less an authority on the dog than Edward C. Ash suggests that this dog is of Mastiff type. One of the dog's names translates to 'black' which, according to Ash, "doubtlessly alludes to the colour." Black, of course, has always been considered the ideal colour for a guarding dog.

This Egyptian dog is shown wearing an almost ruff-like collar and, for generations in Tibet, all valuable Mastiffs wore ruffs as a protection for the throat in the event of a fight. A number of bas-reliefs and terracotta models in the British Museum show dogs which are quite clearly Mastiff types. Assur-Bani-Pal and his attendants preparing for the hunt, Assyrian Mastiffs hunting wild horses, and the relief showing hunters with nets and Mastiffs from the walls of Assur-Bani-Pal's palace at Nineveh, c.668-628BC, all show powerful, strong, heavy-boned dogs, with large heads, albeit not short in muzzle. All are shown displaying great courage and purpose, which are attributes synonymous with the name Mastiff.

As an indicator to the size of these animals, the Mastiffs bringing down the horses, with the aid of huntsmen with spears, are similar in size to the foals. Likewise, the Babylonian bas-relief of c.2,200BC shows a huntsman leading a dog the size of a pony. Also from King Assur-Bani-Pal's palace are terracotta dog models, probably artists' models, which again show the same large, powerful dogs. In the case of the models the dogs are shown

Above: Assyrian bas-relief in the British Museum showing Mastiffs being used on the wild horse. From E.C. Ash, 'Dogs their History and Development', 1927.

Above: Assyrian bas-relief in the British Museum showing Assur-Bani-Pal and his attendants preparing for the hunt. From Robert Leighton's 'The New Book of the Dog', 1907.

Right: Nineveh bas-relief in the British Museum showing hunters with nets and Mastiff. From E.C. Ash, 'Dogs their History and Development', 1927.

with 'hairy manes' which is, no doubt, one of the reasons for Mastiffs at times being likened to the lion. A roughness of coat around the neck of the Mastiff is today an indicator of true type, and the Tibetan Mastiff is, of course, decidedly hairy.

It is believed that all the breeds of Mastiff today, as well as other large breeds, such as the St Bernard, Bernese Mountain Dog, Pyrenean Mountain Dog and others, owe their very existence to the great Mastiff dogs from the East, and Tibet in particular. Marco Polo is supposed to have found in Tibet 'dogs the size of asses', and Turner in his *Embassy to Tibet* mentions seeing a row of wooden cages containing "huge dogs, tremendously fierce, strong and noisy".

THE GREYHOUND INFLUENCE
In 350BC Aristotle listed the most useful known breeds and among them was the Molossian, a large, powerful dog which has, no doubt, played its part in the chain of evolution to our present-day Mastiff breeds. Breeds in Greek art are difficult to identify, for many artists had a tendency to stylise or idealise their subjects. By this age though, the Greyhound was certainly the breed most frequently seen in art.

Both the Greeks and the Romans used large, heavy dogs to help them fight their battles, with the Romans being the first to clad their dogs in protective armour, with spiked iron collars to protect the dog's neck. Some of these ancient war dogs, complete with armour, are depicted on the column of

After Sir Anthony Van Dyck, 18th century English School Portrait of Charles II as a boy with a Mastiff.

Photo courtesy: Sara Davenport Fine Paintings.

Marcus Aurelius in Rome. The practice of putting spiked iron collars on dogs used for guarding continues to the present day in the more remote parts of Europe, the Middle East and Asia.

The arrival of the Middle Ages saw changing attitudes towards the dog which were based on old superstitions in which, in many cases, the dog star, Sirius, was at the centre. Some societies came to hate the dog. As the Middle Ages progressed the dog slowly began to regain importance, aided greatly by the hunt, in which the dog played a fundamental role. By the end of the Middle Ages the dog is seen as playing an extremely important role in the social hierarchy which surrounded the hunt.

Although the Greyhound, or dogs of Greyhound type, predominated, one can argue that there was evidence of a larger,

more powerful dog still being used – the Bayeux Tapestry, showing King Harold setting off with his hawk and hounds, being one such example in art. Bearing in mind that dogs were bred for a purpose, rather than for their appearance, the Greyhound and the Mastiff could easily have been crossed to give strength and stamina to one and speed to the other. As recently as the late 18th century, Lord Orford crossed the Greyhound with the Bulldog to give strength and stamina to the former.

THE ITALIAN FOCUS
Large dogs of Mastiff type were never far from the surface in art and this has remained true since earliest times. In Church art, a number of gargoyles depict dogs of Mastiff proportions and in the *Vision of St Hubert* in the Chapel of Saint-Blaise, Chateau

d'Amboise, the three dogs before the stag are far more Mastiff-like than ever they are like Greyhounds or even Bloodhounds.

The closing Middle Ages and the Renaissance periods saw art being focused on the scholarly areas of Europe, of which Italy could be considered the centre.

Andrea Mantegna (c.1431-1506) was a Northern Italian painter and engraver who, in 1460 became court painter to the Gonzaga family and in their Palace in Mantua he painted frescos of incidents in the lives of his patrons. Most important is the ceiling of the Camera degli Sposi in the Palazzo Ducale which shows a hunting scene of the Gonzaga family which Mantegna completed c.1474. In the scene are two Mastiffs with cropped ears and powerful heads, albeit with muzzles of equal length to the skulls. Mantegna's ceiling, creating an illusion of an opened roof, led directly to Correggio and other masters' exploitation of illusionistic perspective.

Mantegna's frescos gave us units which made up a whole picture – the horse, the figures, the dogs, the bushes in the foreground and the landscape beyond were as one. The same can also be said of the Bayeux Tapestry, the Nineveh bas-relief and other early forms of art, each component contributing to the whole picture.

THE DOG AS AN ACCOMPANIMENT

As the appreciation of 'high art' spread from Italy, and to Northern Europe in particular, and court portraiture became increasingly more popular, we see the dog moving from being part of a balanced picture to become an accompaniment – a means of giving a further dimension to the sitter – one of compassion, understanding, even dominance and power.

The Children of Charles I by the Flemish artist, Sir Anthony Van Dyck (1599-1641), which he painted c.1630 and which is in the collection of Her Majesty The Queen, is perhaps the best known of the early portraits where the dog is an accompaniment. The painting shows the future King Charles II of England resting his arm on the head of a large Mastiff-like dog, which shows that the breed then was just as capable of being docile and friendly as it was ferocious, as had been seen much earlier in art. When it became the fashion in the latter half of the 19th century for artists to copy the works of great masters, Van Dyck's painting was one of those copied the most.

It was Titian (c.1487-1576) who had introduced the dog into portraiture and the practice soon became established, with large dogs of Mastiff proportions playing a leading role. The courts of Europe had their dwarfs and, to emphasise their diminutive stature, they were frequently painted being accompanied by a large dog of Mastiff type. The Spanish painter, Antonio Moro (1517-1575), painted Cardinal de Granville's dwarf, and fellow Spaniard Diego Velazquez (1599-1660) painted the dwarf at the court of Philip IV. The dog in the latter picture, together with the one accompanying Prince Baltasar Carlos in Velazquez' painting of c.1635-36, are both shown as being large parti-coloured animals. Could they be the same type of dog?.

Such paintings only serve to emphasise the fact that for centuries any large powerful dog was referred to as a Mastiff. Throughout Europe the Mastiff was to remain popular in portraiture. In England the painting of Lord Lempster, which is attributed to Sir Peter Lely (1618-1680), shows his Lordship accompanied by a fawn Mastiff, while in Spain, Francesco de Goya (1746-1828) shows two children in conversation over the back of a brindle Mastiff. Both dogs would not look too out of place in the Mastiff ring today.

ANIMAL BAITING

As well as being portrayed as the gentle

Bear Baiting from Richard Pynson's 'Antibassicon,' 1521.

giant, the Mastiff still remained popular in sporting pictures and particularly where baiting was concerned. The German painter, David Kloker Ehrenstrahl (1629-1698), became court painter to the Swedish court of Carl XI and is, today, considered the 'father of Swedish painting'. While at the Swedish Court he completed a number of paintings in the 1670s which showed large Mastiff-type dogs being pitted against bears and other large animals.

His dogs were always painted wearing large, ornate collars, some with spikes to protect their throats. Such collars are reputed to have been popular in Sweden from the older Viking times. Two of four dogs in a painting dated 1674 which shows a bear being baited are credited as being 'very big English Mastiffs'. In Britain the Long Parliament abolished bear-baiting in 1642, but it was revived after the Restoration to be finally made illegal in 1835.

A similar composition to Ehrenstrahl's painting is Abraham Hondius' *Bear Baiting* which he painted in 1650. The large, powerful dogs, which are in a variety of colours and with cropped ears, all wear heavy collars. Dutch-born Hondius (c.1638-1695) moved to London from Rotterdam about 1666 and in his book *Dog Painting* (1840-1940), William Secord observes that Hondius was one of the first foreigners to influence British artists in the field of painting animals.

Hondius' painting, *The Dog Market*, which he painted in 1677, was the direct result of the craze for collecting, and of the new interest in dogs which the new wealthy merchant class in the Netherlands were displaying. The picture shows some thirty different types of dogs, of which the central dog is a large Mastiff, and it is one of the earliest representations in art to show a head of the proportions which are today accepted as 'English' Mastiff type.

MYSTERY AND ROMANCE

From all this art which has survived, it is evident that a type of dog instantly

Lion, one of the many Lyme Hall Mastiffs, by an unknown artist.

The Mastiff from Comte de Buffon's 'Natural History', one of the first complete English versions being published in 1792.

recognisable as a Mastiff was well-established in what was then the 'civilised world'. If we accept as a Mastiff any large powerful dog, bred for baiting, guarding, and in earlier times hunting – a dog bred for a purpose, rather than purity of lineage – then the 'Mastiff' is a very ancient breed, and it is from these dogs that today's Mastiff breeds, now individually identified by their purity of lineage and type, have evolved.

No doubt because of their size, the various tasks they performed over the centuries, and their ancient origins, there is a lot of mystery and romance surrounding the Mastiff. In some small way the breed's association with Lyme Hall near Manchester and the Legh family has helped fuel the romantic image of the breed (see Chapter Five).

In 1604 King James I sent King Philip III of Spain a couple of 'Lyme Hounds' and some years later Velazquez painted the children of his patron, King Philip IV, with a large Mastiff in the foreground. It is tempting to surmise that this dog was

descended from the dogs of Lyme Hall. A copy of this picture, entitled *Las Meninas*, the original of which is in Madrid, hangs at Lyme.

Early evidence of large dogs at Lyme are the two Elizabethan stained glass windows, one in a porter's lodge, the other in a drawing-room, and both show dogs of Mastiff type. By the late 19th century the Mastiffs at Lyme had changed somewhat from the dogs in the Elizabethan windows, although they were still somewhat plain in head, even by the standards of that time. The portrait of Lion by an unknown artist, which hangs in the entrance hall at Lyme, is similar in type to the dogs born in the last litter of Mastiffs to be bred at Lyme in c.1914.

In 1872 the Leghs were granted the baronetcy of Newton and the first Lord Newton chose 'Two Mastiffs proper collared sable' as supporters to his coat of arms.

BULL BAITING

Although one associates Bulldogs with bull baiting and bull running, the Mastiff was pitted against anything, from maimed horses to bears and to bulls. Bull running involving the use of Mastiffs was popular at both Stamford in Lincolnshire and Tutbury in Staffordshire. An exceedingly rare 18th century Staffordshire pottery bull-baiting group, in white lustre, shows a dog of far more Mastiff proportions than the Bulldog of the period. The dog, though, is shown

Exceedingly rare 18th century Staffordshire pottery group.

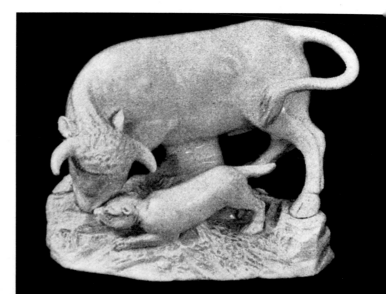

smaller than we would perceive a Mastiff to be, but the bull is shown on higher ground and not crouching, as is the dog, and the Staffordshire potters were never too concerned about perspective.

Edward Alleyn, founder of Dulwich College, held, during the reign of King James I, the patent of 'The Royal Game of Bears, Bulls and Mastiff Dogs'. Evidence that the Mastiff was used for bull baiting well into the 18th century is a poem in Latin and English written by an unknown author. In the five-page preface the author condemns the community for taking too much interest in politics and the pulpit and suggests this evil could be done away with by the encouragement of bull baiting 'throughout the whole Kingdom'.

The dogs used for baiting are called Mastiffs and described as 'keen hard-mouthed curs'. It should perhaps be noted that if Thomas Boreman's *A Description of Three Hundred Animals* of 1736 is any sort of reliable guide, then from the illustrations therein it was hard to distinguish between the Bulldog and the Mastiff of the period.

MASTIFFS IN LITERATURE
In literature the Mastiff has been well illustrated since earliest times. In Richard

Mastiff bitch and puppies from George Turberville's 'Noble Arte of Venerie, or Hunting', 1575.

'The Mastiff' from a woodcut by Thomas Bewick.

Pynson's *Antibassicon* published in London in 1521, a bear roped to a stake is shown being baited by six cropped-eared Mastiffs. George Turberville shows us the more gentle side of the breed in his *The Noble Arte of Venerie or Hunting* published in 1575 (the very title indicates that the breed was still being used for hunting and not just baiting and fighting). In this work a bitch is shown nursing a litter of puppies.

In his woodcut illustration towards the end of the 18th century Thomas Bewick continues to show us a large parti-coloured dog as a Mastiff. The dog is shown against a background of a veritable collection of breeds, including another Mastiff who is obviously looked up to by all the other dogs, for they appear subservient to his superiority.

The opening of the 19th century marked the appearance of what has now become one of the rarest of dog books printed in the English language, one of the most important of all books on dogs in the British Isles and the first dog book to be illustrated with coloured plates and only the second dog book to be published in English. The book is the *Cynographia Britannica* by Sydenham Edwards, who was born in South Wales in 1768 and who died in London in 1819. Edwards was a sporting artist who also

John Scott's engraving of Philip Reinagle's painting of a Mastiff from 'The Sportsman's Cabinet', 1803-1804.

contributed flower paintings for *The Botanical Magazine*. The plates are the most vital feature of *Cynographia Britannica*, which has a publication date of 1800, although some of the plates bear later dates. Well over twenty distinct varieties of dogs are illustrated in the twelve plates and these include the Mastiff, one of which is parti-coloured. The two adults, one shown cropped, are together with a litter of puppies.

Philip Reinagle RA (1749-1833) was one of a family of twelve artists whose father had arrived in Scotland in 1745 as a supporter of the young Pretender. Philip Reinagle became one of the best known of the sporting artists of his era and his dog portraits are some of the most important. It is generally considered that his work is a reasonably accurate representation, rather than just being portraits painted how a patron would wish them to be. His pictures have a fluidity to them, often lacking in the works of earlier artists. In the dog world, Reinagle is best remembered for a series of paintings which were engraved by John Scott (1774-1827) and which appeared

in William Taplin's *The Sportsman's Cabinet* published in 1803-4, and was the third dog book in the English language.

The plate of the Mastiff shows a slightly rectangular dog with a well-developed body, strong, well-muscled limbs and a large square head, albeit the muzzle and skull are of equal lengths. It is the breeders of the last 130 years or so who have given themselves the task of truncating the muzzle of some of the Mastiff breeds. Throughout the latter part of the 18th century it was Bewick who dictated how we perceive dogs to have been at that time. His woodcuts appeared in a number of publications, or were the inspiration for others.

During the early part of the 19th century it was Scott who was at the forefront in dictating how dogs were illustrated. His engravings dominated many publications and in the *Sportsman's Repository*, published in 1820, his engraving of the Reinagle painting which had appeared in *The Sportsman's Cabinet* was still being reproduced as the ideal Mastiff.

We have seen earlier how Mastiffs accompanied man in pre-Christian times, how they have helped man win his battles and how they were used as a means of entertainment in some of the most barbaric sports ever contrived. As so-called civilised man colonised the world, Mastiffs have been at his side. An Indian dog known to New World explorers as the Techichi is illustrated cowering alongside 'an old World Mastiff' in an engraving from around 1800 – evidence, perhaps, that the breed crossed the Atlantic well over 200 years ago.

THE INDUSTRIAL AGE

By the mid-19th century greater ease of communication and anti-cruelty laws first introduced in the early 19th century all contributed to changing attitudes towards animals. Great innovative breeders of livestock turned their attentions towards dogs; dog shows were instituted to assess one breeder's stock against that of other breeders, and the formation of the Kennel Club in April 1873, whose primary aim was record-keeping and overseeing the formulating of Standards, all meant that the world of dogs was to be very different from then on.

LANDSEER AND ANSDELL

With these changes came a new breed of artists who were finally to lift dogs from the status of an accompaniment in art to the subject matter in their own right. At the forefront of all these changes was Sir Edwin Landseer RA (1802-1873). His pictures were frequently anecdotal and his dogs were often given human characteristics. Landseer's influence on the dog in art has been greater than that of any other single artist' and cannot be overestimated.

Landseer was one of the last artists to show us the aggressive fighting side of the breed in his painting *Fighting Dogs Getting Wind*, which he painted in 1818 at the age of sixteen. It shows a parti-coloured Mastiff-type dog victoriously bestriding another dog of nondescript type. The painting was considered to be the first ambitious, independent sporting picture that Landseer exhibited and it was bought by Sir George Beaumont, one of the great collectors and connoisseurs of the age. After observing this picture, one critic of the day wrote: "His [Landseer's] may be called the great style of Animal Painting."

In 1820 Landseer painted an Alpine Mastiff which was more akin to the Tibetan Mastiff than were the other Alpine Mastiffs which he painted in that same year and which are shown resuscitating a distressed traveller – one of Landseer's most famous dog paintings. These are what we today know as St Bernards. As any large dog had been referred to as a Mastiff, perhaps the hairy ones were referred to as Alpine Mastiffs, indicating large dogs from mountainous regions.

Richard Ansdell RA (1815-1885), the only British artist to have had a town named after

The Mastiff, Rajah, a well-known winner and sire in the 1870s, drawn by R.H. Moore.

him, was obviously greatly influenced by Landseer and the style Landseer had made popular. Ansdell's work was often dramatic and monumental, as was Landseer's, and the Mastiff which Ansdell painted in 1841 and which now hangs in the Walker Art Gallery in Liverpool, is similar in type and coat structure to Landseer's first Alpine Mastiff.

In 1865 Ansdell completed a picture entitled *The Poacher*. Monumental in size, it shows the exact moment at which the Mastiff has caught the poacher. The dog stands over the poacher's spoils, between him and a smaller, rangier, black and white dog with cropped ears, presumably the poacher's gazehound/herding dog lurcher. The Bullmastiff was developed as the archetypal gamekeeper's dog and this painting could well be the earliest representation in art of a Mastiff-type playing this sort of role.

GREAT PATRONS

The breed which we today know as the Mastiff had two great patrons who were also great patrons of the Mastiff-types in art and between them they showed us the 'breed' over nearly 300 years. They were Mr E.G. Oliver of Yorkshire, whose wife was considered the leading Mastiff breeder in the United Kingdom between the wars, and Mrs Marie Antoinette Moore in America. Mrs Moore's collecting seemed insatiable. Paintings, bronzes, porcelains, jewellery - if it had a Mastiff on it, then she wanted it. The price tag seemed secondary, although it has to be said that prices then were not what they are today. At one time the bulk of her collection was at Lyme Hall, where it occupied three rooms and a long corridor. Today most of her collection is in the American Kennel Club Museum of the Dog.

The already mentioned Hondius' *Bear Baiting* and the Ansdell *Poacher* were at one time owned by Mrs Moore, as was the rather chocolate-box rendition by William Henry

F.G. Banbury's Mastiff, Wolsey, from Vero Shaw's 'The Illustrated Book of the Dog', 1881.

Hamilton Trood (1860-1899), *A Domestic Scene*, which Trood painted in 1888 and which shows a fawn Mastiff as the central figure in a scene of domestic canine bliss. So too were Edwin Frederick Holt's (op.1850-1905) *In Time of Peace*, painted in 1877, and R.S. Moseley's (op.1862-1902) *Mastiff and Terrier*, painted in 1871.

Both the Holt and the Moseley show heads totally untypical for the period, when the Kennel Club and breeders were struggling to establish the 1-2 ratio of muzzle to skull. These dogs have skulls and muzzles of equal proportions and also lacking width. The dogs, though, are shown with, in the case of the Moseley, a toy terrier, and in the case of the Holt, puppies, to indicate the immense size of the dogs, both of whom have very heavy coats.

A study of the Mastiff in art reveals that heads, just as much as type, have varied over the years, size being the one thing to remain constant. One painting which Mrs Moore

Beaufort, owned by Dr J. Sidney Turner, one-time Chairman of the Kennel Club and driving force in establishing what is considered to be the ideal head in a Mastiff. Turner was an accomplished sculptor and modelled a head from one of his Champions who was considered to have the desired head. Beaufort was painted by Alexander Francis Lydon, and his portrait was reproduced in Hugh Dalziel's 'British Dogs.'

once owned, and which would be considered as a classic modern Mastiff head in art, is an oil on panel by Arthur Wardle (1864-1949) which he painted in 1930. The fawn dog with a black mask and ears looks slightly to the side of the viewer, displaying the characteristic air of grandeur and courage which the Standard calls for. A similar head study was specially painted by Frederick Thomas Daws for Hutchinson's *Popular Illustrated Dog Encyclopaedia* published in 1935.

Oliver's collection showed us, on the whole, much earlier dogs. Allan Ramsay (1713-1784) in his portrait of Charles Edward Louis Casimer, painted in 1745, shows us a dog similar in type to the one Velazquez painted. Richard Cosway RA (1740-1821) was a fashionable portrait

19th century painting on linen with lace surround.

painter, dealer, eccentric, and friend of The Prince Regent. His rather flamboyant portrait of Master Thornton shows the child in the pose adopted by the future King Charles II when painted by Van Dyck. The Mastiff has obviously been copied by Cosway from the same painting.

Sawrey Gilpin RA (1733-1807) painted, in 1780, the Duke of Hamilton's two Greyhounds and his Mastiff, the latter being a large white dog with black patches. Judging from paintings by other artists which have survived, this type of dog seemed a favourite with the landed families of England. A later painting from the Oliver collection, one which portrayed two Mastiffs and a Yorkshire Terrier and which was painted by John Sutcliffe (d.1923) shows us Mastiffs which would be considered as excellent type today.

As we have seen, the only thing which has remained constant about the Mastiff is size. One can, though, see a pattern, so that at certain periods through the centuries there was uniformity of type – the pre-Christian dogs, the dogs of the Middle Ages, the Renaissance, the 18th century, were all dogs, in various areas of the world, looking similar.

Although artists like Wardle, Daws and others did portray the modern Mastiff in Britain, the breed did not receive the attention from the late 19th and 20th century dog artists which other less established breeds did. One exception was George Earl (op.1856-1883). His painting of Barry, one of the Lyme Hall dogs, was presented to the American Kennel Club in 1974. Earl was one of the first artists who specialized in portraits of named show dogs. Earl's study of a Mastiff lying on a path guarding a lady's riding crop and a pair of kid gloves, and with some architectural features beyond, is a classic example of a dog portrait from the second half of the 19th century.

Before leaving these few pictures of the so-

George Earl, 'After The Ride', oil on canvas, 1873.
Photo courtesy: William Secord Gallery Inc., New York.

'My Lady Sleeps'. Etching by Herbert Dicksee.

Siring, a Tibetan Mastiff belonging to the Prince of Wales'. From W.R. Drury's 'British Dogs', 1903

Mastiff by George Vernon Stokes, 20th century animal painter and illustrator.

R.H. Moore recorded many show dogs towards the end of the 19th century. The Dogues de Bordeaux, Cora and Turc, were prize winners at Crufts in 1896.

called 'English' Mastiff behind, one should perhaps look at one of the most sought-after of all 20th century images by collectors of Mastiff art. The print by Herbert Dicksee (1862-1942) highlights the changing fortunes of the Mastiff over the centuries and contrasts greatly with the fighting, baiting image of previous centuries. Dicksee's soft style, sympathetic approach, and hints of solid, almost classical backgrounds were uniquely his, and his Mastiff and child print says all these things, and shows the Mastiff in a situation which owners today expect and get from their Mastiffs.

BREED DEFINITION
As we have seen, with the 19th century, the coming of the industrial age and the

Tibetan Mastiff, Bhotean, painted by Gustav Muss-Arnolt, and reproduced on trade cards by Dwight's Soda in America.

Bullmastiff from a painting by an unknown artist for cards issued in packets of Gallaher's cigarettes.

Dogues de Bordeaux from an early 20th century continental trade card.

Bullmastiff from a painting by Arthur Wardle for cards issued in packets of Wills cigarettes.

formation of kennel clubs came the establishing of breeds. Mastiffs ceased being just large dogs bred for a purpose, they now had to be more clearly defined by type, to reproduce that type and to hold their own in the show ring.

The Mastiff types of Tibet are historically linked to all the Mastiff breeds, and with the opening of Eastern boundaries, Tibetan Mastiffs of the last century found their way into the West. The breed became great favourites with royalty, including King George IV and the Prince of Wales. One of the Prince's dogs, Siring, was brought from India and his illustration was used repeatedly to illustrate true breed type. Sir William Ingram's Bhotean was an import from the Himalayas. Bhotean was chosen by the

American artist, Gustav Muss-Arnolt (1858-1927) to illustrate the breed for a series of dogs reproduced on trade cards by Dwight's Soda in America.

The Dogue de Bordeaux was an established fighting dog in the South of France and was introduced into the United Kingdom by Bulldog breeders and had every promise of becoming established in this country. Cora and Turc won the Open Dog and Open Bitch classes at Crufts in 1896 and their portraits were drawn by R.H. Moore (op.1868-1900). Moore was responsible, perhaps more than any other artist, for recording show dogs in the United Kingdom towards the end of the 19th century. When cropping was stopped in the UK, interest in the breed evaporated but the breed retained a following on the

One of the best-known of the 19th century animalier bronzes, from a model by Charles Valton.

An unusual 19th century spelter variant of the Marly horse with a Mastiff.

Continent and continued to receive some attention from artists.

While the Bullmastiff became established as the gamekeeper's dog, as a breed it received little attention from artists. Arthur Wardle painted the breed for a series of cigarette cards which were given away in packets of W.D.& H.O.Wills cigarettes. An unknown artist also completed a series for cigarette cards, in this case Gallaher Ltd., and the dogs are reputed to have been top winning dogs of the age; the identity of the Bullmastiff, though, seems unknown.

MASTIFF MODELS
The image of a chained guarding dog

appealed to the animaliers working in France and perhaps the best known of the bronzes is a cropped and docked dog in defiant mood by Charles Valton (1851-1918). He studied under Antoine-Louis Barye, the founder of the animalier movement and exhibited regularly at the Paris Salon between 1868 and 1914. Prosper Lecourtier (1855-1924) and Christophe Fratin (1800-1864) also modelled chained, defiant Mastiff types, while Barye (1796-1875) himself modelled a crouching dog ready to attack.

From the mid-19th century onwards it was the common practice for small bronzes to be mounted on desk sets, and a chained Mastiff on its hind legs, reaching forward, lent itself

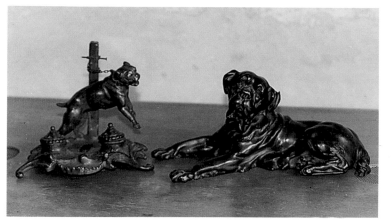

On the left: Bronze desk set with a Mastiff in the manner of Lecourtier. On the right: 19th century recumbent Mastiff.

Partly gilded bronze; the dog is carrying a clock in its mouth, and the base is an inkwell with spaces for wells, sand-shaker, etc.
Photo courtesy: Iona Antiques, London.

Limoges inkstand with recumbent Mastiff.

A pair of Staffordshire Mastiffs c.1855.

admirably to this art form and gave height to the back of the piece.

Not all bronzes portrayed the guarding side of the breed, for many sculptors adopted the characteristic lying position, which those who have owned Mastiffs will know only too well. A bronze familiar to any regular frequenter of the salerooms is the *Marly Horse*, which would have been one of a pair. The work of Guillaume Coustou (1677-1746), these paired bronzes show rearing stallions being restrained by their naked grooms. They were carved in marble between 1740-45 and were originally sited at the entrance of Louis XIV's chateau at Marly, hence their name. They have become one of the most popular groups to be cast in bronze and when spelter became the "poor man's bronze" they became one of the most popular models cast in that medium. One unusual variant of the group in spelter shows a Mastiff-type dog lunging forward at the horse.

Left: c. 1930s Sylvac pottery model of a Mastiff. Centre: 19th century bronze Mastiff in the manner of Lecourtier. Right: French 19th century porcelain pot lid.

Models of Mastiffs were being reproduced in pottery and porcelain some considerable while before their regular appearance in bronze. At about the same time as the baiting piece from the Staffordshire potters appeared, Nymphenburg produced four models of Mastiff-type dogs in porcelain. Three were baiting groups. The earliest, from a model by D. Auliczek, appeared in 1765, and in 1770 the factory produced a sitting dog with cropped ears after a model by F.A. Bustelli.

Early English examples are a cropped and docked dog from the Rockingham factory c.1826-30; a pair almost identical to the Rockingham dog by Samuel Alcock c.1830-45 (there was no such thing as copyright in those days); a pair of Staffordshire cropped but not docked dogs, both sitting under trees which acted as spill vases, c.1855, and a similar dog from the Derby factory from about the same period. All these dogs are shown recumbent, for the potters would have found it difficult to have successfully fired in a kiln a large-bodied dog standing on fine legs.

Towards the end of the last century a number of factories on the Continent producing quality wares produced desk sets with a Mastiff lying along the back. Typical was one made at the Limoges factory in France, with gilt scroll decoration, the top decorated with flowers and a centre jewel-surrounded panel with figures in the classical style. Porcelain and pottery factories sprang up like mushrooms across central Europe and, although their output lacked quality, their wares were cheap and popular. The dog was always a popular subject and many of these models, including those of the Mastiff, have survived to this day and are keenly sought by collectors.

5 THE MASTIFF

By Lyn Say
(With contributions on breed history and breed character by Douglas Oliff.)

There is something attractive about stories which are of historical origin. If repeated to a receptive audience, not only do the stories grow, but they become accepted as facts.

How often have you read, or been told, that when the Romans first invaded Britain, the British fought back not only with their weapons, but with their Mastiffs? How did the Mastiffs first reach Britain? Traditional fables tell us that they arrived via the Phoenicians who traded with Britain for tin. Dr Hadem, a world authority on the ancient Phoenicians states that there is absolutely no evidence that they ever reached Britain. This is also the opinion of R.D. Bennett, head of the Department of Western Asiatic Studies at the British Museum, who, in a letter to me, wrote: "There is no evidence whatsoever to suppose that dogs were brought to Britain by the Phoenicians".

How often when talking of Mastiffs, are you given the quite erroneous statement that the Romans in Britain appointed a Procurator for the purpose of watching over the interests of Mastiffs and exporting them to Rome? The historian Camden who was the originator of the mistake confused the word 'cynoecci' meaning cloth, with 'cynegii' meaning dog. A Procurator was certainly appointed to watch over the production of fine cloth, but in no way was he connected with dog export, or dogs in general.

There is evidence that the Romans did admire a dog which was found in Britain, which they named a 'Briton'. It was a fighting dog – the Roman writer Falicus recommended that: "It was almost worthwhile making the journey to those far shores to obtain one of this breed, as their courage and ferocity is unmatched by any other breed." The Romans also found a breed which they classified as 'pugnace', which, when pitted against the pugnace of Epirus, beat them. From an historical point of view this is of interest, as dogs from Epirus could well have been the basic progenitors of the Neapolitan Mastiff (see Chapter Seven). Strabo (44 AD) wrote of the Celtic use of "war dogs of pendulent ears, lowering aspect and flabby lips".

The Procurator is pure fable, but from Roman written statements it can be assumed that fighting dogs were found in Britain which were likely to have been indigenous. They would not have been the size of the present-day Mastiff, but they were probably the size of a large Bulldog of the old style, and very different from the animal we know today.

It must also be appreciated that the Roman legions moved through Europe with their fresh meat supplies "on the hoof". They would have needed large dogs to protect the

The ancient Mastiff breed has been associated with fighting and guarding throughout its history.

Photo: Anne-Marie Class.

animals from predators, and would most probably have brought these dogs to Britain, where, in due course, they would have bred with the indigenous breeds of the country.

The name 'Mastiff' is thought to be derived from the Middle English 'Mastif' or to be a corruption of the French 'Mastin', but it was a name loosely used to describe any large dog with pronounced guarding or fighting qualities.

In the Welsh Laws of Howel the Good, who died in 950 AD, we read: "There are three kinds of cur, the mastiff, the shepherd dog, and the house dog." The inference is that the Mastiff was kept outside as a guard dog rather than as a companion in the house.

FIGHTING DOGS

Tradition has it that in the 15th century and later, Mastiffs were used as dogs of war and went into battle with their owners, fiercely attacking the enemy. This is something of an exaggeration, but large types of dogs were used in battle. Wearing a collar, fitted with numerous sharp spikes, the dogs were released to attack the horses. The spikes were lethal and wrought havoc on the legs of a horse, often causing such loss of blood that the animal collapsed beneath the rider. Shakespeare was probably aware of this practice when in *Julius Caesar* he wrote: "Cry havoc, and let slip the dogs of war".

In the Forest Laws of Henry III, the

following decree is important for ancient Mastiff history. It states: "Farmers and substantial freeholders dwelling within the forest may keep Mastiffs for the defence of their house, in the same, provided that such Mastiffs be expedited according to the laws of the forest." Expedition consisted of cutting off three claws of the forefeet, thus rendering them incapable of chasing, and pulling down the Royal deer. As a clarification to the law we read: "No other dogs are to be expedited but mastiffs and such curs that are of the mastive kind." Obviously there was more than one kind of Mastiff.

The Stuart and Tudor periods give us many references to the breed as fighting dogs. Shakespeare knew of the breed and its use in

Am. Ch. Iron Hills Warwagon.
The size and weight of the Mastiff appeared to be as variable as his duties.
Photo courtesy: Keith Bushy.

the Bear Gardens of London, but it is William Harrison in his *Description of England*, written in 1587, who painted a detailed word picture of the breed at that time. After describing their use in baiting bull, bear and lion, he writes:

" I say that of the Mastiffs some bark only, with fierce and open mouth. Some do both bark and bite. But the cruellest do not bark at all, or they bite before they bark, and therefore to be more feared than the other.

Some of our Mastiffs will rage only at nigh time, some are tied up both night and day. Some of them likewise are of such jealousy over their master and whatsoever of his household, that if a stranger do embrace, or touch any of them, they will fall fiercely upon him and do him extreme mischief if the fury is not prevented."

THE MASTIFF TYPE

Dr John Kay (1510-1573) a physician, naturalist, and author, under the *nom de plume* of Caius, described the Mastiff as being "vast, huge, stubborn, eager, heavy and burdensome of body, and therefore but of little swiftness". As previously mentioned, the size and weight of these dogs seems to have been as variable as their duties. Caius refers to Mastiffs "of the greater and weightier sort used for drawing water by being placed in a treadmill", or as "baggage dog to transport the tools of tinkers". Other stated duties were for "guarding, carrying, baiting and fighting".

There is a school of thought which considers that the Mastiff of these early periods were 'hunting' Mastiffs built on the lines of a Great Dane or an Irish Wolfhound. As the word 'Mastiff' was so loosely applied to a number of different types, there may be more credence to the hunting theory. What is significant in the description given above is that the animal was a "a mastie that keepeth the house" and "it maketh no matter that he be not swift, for he is but to fight at home and give warning of the enemy"

THE LYME HALL MASTIFFS

No history of the Mastiff could be complete without mention of the most important strain that dominated the centuries – Lyme Hall.

Lyme Hall was the residence of the Legh family from the 14th century to the 20th century. Now National Trust property, it is not used by the family as their main home. The present head of the family, Lord Newton, with whom I corresponded some years ago with reference to the authenticity of the Lyme Hall Mastiffs, informed me that the story from the Battle of Agincourt to the final demise of the dogs during the 1914-1918 war, has always been accepted as factual.

Sir Piers Legh, a staunch supporter of King Henry V, sailed to France with the English forces in their war against that country. At the famous and decisive Battle of Agincourt (1415), Sir Piers was severely wounded. But, on the battlefield, his body was guarded by his Mastiff bitch who refused to give up her precious charge to anyone but an Englishman. Sir Piers died of his wounds, and his body was returned to England together with his Mastiff bitch. She had produced a litter in France which was also transported back to England, and these dogs continued the Lyme Hall line.

The Rev M.B. Wynn, a great scholar and author on the breed and its history, felt that the litter could not have been 'pure' as the bitch had obviously been mated when in France. He dismissed the litter as being 'mongrels'. During this period, it was not uncommon for knights to take their 'dogs of war' with them to battle. The sire of the litter could well have been such a dog, and as the term 'Mastiff' was so broadly used, in an era where pedigrees rarely existed, I have always considered Wynn's dismissal of the pups as 'mongrels' to be a little unfair.

Through the kindness of Lord Newton, I was able to study the records of the family, and there are numerous references to the breed over the centuries. A pair of Lyme Hall Mastiffs was given by James I to King Philip of Spain in 1604. The present accompanied The Oath of the Confirmation of the Articles of Peace, which marked the end of the war between the two countries. Lady Newton in her book *The House of Lyme* considered that the great Velasquez portrait of the children of Philip IV depicts a Mastiff "precisely the same as the Lyme Hall Mastiffs of the present day". The baronetcy of Newton was granted in 1872 and the first Lord Newton chose as supporters to his coat of arms "two Mastiffs proper collared sable".

Int. Am. Mex. Ch. Tamarack's Top Gun, owned by Carole Smith. The breed was quick to gain popularity in the USA.

Photo courtesy: Keith Bushy.

The last of the Lyme Hall dogs was destroyed during the 1914-1918 war as the then Lord Newton considered that the feeding of such animals in that time of food shortages would have been unpatriotic. No doubt other strains were crossed into the Lyme Hall dogs, but Lyme Hall animals were certainly used to build some of the successful kennels of the mid to late 19th century.

Before I close this brief reference to that famous line, let me add that George Earl, one of the great dog portrait painters, produced an excellent painting of Kingdom's dog 'Barry' who was of pure Lyme Hall breeding. Earl was so fascinated by the dog that he followed this original portrait of the dog with two other portraits of the same subject. One of these is in the possession of the American Kennel Club.

FROM 1863 TO THE PRESENT DAY

There is published information that by 1863 the Mastiff had deteriorated due to various crosses. However, there is also evidence that some good specimens still survived in the hands of noblemen. Their popularity was equally evident in America, where there is mention of them in the American Kennel Register 1883, and, by that time, there was in existence an American Mastiff Club.

Dog shows in Britain started in 1859, and in 1860 six Mastiffs were present at Birmingham Show. In 1875 the numbers had increased to the extent that 83 Mastiffs were exhibited at Crystal Palace – a period of increase and popularity comparable to show entries of today. In 1889, 373 Mastiffs were registered. Ten years later this figure was a paltry 18.

In 1872, a number of gentlemen decided to form a club for the breed, The Mastiff Club, with the Rev. M.B. Wynn as secretary; however, one of its rules stated that members could only exhibit at shows permitted by the club and that the judge had to be a member of the club. The members were bound by this rule under penalty of expulsion. This was very unpopular and so the Club's life was short.

The Rev. W.J. Mellor, Dr Forbes Windsor, and Dr J. Sydney Turner formed the Old English Mastiff Club in 1883. A membership fee of one guinea was charged and this stayed until 1973 when it was raised to £2. The original Standard, drawn up by Reverend W. J. Meller, Dr J. Sidney Turner and W.K. Taunton, remains much the same today, except for a few minor changes.

Within ten years, there was a marked fall in popularity; the breed was in a decline, probably due to interest waning. Registrations dropped dramatically by 1900 to only 24, compared to 200 ten years previously. The breed was at a low ebb at the beginning of this century. This period did, however, have breeders' names that are still familiar today – Dr Sidney Turner, Mr Mark Beaufort, Mr W.K. Taunton, Mr R. Cook, Mr C. Court Rice and Mr W. Norman Higgs.

From the turn of the century until the Great War, there was a gradual recovery. Even after the First World War, there were mutterings about the introduction of Bullmastiffs and St Bernards. However, at this time there was a revival of the brindles that had almost become extinct. Registrations for the breed reached 60 in 1913, only to drop again during the period of the war to three in 1918.

Numbers increased during the period between the two wars. Sadly many of these were not pure-bred. I would have my doubts that there are any really true-bred Mastiffs around today. Crescent Rowena, dam of the foundation dog of the Scheerbooms' Havengore kennels, Ch. Bill of Havengore, was out of a cross-bred Bullmastiff, Shirebrook Lady. She was originally registered as a Mastiff in 1921 and re-registered as a correction cross-bred

Bullmastiff in 1922. In the same period Miss Bell (Withybush) bred and owned Ch. Woden, who was by Poor Joe, who also sired the Bullmastiff Sir Roger. The Olivers' Hellingly kennel kept strictly to the pre-war blood lines, their well-known stud dog being Ch. Joseph of Hellingly (formerly of Studland).

BREEDERS BETWEEN THE WARS

By the late 1920s, the breed was again gathering in popularity. The Olivers with their Hellinglys surely must have been a force to be reckoned with, having large kennels with sufficient room to house up to 70 Mastiffs! Mrs Oliver was by then Secretary of the Old English Mastiff Club. Following her husband's sudden death in 1939 she severed all connections with dogs.

In 1923, Mr and Mrs Scheerboom (Havengore) purchased their first Mastiff, Crescent Rowena. From her they bred their first litter and first Champion, the well-known Ch. Bill of Havengore. At the same time Miss Bell (Withybush – a prefix registered after the Second World War) started in the breed and owned a large kennel. The two Miss Blackstones were great friends of hers, accompanying her to many shows. Miss B. Blackstone was secretary of the OEMC from 1964 to 1976. On her retirement as secretary she became a Vice President of the club and maintains a great interest in the breed to this day.

Other well-known breeders at this time were Mr B. Bennett (Broomcourt), Mr L. Cook (Tiddicar) and Mr and Mrs Taylor (Saxondale). Many years later Mrs Taylor was to become the second President of the Mastiff Association, in 1988 and 1989. Last but no means least there was Norah Dicken (Goring), who was secretary of the OEMC from 1932 until 1964, having had her first Mastiffs in the late 1920s.

POST-WAR RECOVERY

At the outbreak of the Second World War, a number of the large kennels were disbanded and much of the stock sent overseas, mainly to America; others were put to sleep. The Scheerbooms had most of their dogs put down, retaining three which, for various reasons, did not reproduce. Only one litter is recorded at the Kennel Club during the war, but the food shortages and rationing would have made it very difficult to feed a Mastiff. Those living in the country who were good shots had the advantage of being able to feed rabbit, which may well have been unpopular, as that was also additional meat to add to the human's rations.

After the war, breeding stock was limited, and sadly several out-crosses were used and the breed lost many of its previously recognised features. Breeding is done on trust, and so it is not possible for me to know exactly what other breeds were used and to give their pedigree names with certainty.

A meeting was held in London in 1946 following an extensive advertising campaign, which included advertising in *The Times*, in an attempt to track down as many Mastiff fanciers as possible. Sadly only 15 people attended. At the time Mr Guy Greenwood was President and he invited them all to the Waldorf Hotel for dinner! A search ensued to trace as many of the breed as possible; 20 to 30 were found, but unfortunately most were too old for breeding, and some were Bullmastiffs and so were rejected. Nora Dickin, Club secretary, went to the USA in search of breeding stock but to no avail.

One dog, reported to have been found wandering during the war, was recognised as a Mastiff, and though there have always been some seeds of doubt, he was registered by the Kennel Club as such. Even if he had been a Bullmastiff, his ancestors would have been strongly Mastiff, as Mastiffs would have still

The De La Tivoliere kennel in France. The problems of keeping large dogs during wartime led to a major decline in the breed.

Photo: Chenane.

been in the five-generation pedigree of the Bullmastiff of the period. He was the sire of Nydia of Frithend, who was to do much to help the revival of the breed.

In 1948 Mrs Mellish, an English lady who had migrated to Canada, hearing of the Mastiff's plight, offered the OEMC two puppies, on condition that two puppies should be returned to her later. The Kennel Club permitted the prefix of OEMC to be registered – a unique decision, something which was never been permitted before or since. OEMC Heatherbelle Sterling Silver went to Mrs Scheerboom, while Miss Bell took custody of OEMC Heatherbelle Portia.

During this time, a number of people had privately imported stock. Mrs Duke had her first Mastiff in Scotland, Raymond of Goring, about 1936 and he lived throughout the war. As no other Mastiffs were living in Scotland at that time, he was never used at stud. Her love of his fine nature led her to play her part in restoring the breed after the war. Mrs Duke and her family then imported Heatherbelle Bearehill Rajah and Heatherbelle Bearehill Priscilla's Amelia; these two were exhibited at the Richmond Show in 1951. The journey from Scotland to London with two Mastiffs could not have been an easy task at that time. They had two litters, but the resultant progeny were not registered. A dog from the second litter was

kept as a companion for many years.

Another of the few people who managed to keep a Mastiff throughout the war was the late President of the OEMC, Mrs Pam Day. She had her first one as a wedding present in 1938, Hermit of Tiddicar, bred by Mr Leonard Crook. She went to Canada after the war to find him a wife, and bought Honey of Parkhurst. However, sadly, during Mrs Day's absence in Canada, Hermit of Tiddicar died. Honey was mated to Mr Hulbert's import Valient Diadem, and a litter of four ensued – the first Hollesley litter to be born. I do not believe Mrs Day was ever without a Mastiff throughout her married life.

THE RETURN OF CCs

By 1953, registrations had improved so much that CCs were again on offer. The late fifties saw the Scheerbooms and Miss Bell as the exhibitors having the biggest kennels.

Greiner Hall Falcon, bred by Stephen and Leah Napotnik.
The brindle colour almost died out, but now some fine Mastiffs of this colour are being produced.

Photo courtesy: Keith Bushy.

Soon there were several more imports from both Canada and America. One of great importance was Weyacres Lincoln, who arrived from the USA in 1953. He was a very important and extensively used stud dog, going back to dogs that had been exported to America pre-war. When he was mated to the Lindleys' foundation bitch, Cleo of Sparry, Jason of Copenore was produced. He also sired many Champions, including Ch. Threebees Friar of Copenore. These were significant stud dogs of the 1950s and 60s.

In 1957, Mrs Rene Creigh (Kisumu) had her first Mastiff, purchased from Mr and Mrs Anderson (Bardayle), who had come into the breed in 1952. Bunty of Bardayle was later mated to Ch. Hotspot of Havengore and they produced Ch. Fatima of Kisumu who, in her turn, produced Ch. Bathsheba of Kisumu. Rene was to be responsible for importing Garstars Eric of Kisumu Canonbury in 1972. Several Kisumus were exported to America, where they certainly made their mark.

Ch. Kumormai Miss Eliza Bennett, bred and owned by Elaine Knight, a top winner in the show ring. *Photo courtesy: Elaine Knight.*

Bill Hanson (Blackroc) had his first Mastiff, Drake of Havengore, in 1956, selected for him by the late Mr F. Scheerboom. Drake went on to win his title. A couple of years later Bill acquired Gypsy of Havengore. Bred together they produced three Champions, Stormy Petrel, English and American Champion Rhinehart of Blackroc, and Falcon of Blackroc who was the first dual titleholder and of great importance to the breed in America. Bill went with them and handled them for Mrs Marie Moore. The early death of Bill was a great loss to the breed.

The numbers were beginning to rise again, and more interest was shown as dog shows were now a regular event. Showing a large breed at this time must have had its complications. Many people took their dogs by train, travelling in the guard's van – those lucky enough to have a car had petrol rationing to contend with.

Mr M.E. Perrenoud, who had had a Mastiff pre-war, purchased Withybush Beatrix and registered his prefix Meps, in partnership with his young son and daughter. Beatrix won two CCs but was not campaigned to gain her title, having been retired for maternal duties. In 1953 she produced a litter of 12 to her grandfather, Valient Diadem. From her second litter, by Ch. Vyking Aethelwulf of Salyng, came Meps Berenice, who was purchased by Marie Moore in America and became the first post-war American Champion bitch. The brindle male, Meps Basil, stayed in the UK and sired that great Mastiff Ch. Hotspot of Havengore. Sadly Mr Perrenoud died in 1959 and the kennels were disbanded. His daughter Marguerite was to continue the Meps lines at a later date.

The Reardons entered the scene in 1954 with the prefix Buckhall. Probably their best-known dog was Ch. Threebees Friar of Copenore, who was the sire of Champions Mr Micawber of Buckhall and litter-brother Lord Jim of Buckhall. They also bred Ch. Master Sirius of Buckhall, owned by Ewart and Tim Williams.

It was these enthusiasts who brought about the revival of the Mastiff, and provided the foundation of today's kennels.

THE BRITISH BREED STANDARD

GENERAL APPEARANCE
Head, in general outline, giving a square appearance when viewed from any point. Breadth greatly desired: in ratio to length of whole head and face as 2/3. Body massive, broad, deep, long, powerfully built, on legs wide apart and squarely set. Muscles sharply defined. Size a great desideratum, if combined with quality. Height and substance important if both points are proportionately combined.

CHARACTERISTICS
Large, massive, powerful, symmetrical and well knit frame. A combination of grandeur and courage.

TEMPERAMENT
Calm, affectionate to owners, but capable of guarding.

HEAD AND SKULL
Skull broad between ears, forehead flat, but wrinkled when attention is excited. Brows [superciliary ridges] slightly raised. Muscles of temples and cheeks [temporal and masseter] well developed. Arch across skull of a rounded, flattened curve, with a depression up centre of forehead from median line between eyes, to half way up sagittal suture. Face or muzzle, short, broad under eyes and keeping nearly parallel in width to end of nose; truncated, i.e., blunt and cut off squarely, thus forming a right-angle with upper line of face, of great depth from point of nose to under-jaw. Under-jaw broad to end. Nose broad, with widely spreading nostrils when viewed from front, flat [not pointed or turned up] in profile. Lips diverging at obtuse angles with septum, and slightly pendulous so as to show a square profile. Length of muzzle to whole head and face as 1/3. Circumference of

Ch. Uberacht of Namous: Crufts CC winner 1988 and 1989.   *Photo courtesy: David Blaxter.*

muzzle [measured mid-way between eyes and nose] to that of head [measured before the ears] as 3/5.

EYES
Small, wide apart, divided by at least space of two eyes. Stop between eyes well marked but not too abrupt. Coloured hazel brown, darker the better, showing no haw.

EARS
Small, thin to touch, wide apart, set on at highest points of sides of skull, so as to continue outline across summit, and lying flat and close to cheeks when in repose.

MOUTH
Canine teeth healthy, powerful and wide apart; incisors level, or lower projecting beyond upper but never so much as to become visible when mouth is closed.

NECK
Slightly arched, moderately long, very muscular, and measuring in circumference about one or two inches less than skull before ears.

FOREQUARTERS
Shoulder and arm slightly sloping, heavy and muscular. Legs straight, strong and set wide apart; bones being large. Elbows square. Pasterns upright.

BODY
Chest wide, deep and well let down between forelegs. Ribs arched and well rounded. False ribs deep and well set back to hips. Girth one-third more than height at shoulder. Back and loins wide and muscular; flat and very wide in bitch, slightly arched in a dog. Great depth of flanks.

HINDQUARTERS
Broad, wide and muscular, with well-developed second thighs, hocks bent, wide apart, and quite squarely set when standing or walking.

FEET
Large and round. Toes well arched up. Nails black.

TAIL
Set on high, and reaching to hocks, or a little below them, wide at its root and tapering to end, hanging straight in repose, but forming a curve with end pointing upwards, but not over back, when dog is excited.

GAIT/MOVEMENT
Powerful, easy extension.

COAT
Short and close lying, but not too fine over shoulders, neck and back.

COLOUR
Apricot-fawn, silver-fawn, fawn or dark fawn-brindle. In any case, muzzle, ears and nose should be black, with black around orbits, and extending upwards between them.

FAULTS
Any departure from the foregoing points should be considered a fault and the seriousness with which the fault should be regarded in exact proportion to its degree.
Note: Male animals should have two apparently normal testicles fully descended into the scrotum.

Reproduced by kind permission of The Kennel Club.

THE AMERICAN BREED STANDARD

GENERAL APPEARANCE
The Mastiff is a large, massive, symmetrical dog with a well-knit frame. The impression is one of grandeur and dignity. Dogs are more massive throughout. Bitches should not be faulted for being somewhat smaller in all dimensions while maintaining a proportionally powerful structure. A good evaluation considers positive qualities of type and soundness with equal weight.

SIZE, PROPORTION, SUBSTANCE
Size: Dogs, minimum, 30 inches at the shoulder. Bitches, minimum 27.5 inches at the shoulder. Fault: dogs or bitches below Standard. The further below Standard, the greater the fault.
Proportion: Rectangular, the length of the dog from forechest to rump is somewhat longer than the height at the withers. The height of the dog should come from depth of body rather than from length of leg.
Substance: Massive, heavy-boned, with a powerful

muscle structure. Great depth and breadth desirable.

Fault: Lack of substance or slab-sided.

HEAD

In general outline giving a massive appearance when viewed from any angle. Breadth greatly desired.

Eyes: Set wide apart, medium in size, never too prominent.

Expression: Alert but kindly. Colour of eyes brown, the darker the better, and showing no haw. Light eyes or predatory expression is undesirable.

Ears: Small in proportion to the skull, V-shaped, rounded at the tips. Leather moderately thin, set widely apart at the highest points on the sides of the skull continuing the outline across the summit. They should lie close to the cheeks when in repose. Ears dark in colour, the blacker the better, conforming to the colour of the muzzle.

Skull: Broad and somewhat flattened between the ears, forehead slightly curved, showing marked wrinkles which are particularly distinctive when at attention. Brows (superciliary ridges) moderately raised. Muscles of the temples well-developed; those of the cheeks extremely powerful. Arch across the skull a flattened curve with a furrow up the centre of the forehead. This extends from between the eyes to halfway up the skull. The stop between the eyes

well marked but not too abrupt. Muzzle should be half the length of the skull, thus dividing the head into three parts, one for the foreface and two for the skull. In other words, the distance from the tip of the nose to the stop is equal to one-half the distance between the stop and the occiput. Circumference of the muzzle (measured midway between the eyes and nose) to that of the head (measured before the ears) is as 3 is to 5.

Muzzle: Short, broad under the eyes and running nearly equal in width to the end of the nose. Truncated, i.e. blunt and cut off square, thus forming a right angle with the upper line of the face. Of great depth from the point of the nose to the underjaw. Underjaw broad to the end and slightly rounded. Muzzle dark in colour, the blacker the better.

Fault: Snipiness of the muzzle.

Nose: Broad and always dark in colour, the blacker the better, with spread flat nostrils (not pointed or turned up) in profile.

Lips: Diverging at obtuse angles with the septum and sufficiently pendulous so as to show a modified square profile.

Canine Teeth: Healthy and wide apart. Jaws powerful. Scissor bite preferred, but a moderately undershot jaw should not be faulted providing the teeth are not visible when the mouth is closed.

Am. Ch. Sillars K.O. Tyson: Number 1. Mastiff in the USA for two consecutive years. Owned by Susie Farber, and co-owned by Beverly Heiser and Roger Barkley.

Photo courtesy: Keith Bushy.

NECK, TOPLINE, BODY

Neck: Powerful, very muscular, slightly arched and of medium length. The neck gradually increases in circumference as it approaches the shoulder. Neck moderately 'dry' (not showing an excess of loose skin).

Topline: In profile the topline should be straight, level, firm, and not swaybacked, roached, or dropping off sharply behind the high point of the rump.

Chest: Wide, deep, rounded and well let down between the forelegs, extending at least to the elbow. Forechest should be deep and well defined, with the breast bone extending in front of the foremost part of the shoulders. Ribs well rounded. False ribs deep and well set back.

Underline: There should be a reasonable, but not exaggerated, tuck up.

Back: Muscular, powerful, and straight. When viewed from the rear, there should be a slight rounding over the rump.

Loins: Wide and muscular.

Tail: Set on moderately high and reaching to the hocks or a little below. Wide at the root, tapering to the end, hanging straight in repose, forming a slight curve, but never over the back when the dog is in motion.

FOREQUARTERS

Shoulders: Moderately sloping, powerful and muscular, with no tendency towards looseness. Degree of front angulation to match correct rear angulation.

Legs: straight, strong, and set well apart, heavy boned.

Elbows: Parallel to body.

Pasterns: Strong and bent only slightly.

Feet: Large, round, and compact with well arched toes. Black nails preferred.

HINDQUARTERS

Hindquarters: Broad, wide and muscular.

Second Thighs: Well developed, leading to a strong hock joint.

Stifle joint: Is moderately angulated matching the front.

Rear Legs: Are wide apart and parallel when viewed from the rear. When the portion of the leg below the hock is correctly 'set back' and stands perpendicular to the ground, a plumb line dropped from the rearmost point in the hindquarters will pass in front of the foot. This rules out straight hocks, and since stifle angulation varies with hock angulation, it also rules out insufficiently angulated stifles.

Fault: Straight stifles.

COAT

Outer coat straight, coarse and of moderately short length. Undercoat dense, short, and close lying. Coat should not be so long as to produce 'fringe' on the belly, tail, or hind legs.

Fault: Long or wavy coat.

COLOUR

Fawn, Apricot, or Brindle. Brindle should have fawn or apricot as a background colour which should be completely covered with very dark stripes. Muzzle, ears, and nose must be dark in colour, the blacker the better, with similar colour tone around the eye orbits and extending upward between them. A small patch of white on the chest is permitted.

Faults: Excessive white on the chest or white on any other part of the body.

Mask, ears, or nose lacking dark pigment.

GAIT

The gait denotes power and strength. The rear legs should have drive, while the forelegs should track smoothly with good reach. In motion, the legs move straight forward; as the dog's speed increases from a walk to a trot, the feet move in toward the centre line of the body to maintain balance.

TEMPERAMENT

A combination of grandeur and good nature, courage and docility. Dignity, rather than gaiety, is the Mastiff's correct demeanour. Judges should not condone shyness or viciousness. Conversely, judges should also beware of putting a premium on showiness.

Reprinted by kind permission of the American Kennel Club.

UNDERSTANDING THE STANDARDS

A Breed Standard is like a blueprint giving a full description of what the completed result should be. So one would imagine, if we are looking at a breed of dog, that the description should be the same worldwide. Just taking two Standards of the Mastiff, we come across several different interpretations of what, presumably, should be the same product. Human nature being what it is, we, in life, frequently put a different view on the same thing. As we cast our eye over a dog, one person may comment that he has adequate bone, another may consider that he is lacking in bone. It is the same animal, but it is seen differently. Many judges faced by brindles will feel there is lack of bone; this is where 'hands on' may prove the point; brindles often give an impression of being fine-boned, when in fact it is the stripes that give a false impression.

There is the view that if it is not in the Standard, it should not be there; however, the British Standard gives no height or weight clause, just "Height and substance important if both points are proportionately combined". The Americans require a minimum height for a male of 30 ins and for a female 27 ins. Does this mean that they go under the ruler and if they do not reach these height they are disqualified? The British Standard under Faults states: "Any departure from the foregoing points should be considered a fault and the seriousness with which the fault should be regarded is in exact proportion to its degree." This leaves it up to the judge's own discretion. The American Standard points out likely faults after each section.

Both Standards are based on the original compiled in 1883. For some reason, over the years, the British Standard has become much shorter than the American one by some 521 words. Both Standards were revised in the early 1990s and the British Standard is now owned by the Kennel Club, as are all British Standards. Both Standards give a similar description, although the American one is probably easier to picture.

GENERAL APPEARANCE

"Large, massive, powerful, symmetrical and well-knit frame. A combination of grandeur and good nature, courage and docility." This is such a good description of what we expect to see. Unfortunately, in the British Standard this is no longer the opening sentence, and "good nature, courage and docility" have been omitted. Both Standards are explicit; however, the final interpretation will rest on each individual's own view. We are looking for a massive frame, with a large head; great breadth of skull, with a broad deep muzzle; giving a square appearance, great spring of rib, with plenty of heart room; broad front with depth, and legs that stand foursquare, well-boned limbs with neat, tight feet.

Above: Am. Can. Ch. Greiner Hall Jedadiah: The Mastiff should present an impression of grandeur, good nature, docility and courage.
Photo courtesy; Keith Bushy.

Below: Forequarters: The legs should be straight and strong, and set wide apart. Photo: Sheila Atter.

Above: The chest is wide and deep. The degree of front angulation should match the correct rear angulation.

Photo: Sheila Atter.

HEAD

As a head breed, this is probably the most important part of the body. One distinctive difference exists between the UK and US Standard. The American Standard calls for "Marked wrinkles which are particularly distinctive when at attention", whereas the UK Standard states, "wrinkles when attention is excited". This would certainly seem to be a personal preference, although in the UK many people prefer the wrinkles to be in evidence all the time. My own feeling is that the whole expression changes when those wonderful wrinkles appear if something of interest is observed by the dog. One sees too many Mastiffs these days that are overdone in head, with surplus folds of skin at the side of the face; sadly, many judges are looking for just such a head.

The British Standard calls for a black muzzle, nose and ears, with black around the orbits and extending upward between them. The American Standard states "the darker the better". The muzzle really should be black and broad and deep, not snipy, narrow nor turned up.

The American Standard requires the ears to be dark in colour, the blacker the better, conforming to the colour of the muzzle. One will often find light ears accompanied by a black muzzle. Brindles frequently, if looked at closely, have brindle ears but these often are not very obvious. The Kennel Club Standard calls for black ears and muzzle.

Both Standards permit a slightly undershot bottom jaw, so long as the teeth do not show when the mouth is closed, the American Standard showing a preference for a scissor

The distinctive black markings include the ears, the muzzle, the nose and around the eyes.

Photo: Anne-Marie Class.

bite while the British Standard asks for a level bite. Considering the importance of depth and breadth of muzzle, it would be very difficult to attain a scissor bite.

COAT
The American Standard goes into more detail of the coat than the British Standard. I am not sure how one interprets "moderately short length". The British Standard gives no mention of an undercoat, requiring the coat to be short and close-lying, but not too fine over the shoulders, neck and back. No mention is made in the UK standard about length, but as it asks for "short coat", presumably that is what is meant.

COLOUR
As far as colour is concerned the UK classifies apricot as fawn and calls it apricot fawn and includes silver fawn (a colour rarely seen these days), fawn or dark fawn brindle – the latter being a bit misleading as it may

Elisgrai Dorset Boy: The wrinkles, when the dog is alert, are typical of the breed.

*Am. Ch. Bereshith Squire Danaher, bred by
Carole Smith.
A beautifully marked brindle showing good size
and substance.   Photo courtesy: Keith Bushy.*

*Monti-de-Lion Brookview: The typical expression
of supreme self-confidence coupled with haughty
dignity.   Photo: Sheila Atter.*

give the impression that apricot brindle is
not acceptable. However, as previously
mentioned, apricot is classed as fawn. The
American Standard gives a better description
of brindle: "Brindle should have fawn or
apricot as a background colour which should
be completely covered with very dark
stripes." Too often what are referred to as
reverse brindles are seen; alternatively, these
could be classed as mismarks – they may
have great patches of lighter coat, with no
sign of any black covering over a large area.
One side of the body can be evenly marked,
the other side looking as if it is a different
dog. The British Standard has no mention of
white; brindles and apricots will often have a
small amount of white on the chest and feet;
sadly it also seems to be creeping in on the
fawns. They can be born with quite a big
white patch on the chest but this usually
fades as they get their adult coat.

THE MASTIFF CHARACTER
There is something essentially English in the
character of the Mastiff. It conjures up the
spirit of England – county cricket with all its
formalities, or the music of Elgar – so correct
and controlled, but with the occasional
discreet glimpse of the private thoughts of a
very private person. So it is with the Mastiff.
It has all the reliability of Old England –
tolerant, slow to anger, even if the tolerance
is founded more on indolence than principle.
If really roused he can be formidable, but
such displays of ire are fairly rare.

The Standard asks for the breed to be a
"combination of grandeur, good nature,
courage and docility". If your only
experience of the breed is from watching
them in the show ring, a false impression
could be given. Few Mastiffs enjoy the show
ring. Some tolerate it better than others, but
most Mastiffs do not possess the show ring
mentality. Any dog of this size and
construction cannot compete against the

Kalcavalier Joshua: The Mastiff thrives on human companionship.　　*Photo courtesy: Betty Baxter.*

The easy-going nature of the Mastiff is a hallmark of the breed.　　*Photo: Desrephany*

smaller, clean-cut outlines of a Dobermann, or a flashy Boxer. Perhaps the dogs realise that they are at a disadvantage, and just go through the formalities to please the owners. As the Breed Standard asks for characteristics, perhaps we should comment on those requirements.

GRANDEUR

This is a wonderfully evocative word. To me it suggests a high degree of self-importance, proudness, supreme self-confidence, coupled with a haughty dignity. Such qualities are not always obvious in the breed today, but if a high degree of proud bearing is present in a dog of such impressive size, then the breed would certainly be able to claim grandeur.

GOOD NATURE

What Mastiff owners can usually claim is that their dogs are very good-natured, especially in their home surroundings.

A dog of Mastiff proportions would be extremely unsuitable for a household if it was not good-natured. I recall the late Mrs Scheerboom telling me how her first Mastiff,

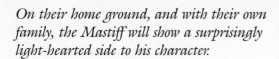
On their home ground, and with their own family, the Mastiff will show a surprisingly light-hearted side to his character.

Photos: Anne -Marie Class.

Crescent Rowena, was devoted to a Siamese cat which was part of the family. The cat always slept with (and usually on) Rowena. When it contracted cat influenza and died, Rowena was quite disconsolate for some weeks.

Another instance of the breed's acceptance of other animals was demonstrated by a famous male, owned by Mrs Lloyd Jones and Mrs Grenwell, who was deeply attached to the Jersey bull owned by the two ladies. He spent much of his time with the bull, who apparently enjoyed the dog's company. Jersey bulls are not usually reliable in temperament, so I presume that each brought out the best in the other.

In my experience the Mastiff is the most easy-going breed, and can be trusted implicitly. He does not need to be relegated to a back room when visitors arrive, as you can be quite confident that the very worst thing he will do is to stretch out on the hearth and monopolise eighty per cent of the heat from the fire.

This good nature has another, and in these days important, advantage. It is a good watch dog in its fashion and the very sight of a Mastiff is sufficient to deter undesirables from coming to the house. A dog of this size which had a mean nature would have to be very carefully housed and monitored.

If brought up with children who have been instructed on how dogs and other animals must be treated, the Mastiff shows a natural affinity to the young and seems to enjoy their company. We can safely award the breed a ninety-eight per cent prize for its good nature.

COURAGE

The Victorian children's books carried stories of Mastiffs coming to the rescue in all sorts of unlikely situations. Such tales were probably fictitious and the word Mastiff was used for any large dog, rather than for a single breed, but it is obvious that in the minds of authors and children, the dog was a heaven-sent lifesaver.

If one takes the average show Mastiff of today as being typical, its appearance in the show ring does not suggest a high degree of courage. Too many slink round the ring, tails between legs, and look thoroughly miserable. It is only when they realise that they are bound for home that they really become animated. It is this lack of animation which puzzles me. Having judged the breed in Scandinavia, Europe and the USA, I find that

Acorn Hills Julip NA, CD, CGC, owned by Jennifer Whitenack: The only Mastiff, to date, to win an Agility title in the USA.

Photo courtesy: Keith Bushy.

Am. Ch. Polaris Oaklane Eloise CD, owned by Nicki Camerra, Lee Brown, and Tim and Vicki Hix, holds the record for the highest Mastiff score in all-breed Obedience competition.

Photo courtesy: Keith Bushy.

a high proportion of the dogs in those countries have a much more extrovert temperament, yet all must have been bred from basic British stock. Perhaps the expertise of the American professional handlers has something to do with it, or it could be that Mastiffs in Britain have an inbuilt modesty which the extrovert foreigners lack!

DOCILITY

This is very closely allied to good nature and, again, one can award the breed a ninety-eight per cent score. I have never been able to make up my mind whether the docility is genuine, or whether it is because a degree of effort is required to be other than docile, and they do not wish to make that effort.

It could well be that within their minds they realise that as one of the giants, they could really crush any upstart, therefore such upstarts are best ignored.

In the crucial post-war period when extinction was a real possibility, many of the owners were quite senior citizens who would have found it difficult to manage any animal of Mastiff proportions which was not docile. Perhaps docility saved the breed, but when shows started again in the post-war period there were one or two Mastiffs who were somewhat 'sparky' with other dogs.

TRAINING

Though not defined in the Standard, trainability in any breed is important and simple 'good citizen' training in a youngster is essential.

As in most other ways, I have found the Mastiff to be rather slow in response to simple obedience, such as coming when called, or realising the meaning of the word No. The breed is not unintelligent but its reactions are extremely slow compared with other breeds within their group. Their reaction to a command to come when called is "All right, I hear you and I will do it in a

Try and see as many adult Mastiffs as possible, in a variety of different situations, before setting out to choose a puppy.   *Photo Anne-Marie Class.*

minute, but in the meantime I just want to...". The dog is usually as good as his thoughts and he will obey when he feels that the time is opportune.

He will do it in his own time and his own style and is not interested in all that immediate response nonsense. He does not have that type of mentality. He is British and prefers to stretch his ample self on a rug and enjoy a peaceful and prolonged snooze until the next mealtime, instead of all that rushing about.

CHOOSING A PUPPY

Do not be in a rush to purchase a puppy. Visit a few shows; club shows usually have a more relaxed atmosphere and breeders have more time to talk to you. Try to get to know the breed; most breeders are accommodating. Visit them at home and they will be happy to talk Mastiffs. See as many of the breed as you can and be sure it is the breed for you, and all your family. If any of you are not sure, then it is not the breed for you.

Contact your national Kennel Club, or one of the breed club secretaries, or the puppy line, for a copy of the Breed Standard. Read and inwardly digest it, so you have a good idea of what your chosen breed should look like at maturity. Club secretaries usually know who has puppies available and they will point you in the right direction.

Look into the special needs of owning a large dog and consider your ability to meet them. Though Mastiffs are not given to roaming, it is advisable, especially when they are young, to have an area that is secured. Some are great diggers, so keep a check on the exercise area; and during their teens some will have a go at jumping gates and fences. These are things you should be aware of and make allowances for.

If you are not sure, see adults first – a litter of puppies can be so appealing. Mastiffs are prone to drooling, and like to share it with everyone. In my experience, children, and little boys in particular, find this quite offensive. A towel at the ready soon mops it up, but remember, you will have to live with it and it can have quite a disastrous effect on polished furniture.

If you want to show, or to show and breed, make this clear at the start. A breeder is lucky to get one or two that are show specimens in a litter; there are bound to be some that are not show quality. That is not to say that there is something wrong with them; they are just lacking in some show point. Many people purchase a puppy with no intention of showing – but then they get interested in the breed and join the breed clubs, they go along to a club show and they are hooked.

MALE OR FEMALE

Male or female is a personal preference, often determined by what is available. The males are larger and, unlike many other breeds, they are not given to roaming; they eat more, but are normally just as loving and gentle as the girls. You should be able to tell if they are entire from about seven weeks of age.

If you are planning on breeding, then you should know that Mastiff bitches can be difficult to get in whelp, and are fussy about the chosen stud, especially if you have a male of any breed at home who they fancy! They will have to be contained during their seasons. They normally have the first one at about fourteen months, then at six to seven monthly intervals. A few will be once-a-year girls. Mastiffs are usually very good at keeping themselves clean.

VIEWING A LITTER

No breeder worth their salt will sell you a puppy guaranteeing it will become a Champion, despite some of them thinking all their geese are swans. Purchasing a puppy with show potential is no guarantee that it will turn out that way; likewise, the pet puppy can turn into a stunner and the breeder will be urging you to show it. When you visit a breeder, be prepared for a grilling – most of us are very dedicated and only want the very best for our pups.

You should see the pups with their dam, and, though this is not always possible, try and visit them more than once. Try also to see the sire – you may be lucky, and he is on the premises. If not, the breeder will be glad to let you know where you can go to see him.

Check with the breeder if the parents have been X-rayed for hip and elbow dysplasia. This condition affects many of the large, heavy breeds and scoring is a method of monitoring the condition. Good hips do not always guarantee good hips in the progeny;

There is no substitute for good temperament, and this should always be a top priority.   *Photo: Nash.*

Watch the puppies interacting with the adult dogs to get an idea of individual personalities. Photo: Anne-Marie Class.

parents with a high score can produce low-scoring offspring. Some breeders also make use of eye tests.

Mastiffs of today differ from their forefathers very little; they are noted for their docility and benevolence. They give an impression of tremendous strength, with a large, square, broad-muzzled head, huge limbs and an impression of power.

ASSESSING A PUPPY
Do not expect a breeder to allow you to examine the pups until they are five to six weeks of age; by then they will be less reliant on their dam and beginning to take quite a lot of interest in their surroundings. A puppy should look like the finished version in miniature; their feet can look enormous, as can the ears – do not worry, they will grow into them.

Look for all-over squareness in the head, a long body, with good bone and tight feet. Make sure the toe nails have been kept

Look for squareness in the head, a long body and tight feet.   *Photo: Nash.*

There should be depth of chest and the legs should be set well apart.   *Photo: Nash.*

trimmed and beware the pup that is down on its pasterns. Feet should be neat and well-arched and the toe-nails black. Avoid over-fat puppies; at eight weeks they should be comfortably plump, active and interested.

A slightly overshot jaw at this age will come right as the lower jaw continues to grow. The muzzle should be deep and broad, short but not puggy. Broad under the eyes, the stop is apparent at birth but seems to disappear and then return at about seven to eight weeks. Avoid long and narrow or snipy muzzles. As far as eyes are concerned, the darker the better, and, though probably in the puppy they are still blue, the darker blue the better. No droopy eyelids, and no bulging eyes or eyes set too far apart. Ears at this stage will be rather large – this is normal – and placed high on the side of the head, flat and close to the cheeks. They should be thin to touch, not leathery. There should be wrinkle on the forehead, showing when the dog's interest is alerted; too many wrinkles can cause eye problems and infection in the folds of skin around the head.

There must be depth of chest, with legs set wide apart and strong straight limbs. Shoulder placement at this age can be difficult to assess with any degree of accuracy. The back should be long and level with a good rib cage. The British Breed Standard does not give a weight or height clause, just the larger the better; this should be made up from depth of body, not length of leg. Size at this age will change, and the biggest in the litter may finish up the smallest. Do not be tempted to give additional rations to make the puppy bigger; you can do more harm than good, and the same applies to supplements.

Feathering on the tail, legs and ears is a sign of a woolly coat and, although it can be very attractive, it is not correct and if you want to show or breed, dogs with incorrect coats are not for you. You may be surprised

Most important of all: take time when making your choice, for you will be responsible for the puppy for the entirety of its life.

Photo: Anne-Marie Class.

to find some judges do give them high honours.

Colour is usually a personal preference. Some of the whole colours, if they have good pigment, may have a donkey stripe down the back. This will clear as the puppies get older, and the ears will get darker, if they have black inside the ears. Puppies are born almost black, and apricot and brindles can be quite difficult to distinguish between for the first few days; as they grow they get lighter. Many of the fawns can be almost salt and pepper and appear to have a dirty look. The light

fawns with black mask and ears are much more desirable.

It is important to watch them at play; puppies in all breeds will have a violent game between themselves and then go off into the deepest sleep. Most will be inquisitive and, if you sit with them, they will be crawling all over you, and the hesitant one, given a bit of extra fuss, will join in. Shyness can be a problem; unfortunately it sometimes does not show until puppies are over a year old and they will suddenly change from being everyone's friend, to being more selective.

6 THE BULLMASTIFF

By Douglas Oliff

A certain degree of historical snobbery exists among owners of many breeds of dogs. Some delude themselves into thinking that their particular breed has, over the centuries, maintained the same form, colour and mentality that it has today. Others feel that breeds which are "man-made" are second-class in terms of canine hierarchy.

Every breed is man-made, some to a greater extent than others. Left to her own devices, an on-heat bitch would mate with any capable dog. Man plans and controls the breeding of animals, usually in the hope of improving the originals or to attempt to develop and perpetuate characteristics in the progeny. It is an ongoing process of attempting to improve on the mental and anatomical design and to fix this design so that it can be perpetuated. To take a simple analogy, Henry Ford's original Model T car, which was revolutionary and much sought-after in its heyday, could hardly compare with today's models of the same firm, yet the purpose for which both were designed remains the same. The fact that the Kennel Club did not open a section in the "Any other variety" registration for the Bull-Mastiff until 1924 has been considered by many to suggest that this is a modern man-made cross breed. Before accepting such opinion we should consider references to the breed prior to 1924.

EARLY HISTORY

In the Forest Laws, enacted in the reign of King Henry III, we find the following reference to the Mastiff:

"And therefore farmers and substantial freeholders dwelling within the forest may keep mastiffs for the defence of their homes within the same, provided that such mastiffs be expeditated according to the laws of the forest. The way of expeditating mastiffs is done after this manner. Three claws of the fore feet shall be cut off by the skin by setting one of the forefeet upon a piece of wood, eight inches thick and a foot square and, with a mallet and chisel of two or three inches broad upon the claws of the forefeet and, at one blow, cutting them clean off. And this expeditating (by some called hambling or lawing of dogs), ought to be enquired of by Regarders of the Forest every third year. And to prevent such as are not expeditated and the owners of them amerced three shillings for keeping such dogs so outlawed".

As with current legislation there were exceptions and definitions to the law. If the property of a Prince of Royal blood, Mastiffs were exempted, as were other breeds of dog, but one sentence is of historical significance. It states "no other dogges are to be expeditated but mastives and such curres that are of the mastive kind." What were these "curres of the mastive kind"? As the reason

95

Ch. Azer Of Oldwell: The Bullmastiff – powerful, strong, active and alert.

for expeditating was to prevent the dogs from pulling down the Royal deer, they must have been similar to the Mastiffs, strong and determined animals. Could they have been the root from which both breeds evolved over the centuries? By crosses with large hounds the Mastiff increased in size, while others evolved as a smaller, but heavily built animal, to form the rudimentary Bulldog. It is impossible to authenticate such theories, but in Henry III's reign both Mastiffs and Mastiff-types existed in such numbers as to merit expedition.

Moving forward some centuries, there are important references to the fact that crosses between Mastiffs and other breeds, chiefly Bulldogs, were not uncommon.

Bewick, the famous wood-engraver (1753-1828), wrote in his *History of Quadrupeds* that "the Mastiff in its pure and unmixed state is seldom met with. The generality of dogs by that name seem to be compounded of the Bulldog, Danish Mastiff and Bandog."

Buffon in his *Natural History* 1755 wrote: "The Bulldog produces, with the Mastiff, a dog which could be called "the strong Bulldog", which is much larger than a normal Bulldog but approaching the Bulldog more than the Mastiff."

In his introduction to his book *Anecdotes of*

Int. Dutch Ch. Bunsoro Red Flag, bred by Mrs F. Harris. Note the squareness of the skull, the deep brisket, and the overall deep chest.

Dogs (1858) Edward Jesse wrote: "I had forgotten to mention a bull-and-mastiff dog which I had called Grumbo. He was the first four footed companion established in my confidence. I was then very young and, of course, inclined to anything like a row. Grumbo, therefore, was well entered in all kinds of strife – bulls, oxen, pigs, men, dogs, all came in turn as combatants, and Grumbo had the oddest ways of making men and animals the aggressors I ever knew. He seemed to make it a point of honour never to begin but, on receiving a hint from me, someone of his enemies was sure to commence the battle and then he, or both of us, would turn to as an oppressed party. I have seen him walk leisurely out into the middle of a field where oxen were grazing and then throw himself down. Either a bull or the oxen were sure to be attracted by the novel sight and come dancing and blowing round him. All this he used to bear with the most stoical fortitude till someone more forward than the rest touched him with the horn. Grumbo then had one of them by the nose directly. Grumbo got tossed in the air and some beast would get pinned by the nose, lie down and bellow. So it would go on until Grumbo and myself were tired and our "enemies" happy to beat a retreat. If he wished to pick a quarrel with a man he would walk listlessly before him till the man trod on him and then the row began. Grumbo was the best assistant in the world for catching delinquents.

"As proof of his thoughtful sagacity, I give the following fact. He was my sole companion when I watched two men steal a quantity of pheasant eggs. We gave chase but, before I could come near them, with a two hundred yards start on me, they fled. There was no hope of my overtaking them before they reached the village of Harlington, so I gave Grumbo the job. Off he went but in the chase the men ran up a headland on which a cow was tethered. They passed the cow; Grumbo stopped and, to my horror, contemplated a grab at the tempting nose. He was, however, uncertain as to whether or not this would be right and he looked back to me for further assurance. I made the sign to go ahead and he understood it, for he took up running again and disappeared down a narrow pathway through orchards to the houses. When I turned the corner, to my infinite delight, I found him placed in the narrow path, directly in front of one of the poachers, with such evident determination of purpose that the man was standing stock still, afraid to stir either hand or foot. I came up and secured the offender and bade the dog be quiet."

The cross between Bulldogs and Mastiffs was well-known to General W.N. Hutchinson, an authority on gundogs. He wrote: "Bulldogs have good noses. I have known a cross between them and the Mastiff being taught to follow the scent of a man almost as truly as a Bloodhound."

We could add more instances in which old writers have confirmed the existence of Mastiff/Bulldog crosses, but those already mentioned should help to dispose of the assertion that the Bullmastiff is the product of crosses made in the first quarter of the present century.

Victor's Ultimate Imposter, owned by Mr and Mrs A. Tier. The gamekeeper's dog – a role that required a guard dog of size, courage, spirit and determination.

THE GAMEKEEPER'S DOG

During the latter part of the 19th century, a period in which the Industrial Revolution plus the might of the British Empire brought great prosperity to some sections of society, a new class of wealthy manufacturers became established. The extent of their wealth was demonstrated by the creation of sporting estates with the stolid Neo-Gothic Victorian residence as the centrepiece. Domestic staff were easily obtained and poorly paid. Alongside the affluence of the estate-owning class was a section of Society for whom extreme poverty was the accepted style of living. To survive in country areas, poaching became rife despite the knowledge that, if caught, penalties would be excessively harsh. In the majority of instances, the poacher was driven by the desperate needs of himself and his family. It fell to the lot of the gamekeeper not only to breed, rear, feed and maintain his master's game, but to protect it from theft by predators both human and animal, most of which occurred at night. For his nocturnal patrols the keeper needed a protective guard dog of size, courage, spirit and determination, capable of moving at a good speed over comparatively short distances, plus a good nose and silence when on the trail.

The dog's function was to knock down the poacher and hold him down until the keeper could come along and apprehend him. The dog was not designed as an attack dog but, having had many years of Bullmastiff ownership, I cannot imagine that such a dog would just stand over the poacher and wait for the gamekeeper. I should imagine that, if the poacher became violent, the dog would reciprocate.

You may wonder why the Mastiff/Bulldog cross had been chosen. Over the centuries the Mastiff was acknowledged as a superb guard, but its size made it somewhat slow and cumbersome. Many realised that, if crossed with a Bulldog, not only would the progeny be more agile, but the spirit of the animal would be enhanced, rather than reduced, by the crossing. There were no pedigrees kept as such. Keepers probably added a dash of Bloodhound or Great Dane, but "The Gamekeeper's Night Dog" became an essential to many sporting estates. In the early part of the present century the popularity of such a dog was well-established. There was little emphasis on type; courage and function were the essentials but, at the same time, the animal had to be intelligent and biddable to the keeper and his immediate family. Undoubtedly the dogs were a pretty tough lot to anyone other than the handler. Pedigrees, where they existed, meant nothing and, in many instances, were word of mouth and unrecorded. What was required was a working guard dog with strength, courage and few inhibitions.

The 1914-18 World War, followed by a period of depression of the late twenties and thirties, brought social changes. The

98

Ch. Tailwynde's J Paul Get 'Em: The stud force behind the world famous Tailwynde line.

experience of the Army, and fighting abroad, considerably altered the attitude towards the social structures of many who returned from the war. One of the products of war was to demonstrate how foreign breeds such as the Alsatian (now called German Shepherd Dog) could be used in their role as guard and watch dog. It was probably this realisation that prompted a few in Britain to realise the coming need for a guard dog whose temperament could be attuned to a more domestic role, but without loss of efficiency. The Bull-Mastiff began to take on a new role.

THE MOSELEY BREEDING PLAN
Mr S.E. Moseley sensed the mood of the times and the possible development of a market for the breed. He was a Staffordshire man and lived most of his life at Burslem. He was basically a smallholder but had long experience with dogs, his main breed being Cocker Spaniels, but he also kept Mastiffs and a few Bloodhounds. He had been breeding Bullmastiffs for some while using the prefix "Hamil". This was the name of a village which was his previous home. Realising that it would not be long before the Kennel Club would accept the BullMastiff as a pure breed, Moseley took active steps to ensure that, when this occurred, he would have a strong hand in the breed.

Although a smallholder, he had quite a number of bitches out on breeding terms and so was well placed for expansion. His advertisements placed great emphasis on how he produced "set type which breeds true". He also made great claim to his rigid principles of breeding only from Mastiffs or Bulldogs which had given him "total eradication of the St Bernard and Great Dane crosses". His formula, which was oft repeated, was for 60% Mastiff and 40% Bulldog. Unless there have been recent changes, these proportions are still quoted in the American Breed Standard under "general appearance".

I will be kind and describe the formula as a fine piece of imaginative writing, but it is highly unlikely that it would "set type" or "breed true". His aim was to fix proportions, but anyone with even an elementary knowledge of animal genetics would today see that the method outlined would be highly unlikely to produce the requisite result.

The Moseley formula was: "Taking a Mastiff bitch and a Bulldog, I produce a 50/50. A bitch of these I mate to a Mastiff dog and which gave me a 75% Mastiff, 25% Bull bitch which I mate to a 50/50 dog. A bitch from this litter is 62.5% Mastiff, 37.5% Bulldog. I mate this to a 50/50 dog and a bitch from this litter I put to a 62.5% Mastiff, 37.5% Bulldog, which gives me my ideal 60% Mastiff. I established my Farcroft strain and the BullMastiff a standard breed of set type which breeds true – like produces like. This is fixing a type not merely breeding a cross breed."

As most show judges today complain of the great variety of types which we have in the breed and as nearly every Bullmastiff in the world goes back to Farcroft Fidelity, I have a feeling that our founding father did not get his calculations quite right.

As an interesting aside, some years ago, when I was running a rally for Bullmastiffs and Mastiffs, a Mastiff owner asked me what I thought of her young dog and proceeded to get him out of the car. He was a clear fawn, strongly boned, black muzzle, strong head, level mouth and a first-class mover. I was greatly impressed and remarked that I was unaware that she had Bullmastiffs, but who was his breeder? She replied "Me". This puzzled me, and then she told the story. She had a ten-month-old Bulldog puppy of the modern "puffing billy" type and one of her Mastiff bitches came on heat unexpectedly. As accommodation was tight and the bitch had been on heat three months previously, she put her in with the Bulldog; in fact she explained that they got on so well together that she left them in that accommodation for the next six weeks. About this time she noticed that the bitch was thickening up in the abdomen so she took her to the vet. To her utter surprise and dismay he told her that she was in whelp and that, on manipulation, he could feel at least three puppies. These were duly produced, three bitches and one dog. All looked exactly like Bullmastiffs; the bitches were given away to friends but the dog puppy was so full of self-confidence and vitality that he was retained as a pet. No one believed that he was from a Mastiff bitch. I wonder how, as one of the Moseley 50/50, he would have bred on. The breeder went to live abroad shortly afterwards and I lost touch.

GROWING RECOGNITION

The Bullmastiff, having proved itself in its capacity as a gamekeeper's guard, even normally conservative authors, such as Robert Leighton in his *Complete Book of the Dog*, wrote in 1922: "The most popular of all half breeds as a watchdog is the Bull Mastiff who is almost worthy to be called a distinct breed." These were quite prophetic words and did not go unnoticed.

Count Hollander, a specialist in bull breeds, wrote in *The Kennel*, March 1911 issue, under the heading 'An unrecognised

Fin. Int. Ch. Anelma: Bitch CACIB at the World Show 1998.

breed of British dogs': "The public know very little of the qualities of the Bull-Mastiff and, what is more, that it has been in existence for some considerable time. It is useless to make an appeal for this dog from a sentimental point of view. I do so quite conscientiously knowing that this dog is the bravest, the most perfect guard and protector in the world." He goes on to qualify his opinion: "Mr. Biggs of Osmaston Hall, Derby, owns some wonderful specimens and is very interested and keen. On more than one occasion he has owed his life to his dogs. Osmaston Daisy and Osmaston Grip have taken more poachers between them than any other dog living."

Commenting on their tracking ability he continues: "I was baffled to find out whence they get their speed and wonderful noses, as neither the Mastiff nor the Bulldog could be looked upon as very fast dogs or of possessing wonderful scent. Personally I think at times that the strain of Bloodhound has been introduced and that the old fashioned Bulldog was used and not the modern dog." He concludes: "I hope I shall have interested many who will look into the claims of a dog that is not only all British, but combines wonderful pluck and endurance with the gentleness of a lamb and whose only aim is, if necessary, to be allowed to take its death saving its master or mistress. One cannot buy devotion but the next best thing is to buy a Bull-Mastiff."

Count Hollander was probably not unaware that some of the Osmaston dogs were from half Bloodhound, half Mastiff crosses.

Dogs of the old "Night Dog" types were still being bred in the Midlands and Black Country, areas which always were (and still are) bull breed strongholds. London had its followers of the old type of guard dog, Mr Pierce MRCVS of Shireland Road, Paddington, being one example. His

advertisements for sale or wanted, contained such epithets as "game and most active" or "savage". Incidentally Mr Pierce was of the opinion that no dog fit for his job should weigh much over 90 lbs.

THORNEYWOOD TERROR
In the period prior to the 1914-18 war, Mr W. Burton of Thorneywood, Nottingham, was breeding "Night Dogs" mostly of the Mastiff and Bulldog extraction and exhibiting them at events at which the guarding abilities of the dogs could be demonstrated. One must realise that, until 1925, there was little interest in these dogs as show dogs. They were very much working dogs with the highly tuned mentality of an active guard. Mr. Burton's most famous exhibit was Thorneywood Terror, a 90lb brindled lethal weapon. Like many of the old-time Night Dog breeders, the pedigree of Thorneywood Terror was not recorded by his owner, but progeny of the dog were registered. Terror toured Britain in a barred iron cage and demonstrated his abilities as a guard. Wagers were taken at the events and money offered to anyone who could escape from a heavily muzzled Terror, when released from his cage.

Am. imp. Eng. Ch. Blazins Jubullation Of Jobull JW.

Apparently Terror never missed his "victim" and could down the man with consummate ease and, one imagines, with a degree of ferocity. Mr. Burton was well-known at that time as a breeder and trainer of such dogs.

THE FIRST BREED STANDARDS

The British Bullmastiff League, not long after its formation, took the National Bullmastiff Police Dog Club's Standard, but made minor modifications here and there. It will be noted that this Standard, although differing from the current one in some respects, still has much of the breed requirements today.

General Impression
The Bullmastiff is a powerfully built dog, symmetrical and showing great strength. His temperament combines high spirits, reliability, activity, endurance and alertness.
Dogs should be 25 to 27 ins. at shoulders and 90 to 110 lbs. in weight.
Bitches 24 to 26 ins. at shoulder and 80 to 90 lbs. in weight.
Soundness and activity most essential.
Skull should be large and square, with fair wrinkles and may measure the height of the dog, it should be broad with good cheeks.
Muzzle not more than 3.5 ins. long, deep and broad.
Nostrils large and broad.
Flews not pendulous, stop moderate, mouth level, favouring projection of the lower rather than the upper incisors.
Canine teeth large and set wide.
Eyes dark and of medium size, set apart the width of the muzzle with furrow between. Light or yellow eyes most objectionable.
Dark mask essential.
Forehead flat, ears "V" or folded back, set on wide and high, level with the occiput, giving a square appearance to the skull, which is most important. They should be small and denser in colour than the body.
Neck slightly arched, moderate length, very muscular and almost equal in circumference to the skull.
Chest wide and deep, well set down between forelegs.
Shoulders muscular and sloping.

Girth may be one third more than the dog's height.
Ribs arched, deep and well set back to hips.
Back short, giving a compact carriage.
Loins wide and muscular, with fair depth of flank.
Arms powerful, elbows square, forelegs straight, well boned and set wide apart.
Pasterns straight.
Feet not large with well rounded toes well arched (cat feet), pads hard.
Hind legs strong and muscular with well developed second thigh, denoting power but not cumbersome.
Hocks well bent, cow hocks or splay feet decidedly objectionable.
Tail set high, strong at the root and tapering, reaching to the hocks, straight or curved but never carried hound fashion.
Coat short and dense, giving weather protection.
Colour – any shade of fawn or brindle.

This Standard was unaltered until 1937 when the main change was in the weight; the dog's weight became 100-125 lbs and the Standard weight for bitches 90 to 110 lbs. Further changes of the Standard occurred in 1943, again in 1956 and in 1994. At the time of writing there are suggestions that the Standard should again be altered due to what some consider to be ambiguous wording.

One must take into consideration the fact that, in the post-recognition era, there was a drawing together of a multiplicity of types and sizes in the breed. The conventions of shows and show techniques were irrelevant when, in some isolated woodland in the early hours of the morning, an assailant was about to attack the gamekeeper with knife or cudgel. These early dogs gave obvious indications of their previous functions and, in some quarters, were labelled as "Bad Mastiffs not Bull Mastiffs". They were not the type of dog to be trifled with and, as we are aware of the fact that not just Bulldog and Mastiff went into the early breedings, type was extremely variable. The fact that a Breed Standard was drawn up is proof that changes were being contemplated and that the show ring was a useful form of publicity and trade.

THE FARCROFT INFLUENCE

The National Bullmastiff Police Dog Club under the guiding hand of Mr Moseley, encouraged members to exhibit their dogs and had quite an impressive bronze medallion struck showing a Bull Mastiff head in relief and the name of the club in enamel. I have one of these medallions in my collection and, although the head is not quite what would pass as a winner today, it is recognisably a Bullmastiff. In one of his booklets, Mr Moseley states that this head study is of Farcroft Fidelity.

Although Mr Moseley's formula for the cross breeding, which was the foundation of his Farcroft Kennels, has something of a fairy tale element about it, he brought the breed out of the shadows of the night and into a blaze of publicity. He foresaw a market and was determined to develop it. It can truthfully be said that every Bullmastiff in the world today has at least one Farcroft as an ancestor. He clearly understood the power of publicity and advertising. "Faithful and fearless, but not ferocious" was how he described the Farcrofts; this caption appears on his headed notepaper. I have one of his letters, which is interesting as the notepaper serves a dual purpose. The front is for the letter and the back is a pedigree form – obviously Mr Moseley studied economy. The heading on the notepaper reads: "S.E. Moseley, Breeder, Trainer, Exhibitor, Exporter. Author of *Bull-Mastiff History*, Standard type and utility with illustrations and reviews and hints on training including tracking". A portrait of a young girl holding a BullMastiff graces the top left-hand corner of the page.

The pedigree on the back of the letter refers to "Sorrel of Lyndorgan" registered 21.8.31 Gazette 618. The sire was Farcroft Formative, the dam Farcroft Staunch. An attached sheet reads: "Farcroft Tenacity is bred exactly the same way as Farcroft

Staunch. There were eight sisters – Farcroft Staunch, Leech, Patrol, Tenacity, Vigilant, Trailer, Fearless and Quest."

In order to keep up with the very considerable demand for stock, Farcroft had dogs out on breeding terms. At home there were a few Mastiffs, German Shepherd Dogs and Cocker Spaniels. There was a team of Bull-Mastiff stud dogs housed at Farcroft which were extensively advertised at the time and were very well used.

The claim to be "Author of Bull-Mastiff History etc." is quite true, but the booklet consisted of sixteen pages, most of which are taken up with adulation of Farcrofts. Business acumen was a Moseley strong point but

Ch. Copperfield Capt. Bailey: "Faithful and fearless, but not ferocious".

Photo: Pamela Jeans-Brown.

modesty rarely appears on any of the pages. In my copy (the booklet sold for one shilling – 5p in modern currency) the front cover has all the Moseley publicity plus a portrait of Farcroft Fidelity. The author states that he was "The originator of the breed in the accepted type" and that "Every challenge certificate winner carries 'Farcroft' blood." It goes on to claim that he is "The oldest breeder-trainer and the largest kennel of true type Bull-Mastiffs in the world". The booklet announces that Farcroft is under Royal Patronage and that Farcroft dogs are "Big enough to be powerful but not too big to be active".

In the Farcroft heyday bitches were usually sent for mating duly crated and despatched by train. After successful mating the bitch was again crated and despatched home by train. A condition at Farcroft was that bitches were only received at the owner's risk, but "every care will be taken under my personal supervision". All fees were to be pre-paid and the return carriage remitted at the time of advice of the bitch's despatch. Moseley often selected which of his stud dogs should be used and, in order to guide him in such selection, he requested that the owner forwarded a copy of the pedigree. He made a price reduction in stud fees of half a guinea for bitches which had been purchased from Farcroft and a further rebate of half a guinea to all members of the National Bullmastiff Police Dog Club.

With such a potentially lucrative business, plus the run of show wins, it is not surprising to read that Farcroft had its critics. In *Sports and Fancies* Christmas edition in 1930 one reads: "One cannot be altogether surprised that Farcroft's successes have planted that arch fiend, jealousy, in the hearts of some of Mr. Moseley's would be supplanters, who would usurp, rather than take a more honourable course, of place by merit. He is the generally accepted originator of the breed and, to him, the fancy owes its progress and fixing of a true standard type."

That the Bullmastiff, as a pure breed of fixed type, owes its inception to Mr Moseley, is shown by a glance through the pedigree of any prominent winner, where invariably its foundation was laid at Farcroft.

As Farcroft Fidelity was the first Bull-Mastiff to win a first prize, present-day readers will probably wonder about his overall size. According to his owner/breeder, Fidelity, at three years of age, stood 28 inches at the shoulder, weight 116 lbs, chest girth 40 inches, neck and skull 26 inches, muzzle circumference 16 inches and forearm 11 inches. He is "straight and active as a terrier". The National Bullmastiff Police Dog Club advocated dogs to be 26 to 28 inches at the shoulder and 90 to 110 lbs in weight, bitches 25 to 27 inches at the shoulder and 80 to 90 lbs in weight.

The breed's first Champion was the brindled bitch, Farcroft Silvo, bred by Mr Moseley in 1925 from Hamil Grip out of Farcroft Belltong. As already mentioned, Moseley used the prefix "Hamil" in his early days, the name being adopted from a village near Burslem. Pedigrees at that time, especially for cross-bred animals, were probably very much word of mouth and so it was not surprising that many good dogs went unregistered. Their function was utilitarian and not primarily for breeding or exhibition. The dam of Farcroft Fidelity, Farcroft Faithful, died in a poaching affray on the Yorkshire Moors. Writing to Mr Moseley requesting a puppy of the same strain the owner said: "The kiddies wanted her brought home, so I carried her for two miles over the moors and buried her where we can see the grave of the best pal man or child ever had. True to death."

Farcroft gradually wound down and its owner died in 1937. As we said previously, S.E. Moseley did not "invent" the breed, as proven by the references of historical significance. What he did was to see the potential of breeding an animal derived from two of the great British guard breeds but without some of the disadvantages of either. Fashion has changed the Farcroft concept but, without Farcroft, we may not have had the prototype from which the changes have been made.

THE BULLMASTIFF BREED STANDARDS

The content of the Breed Standard is of paramount importance to any breed. One should consider it to be the blueprint, or pattern, not only for breeders, but for judges at any level. To a major extent the Breed Standard reflects the type of work for which a breed was intended.

The Bullmastiff was never intended to be an 'attack' dog. Its function was to knock down and hold. If the basic mechanics of such an action are applied, the animal obviously needs size and weight, especially weight in the forequarters. It needs plenty of thoracic capacity for lung and heart room, and four strong legs with well-muscled hindquarters to be able to allow it to spring and knock its adversary over. The Standards ask for "powerful build, great strength, soundness and activity" but "not cumbersome". Can a lightly-built animal, no matter how apparently sound and not cumbersome, satisfy the requirement of "powerful build and showing great strength." It is very doubtful.

THE BRITISH BREED STANDARD

CHARACTERISTICS
Powerful, enduring, active, reliable.

TEMPERAMENT
High spirited, alert, faithful.

HEAD
Large, square with fair wrinkle when interested.

EYES
Dark or hazel and of medium size.

EARS
V-shaped, folded back.

MOUTH Level desired, but slightly undershot allowed but not preferred.

NECK
Well arched, moderate length, very muscular.

Ch. Dixson Of The Green. Winner of 15 CCs, twice BIS All Breed Championship Shows, five times BIS Bullmastiff specialist Championship Shows, three time winner of Working Groups at All Breed Championship Shows, winner of the Pedigree Chum Championship Stakes 1998.

FOREQUARTERS
Chest deep, wide, well set down between the forelegs with deep brisket.

BODY
Back short and straight giving compact carriage, but not so short as to interfere with activity. Roach and sway backs highly undesirable.

HINDQUARTERS
Loins wide and muscular with fair depth of flank. Hind legs strong and muscular with well developed second thighs.

FEET
Well arched and cat-like with rounded toes, pads hard, dark toe nails desirable, splayed feet highly undesirable.

TAIL
Set high, strong at root and tapering, reaching to the hocks, carried straight or curved but not hound fashion, crank tails highly undesirable.

GAIT/MOVEMENT
Movement indicates power and sense of purpose. When moving straight neither front nor hindlegs should cross or plait, right front and left rear leg rising and falling at same time. A firm backline unimpaired by powerful thrust from hindlegs denoting a balanced and harmonious movement.

COAT
Short, hard, weather-resistant and lying flat to the body. Long, silky and woolly coats highly undesirable.

COLOUR
Any shade of brindle, fawn or red; colour to be pure and clear. A slight white marking on chest permissible. Other white markings undesirable. Black muzzles essential, toning off towards eye, with dark markings around eyes contributing to expression.

SIZE
Height at shoulder: dogs: 63.5 to 68.5 cm, 25 to 27 inches; bitches: 61 to 66 cm, 24 to 26 inches. Weight: dogs: 50 to 59 kg, 110 to 130 lb; bitches: 41 to 50 kg, 90 to 110 lb.

NOTE: Male animals should have two apparently normal testicles fully descended into the scrotum.

Reproduced by kind permission of the Kennel Club.

THE AMERICAN BREED STANDARD

GENERAL APPEARANCE
That of a symmetrical animal, showing great strength, endurance, and alertness; powerfully built but active. The foundation breeding was 60% Mastiff and 40% Bulldog. The breed was developed in England by gamekeepers for protection against poachers.

SIZE, PROPORTION, SUBSTANCE
Size: Dogs, 25 to 27 inches at the withers, and 110 to 130 pounds weight. Bitches, 24 to 26 inches at the withers, and 100 to 120 pounds weight. Other things being equal, the more substantial dog within these limits is favored.

Proportion: The length from tip of breastbone to rear of thigh exceeds the height from withers to ground only slightly, resulting in a nearly square appearance.

HEAD
Expression: Keen, alert, and intelligent.
Eyes: Dark and of medium size.
Ears: V-shaped and carried close to the cheeks, set on wide and high, level with occiput and cheeks, giving a square appearance to the skull; darker in color than the body and medium in size.
Skull: Large, with a fair amount of wrinkle when alert; broad, with cheeks well-developed. Forehead flat.
Stop: Moderate.
Muzzle: Broad and deep; its length, in comparison with that of the entire head, approximately as 1 is to 3. Lack of foreface with nostrils set on top of muzzle is a reversion to the Bulldog and is very undesirable. A dark muzzle is preferable.
Nose: Black, with nostrils large and broad.
Flews: Not too pendulous.
Bite: Preferably level or slightly undershot. Canine teeth large and set wide apart.

NECK, TOPLINE, BODY
Neck: Slightly arched, of moderate length, very

Am. Ch. Blackslate's Boston Brahmin: A Best in Show winner, now aged thirteen – a great age for the breed.

muscular, and almost equal in circumference to the skull.

Topline: Straight and level between withers and loin.

Body: Compact. Chest wide and deep, with ribs well sprung and well set down between the forelegs.

Back: Short, giving the impression of a well balanced dog.

Loin: Wide, muscular, and slightly arched, with fair depth of flank.

Tail: Set on high, strong at the root, and tapering to the hocks. It may be straight or curved, but never carried hound fashion.

FOREQUARTERS

Shoulders muscular but not loaded, and slightly sloping. Forelegs straight, well boned, and set well apart; elbows turned neither in nor out. Pasterns straight, feet of medium size, with round toes well arched. Pads thick and tough, nails black.

HINDQUARTERS

Broad and muscular, with well developed second thigh denoting power, but not cumbersome. Moderate angulation at hocks. Cowhocks and splay feet are serious faults.

COAT

Short and dense, giving good weather protection.

COLOR

Red, fawn, or brindle. Except for a very small white spot on the chest, white marking is considered a fault.

GAIT

Free, smooth, and powerful. When viewed from the side, reach and drive indicate maximum use of the dog's moderate angulation. Back remains level and firm. Coming and going, the dog moves in a straight line. Feet tend to converge under the body, without crossing over, as speed increases. There is no twisting in or out at the joints.

TEMPERAMENT

Fearless and confident yet docile. The dog combines the reliability, intelligence, and willingness to please required in a dependable family companion and protector.

Reproduced by kind permission of the American Kennel Club.

DISCUSSING THE STANDARDS

CHARACTERISTICS

The leading word is "powerful". As for "active" – does this mean in mind, body or both? A true watchdog is always watching, listening, smelling and then acting on what it has seen, heard or smelled. As regards the word "reliable", my interpretation is that one can rely on the dog to react in the required manner for which he has been bred and kept.

If we look again at the word "powerful" as applied to the dog, it is suggestive of size, strong bone, ample muscular development, overall strength of constitution, together with

Ch. Dajean Goldust The Poachersfoe: The UK's breed bitch CC recordholder with 21 CCs, Top Bullmastiff 1992, Top Bullmastiff bitch 1993.
Photo: Carol Ann Johnson.

Am. Ch. Ladybug's Lady Caitlin TD: This owner-handled bitch was a prolific winner in the show ring, winning seven All Breed Best in Shows and two National Specialties. She was No.1 bitch 1989-1992 and the No. 2. Bullmastiff 1991 and 1992. She was the fourth dog in the breed's history to win the Tracking title.

the mentality to co-ordinate and use those physical attributes to advantage.

TEMPERAMENT
"Faithful" needs no explanation and is a characteristic which most Bullmastiffs possess in excelsis. "High spirited": here I give the dictionary definition – "showing courage, mettle, or enterprise". For "mettle" the dictionary definition is "the stuff a person or animal is made of in regard to spirit, courage or endurance". Not every Bullmastiff being shown at the present time quite comes up to the definition of high spirits.

HEAD
Most owners and judges would agree that this is a "head breed", i.e. the distinctive head is one of its most important features. A plain head rarely shows sufficient wrinkle, even when the dog is interested and must, therefore, be considered a fault. On the other extreme is a head which is over-wrinkled to such an extent that it typifies a Dogue de Bordeaux rather than a Bullmastiff.

The muzzle length in relation to the skull is important. No one wishes to see a return of the long, weak muzzle which was prevalent before the war. One could say in its favour that it was functional but, at the same time, could such a muzzle fulfil the requirement of "square when viewed from every angle"?

The ultra short muzzle is also wrong, as such a muzzle could give breathing difficulties and reduce function. I think that the English wording of the muzzle to be "approximately" one third of the length of the skull, gives breeders and judges a degree of flexibility.

On the subject of muzzles, it is not always appreciated that these, too, must be square if the requisite squareness of the head is to be achieved. In many otherwise attractive heads there is a tendency for the muzzle, when

TWO FRENCH RESIDENTS

Copperfield Clara Peggotty: Viewed from the front, the muzzle must be square.
Photo: Berthou.

A good head showing excellent pigmentation.
Photo: Berthou.

viewed from the front, to be triangular due to a falling away beneath the eyes. The length of muzzle will change as the puppy grows and matures but, unless the muzzle is broad and full under the eyes (which can be easily felt), this triangular tendency will remain even in the mature head.

EYES

There are some judges and breeders who feel that the eyes should be almost black, but this is not a requirement of the Standards. "Hazel" can be described as either a greenish brown or, more correctly, as a "reddish brown". The word dark obviously means "dark brown". I have known instances where, in a young animal, eyes looked too light but darkened to an acceptable colour by the age of two. A really yellowish green in a puppy rarely, if ever, darkens to the requisite colour.

A "medium sized" eye is called for. Quite a proportion of exhibits today have eyes which appear to be too large; on careful scrutiny,

however, it will be noted that the size of eye fits the Standard, but, as it is not deeply set, it will appear to be larger than it should be. A roundish, somewhat protruding eye spoils the intense expression which typifies the breed; but, at the same time, a proportion of breeders claim that such an eye-setting rarely has entropion, a painful condition which sometimes affects the deeply set eye.

EARS

This, to me, is the most baffling part of the Standards' requirements. I cannot see how a V-shaped ear can remain V-shaped if "folded back". One presumes that a "folded back" ear is one in which the ear has a fold in the V, so that part of the inside of the ear is visible, whereas in the true V it is not. Small dark ears, correctly placed on the skull and carried in a V touching the cheeks, greatly enhance the overall squareness of the skull which is of such importance in the breed.

Ch. Bunsoro Red Sails: A typical Bullmastiff head showing the correct squareness of muzzle.
Photo: Dalton

MOUTH

If we consider the progenitors of the breed, neither of which have level bites, is it practical to ask for a level bite in the Bullmastiff and why is it desirable? I would query the mechanical efficiency of a level bite. The wear on teeth in such a formation would be excessive. Perhaps our founders wanted a "scissors" bite which would have had better mechanical efficiency. The slightly undershot bite is quite efficient, provided that the underjaw is wide, the canine teeth well-spaced and the incisors strong and evenly spaced in a straight line between the canine teeth.

When the underjaw is so undershot as to make it difficult for the animal to contain its tongue this must be penalised as a fault. A broad underjaw, with strongly set teeth and slightly undershot, often gives the head an expression of strength and determination. A slightly overshot lower jaw in a puppy often becomes a level bite in adulthood, whereas a badly undershot jaw in a puppy usually becomes worse as the animal matures.

NECK

Nothing enhances the Bullmastiff profile more than a good, well-arched neck, sweeping back into well-placed shoulders. Short stuffy necks are usually accompanied by straight shoulders.

FOREQUARTERS

If asked what fault is the most common in Bullmastiffs today I would say that it was lack of correct forequarters. If the original purpose of the breed was the ability to down a man and hold him down, such action would, to a major extent, call for a strong front which would be the point of impact between dog and "victim". In so many otherwise attractive exhibits there is a lack of width of chest, depth of brisket and overall hard muscular development of the forequarters. If viewed from the front the brisket should come down in a U formation to the level of the elbows. Far too many lack this essential, often to the extent of the U formation being inverted in what some call a "Gothic window" formation – which is quite an apt description.

BODY

I think that the compilers of the Standards really meant short and level rather than short and "straight" – a "crooked" back would certainly be an anatomical phenomenon. In practically every standard for dogs of the Mastiff group a long back is required. At the present time many Mastiffs in Britain are being criticised for being short in the back and rightly so if judged to their Standard. What I think is important and often overlooked in the Bullmastiff Standard, are the words "but not so short as to interfere with activity". The word "activity" features throughout the Standard and the very fact that it is used as a qualifying condition to the words "back short" seems to be overlooked by too many.

What benefit would there be in a very short back, other than the fact that some would admire it in the show ring? It could be a great disadvantage to a breeding bitch by reducing her capacity to carry a litter and would look disproportionate in a substantially built dog. One should ask oneself why the racehorse is long-backed and why the short-backed riding cob could never compete in a steeple chase. To shorten the back to a major degree would be a retrograde step from many points of view.

HINDQUARTERS

There is no mention of the degree of angulation in the hind limb except that the hocks should be moderately bent. All too often owners and some judges fail to realise that the dog drives off its hocks and the lower the set of hock the greater the drive. Hocks are a very important factor in the geometry of the hind limb.

FEET

Feet vary considerably at the moment. Many tend to be flat and spread which is often the

A good wide front, straight forelegs and correct depth of brisket.   *Photo: Sheila Atter.*

result of under-exercise. It is not always appreciated that one of the best exercises for a dog's front feet is to give it large marrow bones to chew. The amount of "toe work" which the animal does in holding, moving and turning the bone around is far more than can be achieved by a long walk.

A comparatively new fetish is for black toenails. The British Standard asks for dark not black toenails and does not insist on this but calls it "desirable". I have known instances when judges (who should know better) have criticised an exhibit for not having black toenails. The reason why a dark toenail is advocated is that light or poorly pigmented nails are much softer than their dark-coloured counterparts. As most of us have the unenviable task of periodically clipping toenails, I would have thought that a

Wyburn Mister Syreshan: The outline of a young male.

Photo: Leigh.

Ch. Graecia Mercury: The back should be short and straight.　*Photo: Sheila Atter.*

lightly coloured and therefore softer nail which, in all probability, would be self-regulating as regards length, would be a distinct advantage.

TAIL

Tail faults are common. One of the most prevalent faults is that, due to a steeply set pelvis, the root of the tail is set too low. The tail is an extension of the spine and its root should reflect this, hence the Standards' requirement of set high and carried straight. In normal circumstances and especially when moving, the tail should be carried at the same level as the spine. The words "or curved" means that the end of the tail may have an upward turn. On no account should the tail be carried "hound fashion", i.e. at nearly a 90 degree angle to the spine – there are quite a few dogs which do this.

The vexed question of crank tails has been with us for many years. There are minor cranks in many tails which are not noticeable unless the hand is run down the tail from the base to the tip. A common crank is very high up and near the root of the tail, which is almost imperceptible except when the dog wishes to wag or raise its tail and the

Blackslate's Dream Chaser, imported from the USA by John and Muriel Bisatt. Despite its size, the Bullmastiff should appear ready to spring into action.

restricted tail movement becomes obvious. When judging Mastiffs over the years I have found that in this breed there are many kinks or slight cranks in the tail – and these, as so often in Bullmastiffs, are usually the animals with the strongest heads.

GAIT/MOVEMENT

Movement in any breed is indicative of the anatomical construction required by the Standard and must be specifically assessed. A Bullmastiff which moves with the stilted hind action of a Chow, the rolling movement of an Old English Sheepdog or the high stepping action of a Poodle, would be quite untypical. The straight hindquarters of the Chow produces the typical Chow movement required by the Chow Standard. In the Bullmastiff we have long battled with straight hindquarters and I am pleased to say that, to a major extent, such battles have reduced the incidence of the straight hind legs. All that we ask for is that the front and the hind legs follow a straight line and do not cross or plait and that the backline is unimpaired by a powerful thrust from the hind legs.

Correct movement is an essential in any breed and, as already mentioned, the anatomical construction is linked with movement, but so are such factors as body condition and overall general health. The

correct diet, the amount of regular exercise and the type of such exercise are all contributory factors. Overweight dogs, heavy with fat and lacking in muscle tone, cannot be expected to move enthusiastically, neither is it logical to expect a dog at the top of the height/weight scale of the Standard to be able to move as quickly as one of lighter construction and at the bottom of the Standard's size requirements. Many Bullmastiffs move very closely at the hind end and one sees a growing tendency for some to move with a loose "flapping" of the pasterns in the front.

COAT

This is self-explanatory and befitting for such an outdoor working breed.

SIZE

There is a practical degree of latitude in the maximum and minimum heights and weights of the breed. It would be an interesting exercise to weigh and measure a cross-section of the winning exhibits. My guess is that some of the biggest would tip the scales but, at the same time, some of the smallest would be marginally under the requisite minima. We need to avoid breeding Bullmastiffs which almost reach Mastiff proportions but, at the same time, we must never reduce the breed

Ch. Patchings August Lady: (Pitmans Major – Maggie of Pitmans), owned by Linda and Robert Wade. The fawn colour may be quite pale.
Photo: Roy Sainsbury.

Zingara De Castro Castalia At Murbisa (Blackslate's Mr Heartbreaker – Oddrock Sarah), imported from Spain. Owned by John and Muriel Bisatt. Brindle markings may be dark, but they must be distinct.

Kingsreach William Rufus (Kingsreach Thundercloud – Bunsoro Forever Amber), owned by Di Williamson. A deeper red-fawn.

Wyburn Just-So (Wyburn Rustler – Maxstoke Miranda), bred by Miss C. Risdale: Well up to size, and combining a powerful but active build.

to the size of a Boxer. It is far easier to lose size in animal breeding; it is often an uphill battle to try to regain it.

THE BULLMASTIFF CHARACTER

The brief summary given in the Breed Standard under "Characteristics" is: "Powerful, enduring, active and reliable". Under "Temperament" we find: "High-spirited, alert and faithful".

This is an accurate summary of the breed both physically and mentally. When dealing with the Bullmastiff one should never lose sight of the fact that the breed was created as a hybrid of the two oldest British guarding and fighting breeds. It was developed to do a tough job of work and to give a good account of itself in any role where courage and strength were almost literally a matter of life and death.

Over the past half-century these original services and functions have almost disappeared and, in any case, would not be tolerated by modern legislation. The fact that the breed is rarely put to the test nowadays does not (or should not) mean that its capabilities have, in any way, diminished. It must remain a spirited guard dog but one has to admit that the old level of aggression, which was difficult to disguise and control in the dogs of the early 1930s, would be unacceptable to most owners today.

The breed has a natural affinity for children, especially if reared with a child who is correctly instructed in the dog/child relationship necessary with any breed. It is normally a quiet breed, barking only when there is a real need of sounding the alarm on the approach of strangers, or some unusual noise in the immediate area. The Bullmastiff has very acute hearing, good vision and a surprising scenting ability. No breed needs more human contact if its intelligence and devotion is to be developed. They all seem to enjoy physical human contact, such as being

able to lean against the owner's legs. Once this deep liaison has been established, the Bullmastiff develops a desire to please and will often show great contrition when it realises that some misdemeanour has displeased the human object of its affection. Over the years I have found that bitches are easier to live with than the males. There is a tendency amongst males, which have reached puberty, to become intolerant of other male dogs. This can cause some difficulty, as the Bullmastiff is often very territorial and resentful of any stray dog trespassing on his property. Care should be taken if a visitor to

Germ. imp. Eng. Ch. Hurry vom Frankental: The weight and power of a Bullmastiff makes it a formidable opponent.

Jobull's Tornado of Frankental (Ch. Hurry vom Frankental – Ch. Blazins Jubillation of Jobull.) Intelligence and devotion are both highly developed.

Am. Ch. Blackslate's Boston Blackie: A sire of international influence. He was bred in the USA, travelled to Scandinavia, through Europe, particularly Germany and Spain, and returned to the USA, leaving offspring in every country he visited.

the Bullmastiff owner's house decides to bring their own dog on the visit.

As the breed becomes increasingly "civilised" I sometimes wonder whether "activity", "high spirits" and "alertness" have also been somewhat diminished. To walk past the show benches today and see the exhibits peacefully dozing and often unattended, is a very different scene when compared with the Bullmastiff benches, even as recently as the 1950s, when there were always a few spoiling for a fight.

There are breeds which may be larger than this one but few which have greater strength and stamina. A well-built Bullmastiff in peak, hard condition is a very formidable adversary, which is why the owner must always be in control of the dog, who will accept this subservient relationship. Some unpleasant accidents could occur if the roles became reversed.

CHOOSING A PUPPY

Anyone proposing to purchase a Bullmastiff, especially if they have no previous experience of the breed, would be well-advised to attend a few shows in which breed classes are scheduled. This will give an indication of size, especially the quite noticeable size difference between the sexes. Talk to some of the exhibitors about the nature and attitude of the exhibits. Compare the colours and consider which of the three colours is the most attractive to you. Having done the rudimentary spadework, look through the advertisements of the dog papers and visit the premises of a breeder advertising puppies for sale. For a complete novice to buy a puppy from a "Free Ad" type of paper is courting disaster. A UK breeder, licensed by the local authority under the breeding of dogs act 1973, must have satisfied the conditions and regulations regarding health and wellbeing of the kennel inmates and should, therefore, be a reliable source. The

The Bullmastifff has a natural affinity with children – but take care that babies and small children are always closely supervised.

dam should be at the kennels, so ask to see her. The sire may be owned by someone else and not readily available. If you know someone who has a fair knowledge of the breed, or is conversant with what constitutes good anatomical construction of a puppy, invite this person to accompany you.

If you are inexperienced with the breed, I would not recommend that you take anything but a puppy, especially if you have children. An older dog unaccustomed to children can, on very rare occasions, present problems.

It is common sense, especially if the kennels are some distance from your home, to make a definite appointment to see the

If you are planning to show your dog, essential points of conformation will need to be assessed.

A litter of 14 puppies sired by Am. Ch. Oakridge Fresh Prince ex Can. Ch. Blazins Tiara of Nytestock. Bred by Amy and Lanson Hayword.

Photo: Lynn Murphy.

A healthy puppy should be well-covered, but not obese. Photo: Anne-Marie Class.

litter. Kennel owners are busy people but are usually willing to give time to anyone seriously interested in the breed. Note the condition and temperament of the dam. Bear in mind that she has produced and fed a litter and cannot be expected to be in show condition. A bitch will often shed her coat after rearing a litter but there should not be any obvious signs of ill-health. Note the temperament of both the parents and the puppies. If they shy away or run and hide – forget them. They are likely to develop into nervous adults. A well-nurtured puppy should not be fat but certainly should not be showing its ribs. If pot-bellied, it is probably worm-infested.

Avoid any puppy with weeping eyes or discharges from the nostrils, irritation of skin in the ear channel, crank tail, lack of pigmentation (black muzzle, dark ears), badly undershot or overshot lower jaw, excessive white markings, light or "flat" bone in the limbs, bent front limbs, greenish or yellowish eyes, long or excessively woolly coat. If pigmentation of muzzle and ears is poor, never believe the old favourite tall story

Pictured (left to right): Kingsreach Forester, Kingsreach Border, Lord, Barclaydoons Lilybelle, Kingsreach Tapestry, Kingsreach Mystic Prince and Kingsreach Lady Hawke.

that pigmentation will come – it is more likely to get poorer, not better.

If the parent stock satisfies you, choose the puppy which possesses fewest of the faults listed above; look for one which stands four-square on strong legs, is self-assured, has plenty of distance between the forelegs, and evidence of a depth of brisket. Study the distance between the eyes. The wider the distance, the greater the possibility of the development of the requisite wide skull and good expression. Ask for a copy of the pedigree, the Kennel Club registration and transfer form, a history of inoculations and worming to date, and, most importantly, a diet chart. It is essential that the feeding regime to which the puppy is accustomed is maintained during the initial period of new ownership.

A LASTING DEBT

No chapter on the Bullmastiff could be considered to be complete without expressing appreciation of those great breeders who, by perception and perseverance, laid the foundations of the breed and, to a major extent, brought their principles to fruition.

Mr C.R. Leeke of the Bulmas kennel, working chiefly from Farcroft stock, bred and fixed the modern head type. His advertisement: "Always A-Head with Bulmas" was no idle boast. Although in latter years with deteriorating health, he still found what he described to me as "peace and solace" when sitting alone with a growing litter of Bullmastiffs – a breed to which he had been devoted for major part of his life.

Mr E.L. Terry founded his successful Buttonoak kennel on the best Bulmas stock and successfully campaigned it throughout Britain, taking major honours in the show ring. Mr Terry consolidated many aspects of Bulmas.

Finally, Mr Harry Collliass and his wife Beryl, now in their nineties but still owning dogs of the famous Oldwell prefix, and with the assistance of their daughter Anne, breeding the very occasional litter, made a worldwide impact. Although Mr Colliass has lost his sight he is still mentally astute and can easily recall his career in the breed. Oldwell originated on the combination of Buttonoak and Marbette, then owned by Mrs Millard and her daughter. Through careful line breeding a consistent type was established, and this type is still being sought in many parts of the world.

Bullmastiff breeders and exhibitors today owe much to these three stalwarts of the breed.

7 THE NEAPOLITAN MASTIFF
(Mastino Napoletano)
By Douglas Oliff

In the Assyrian section of the British Museum is the Nineveh bas-relief, sculpted about 850 BC, which is in a remarkable state of preservation. The animal portrayed is a long-backed, heavy-fronted, massive dog, with a thick neck, being led on a double rope by a handler whom the dog certainly dwarfs. The head shows a short, truncated muzzle, folds of skin on the cheeks and a pronounced dewlap. The tail is curled up over the back, which may or may not be artistic licence. Those familiar with the Neapolitan Mastiff today will recognise the long stride of the foreleg, which is typical, and can be seen in the best contemporary specimens.

EARLY HISTORY

Did such dogs exist over two thousand years ago? We can prove very little. It is possible that the sculptor just imagined that such a dog existed. However, there is such realism in the animal, and such presence and power, that it seems more likely to be from life rather than imagination. What was this ancient giant dog of the Middle East, and what were its origins? It is known that the Greeks and, later, the Romans, admired the ferocious Mastiff-type dogs which were not uncommon in the Middle East. It seems that the word 'Molossus' was used in Roman times to describe any large, formidable guard dog, and such animals were kept in the grand Roman houses for that purpose. One writer has suggested that the dogs were also kept in the Roman temples where "they could distinguish the pious from the idlers, and the Romans from the barbarians". This, I think, is colourful imagery but cannot be seriously considered.

In the fourth century BC, there was a Greek state called Epirus, close to Corfu. The rulers called themselves 'Molossians' and Alexander the Great's mother was of this dynasty. History suggests that when Epirus was overrun by the Roman forces, among the plunder were dogs whose great size and physical power made them worthy imports to Rome for fighting in the arena. We have no proof that this took place, but we know that the Romans had an infallible eye for the appropriation of anything which would add to their glory. As the arena was one of the great pastimes, a superior, or a larger, fighting dog which existed in a conquered country would have been exported to Rome. What is possibly of historical significance is that some of the Greek encyclopaedias, as recently as the turn of to 20th century, listed among the dog breeds the 'Molossian of Epirus'.

What we can safely assume is that before the Second World War a large, heavy guard dog existed in Italy, more especially in the

Ch. Azzura, bred by Carlo Nicoletti in Spain. There are records of large guard dogs that were used on the grand estates, around the Naples area.

region of Naples. It was used as a guardian of some of the grand estates, but also was owned by traders and other members of society. These dogs were more of a type, not a breed, but were generally known as 'Molossian', a term which covered many dogs with guarding abilities and large size. As with the Mastiff in Britain, I have no doubt that the 'Molosser' group contained butchers' dogs, fighting dogs, guard dogs – in fact, any large dog of spirit.

After the war these dogs, which had been owned by a minority pre-war, had become so numerically weak that they were considered by many to be extinct. It should be realised that, even pre-war, the gene pool available to these dogs in a pure form was extremely limited, and the resultant inbreeding probably carried genetically inherited defects, which would have added to the parlous position in which the breed found itself.

RECONSTRUCTION

In 1946 a small nucleus of enthusiasts began to collect data about any living 'Molossians', hoping to establish the breed's existence in a recognisable form. A few animals of vastly differing types and degrees of soundness were located. Their one common feature was something of the spirit of the pre-war dogs. This rather heterogeneous collection was exhibited at the 1946 dog show in Naples, but their impact was not sensational. It was at this show that Piero Scanziani, a dog fancier and journalist living in Naples, was inspired to fight for the cause of the 'Molossian' and to try to save from extinction a breed which was so much part of the Italian heritage.

Scanziani must have realised that to find the breed in a pure form was unlikely, but he knew Naples and the surrounding countryside well, and believed that, with careful selection, it should be possible to reconstruct the old breed, even from such specimens as had already been located. He managed to find three dogs, a male and two bitches, from which to start a reconstruction.

In 1949 he exhibited Guaglione at Naples, and created a sensation in the Italian dog press and dog-owning public. The dog went on to become the first Champion of the breed – but under what breed name? From the old generic term 'Molossian', the recreated breed was to be called the Neapolitan Mastiff or, in its country of origin, Il Mastino Napoletano. Although the name was new, the forebears of the breed were as Italian as the Bay of Naples. The threat of extinction had receded.

To re-establish a breed is not an easy task. It is doubtful if any pedigree records existed in an official form, and, as mentioned earlier in the chapter, unsoundness due to some years of neglect must have been an added problem. In a war-ridden country it was difficult enough to feed the human populace, and the level of nutrition of the dogs must have been fairly low, especially for dogs which were considered to be a guarding 'commodity' and not a house pet.

BREED DEVELOPMENT
In the early days of the breed's emergence there was a difference in concept between breeders in Southern Italy and those of the North. The main argument was about what constituted true type.

The South, which had been the home of the Mastino for centuries, wanted a strong guard dog and had few aspirations for the production of a show dog. Their concept was for a somewhat tough, broad, heavy, low to the ground animal whose function was the defence of persons and property. A small pocket of such dogs existed which were extremely inbred, and possessed disproportionately short, but heavily boned legs, giving such animals a somewhat grotesque appearance. This strain became known as 'Zacarro', which was the name of the breeder whose family had, apparently, owned dogs of this type for many years.

I am not suggesting that all the Southern

Italian breeders owned, bred or even advocated this extreme of type, but the Northern Italian breeders, even in the early days, envisaged a heavy dog combining type, weight, breadth and correct balance. Obviously some of the more progressive breeders realised the show potential and ownership appeal of this unique new development. The disagreement continued over the years but has now, to a major extent, subsided, yet it is still present in the breed diehards.

In 1958 a man who was to strongly influence the breed, and to develop it further, made up the first of his many Champions and International Champions. This breeder was Mario Querci, who owned a small business near Florence, and the dog was his Sahib 1. In the same year he made up his first Champion bitch, called Susi, and began registering dogs under his prefix Ponzano in 1963.

Ponzano, by virtue of the owner's breeding skills and the numerical strength of the kennel, had worldwide influence. The head type of the latter years of the kennel's existence was different from the rather plain-

Fruit D'Amour Hélène bred and owned by Andrea Spiriev: There was a major split between breeders when trying to establish a true type.

headed days of Sahib 1, but I do not think that Querci would have appreciated some of the excessively over-wrinkled skin and hanging flews which one sees today in some kennels.

Dr G. Benelli, a wealthy industrialist living near Florence, owned a well-known kennel of high class show terriers. Dr Benelli was an international judge and a regular visitor to Crufts. Under the affix del Canadoro, Neapolitan Mastiffs were added to the breeds in his extensive kennel, probably in a dual-purpose role, firstly as part of his Italian heritage and secondly as guardians of the estate, which had a small herd of wild pigs as well as deer. His first Champion was Marcantonio di Ponzano, in 1968, followed in the same year by three more from Ponzano – Giara, Frusta and Quintiliana.

Another kennel of importance in the development of the breed is della Grotta Azzura, which is still active. One of the great influential sires produced in this kennel was Ch. Falco della Grotta Azzurra who became a Champion in 1976. Falco was extensively

Representatives of the famous Ponzano kennel, owned by Mario Querci, who was instrumental in bringing about world recognition of the breed.

used at stud and his influence for the betterment of the breed is legendary. It is impossible to comment on every Italian breeder but one should not overlook the good work of such enthusiasts as Guido Vandoni, and Antonio di Lorenzo of dell'Alta Fiumara, whose El Gavilan dell'Alta Fiumara features in some of the USA pedigrees today.

THE NEAPOLITAN IN BRITAIN

The first importer of the Neapolitan into the UK was Trevor Lewis of the Kensington Dog Bureau in London, who did a lot of trading with Italian dog fanciers, chiefly with toy breeds. A fluent speaker of the language, as his mother was Italian, he was very familiar with the Italian scene.

In a boarding kennels owned by a client he noticed two large Mastiff-type animals of what, to him, was an unrecognisable breed. The kennel owner informed him that they were Mastini, and had been left by a client who now said that he did not wish to have them back, and that they were for sale. Lewis bought the pair, a mahogany registered as Kronos della Presse, and a black bitch called Ursula. Kronos was a quite even-tempered animal, a good guard but very biddable. Ursula had all the old Italian fire and mentality of her forebears. The pair were housed together and mated, but Ursula did not conceive.

The dogs were passed to a Mr N. Homfray, under a breeding terms arrangement. Ursula then conceived and had a big litter, some black, some mahogany and some blue. This was the first Mastino litter to be born in Britain. A few puppies were sold in Britain, but most went abroad. Trevor Lewis imported several other Mastini which again were housed at the kennels of Mr Homfray.

In the mid-1970s I used to organise what was basically a Bullmastiff teach-in and social occasion but, to make it more interesting, I normally invited another Mastiff-type breed to

Clever Duke At Bronorn, owned by Mrs V. Roach in the UK.

Photo: Carol Ann Johnson.

share the day with us. I managed to persuade Trevor Lewis to allow Mr Homfray to bring along some Mastini to what was the first public appearance of the breed in Britain. When I saw that the chosen examples of the breed were Ursula and an eight-week-old litter of puppies, I will admit that I viewed the forthcoming event with some trepidation. However, Ursula was kept on her lead and, surrounded by her offspring, behaved impeccably.

One of Ursula's daughters from her first litter by Kronos, and owned by a Mrs Bacchus in Wiltshire, had been mated back to her sire, as he was virtually the only male in Britain. A litter resulted with some black, like the mother and grandmother, some blue and some mahogany. The Kronos and Ursula combination always seemed to produce these colours. Mrs Bacchus had some difficulty in selling the puppies as she wanted them to go to responsible clients who would realise that these dogs needed a great deal of understanding. Two black bitch puppies remained unsold at nine months, and I was asked if I could help in any way, otherwise they would have to be put down, especially as one of them was somewhat out of hand.

In the company of Dr A. and J. Clark who had become very interested in the breed, I went to see the two puppies, registered as Rosemaund Paula and Rosemaund Netta. Paula, who was a good specimen and quiet-natured like her sire, was chosen by the Clarks and became the foundation of the Kwintra kennels. As, at that time, I had quite enough Bullmastiffs and a few Mastiffs, I declined the offer of taking Netta, but then, realising that the only alternative was having such a vital animal put down, I changed my mind the next day and collected her.

In 1981 Dr Clark imported Winner of Colosseo Avallu from the German kennel of Frau L. Denger. Winner was an impressive blue-grey of very good type and size. The main reason for his purchase was as a future mate for Rosemaund Paula. He was impeccably bred, as not only was he a grandson of Enea di Ponzano, who had sired much high-quality stock for Frau Denger, but his pedigree showed him to be line-bred to one of the greatest early stud dogs, Falco della Grotta Azzura. In due course, Winner was exhibited at shows in Britain and created a great deal of interest in the dog showing scene. Few judges had even seen the breed and fewer still had the necessary breed knowledge to assess him accurately.

In due course he was mated to Rosemaund Paula and a litter was produced. Half were blue or blue grey and the others were black. A male blue-grey, Kwinta Herca, was retained, together with a black bitch. Herca was a much calmer dog than his sire and grew on to be a very well-proportioned Mastino, who sired quality stock chiefly from bitches which Dr Clark imported from Italy and Germany. In its heyday Kwintra housed nine or so adults and, although the numbers bred were not extensive, it was from this kennel that the foundation stock for the first kennel in New Zealand was obtained. The last of the Kwintra bitches died comparatively recently at the age of eleven. My present seven-year-old house dog is a descendant of Dr Clark's first Mastino and is probably the only remaining dog of that strain in Britain today. She was bred in New Zealand from the imported British stock and came back to Britain as a puppy.

USA

The prime mover in introducing the breed to the USA was the late Michael Sottile of New Jersey who in 1973 founded The Neapolitan Mastiff Club of America. Several well-known figures in other breeds became interested but none had Neapolitans for any length of time.

In more recent years the most active and authoritative owner and breeder is Dr Sherilyn Allen with her Ironstone kennel. She based her breeding programme on Italian imports, especially those of the Dell'Alta Fiumara of Antonio di Lorenzo. Dr Allen considers that the Mastino is not a breed for everyone, as their minds and reactions are as individualistic as their physical appearances and one must be aware of that.

The breed population in America is quite high but development is hampered by the AKC's unwillingness to add the Neapolitan Mastiff to its list of accepted breeds. The breed can only be exhibited in Variety Rare Breed classes. In Britain the KC allows breed classes, as the Neapolitan is accepted on the list of registered breeds. The present disadvantage is that the KC Interim Standard is rather basic and very few judges are fully conversant with what constitutes true breed type.

GERMANY

In the 1970s and 1980s Germany had a tremendously important collection of Neapolitan Mastiffs with many highly prized specimens imported from the best Italian breeders. Herr Didion of Neunkirken had an impressive collection of dogs which, had they been extensively used at stud could have made Germany the country to seriously rival Italy for breed quality. Otto Kleemeyer won Best in Show at a Molosser Club show and had great enthusiasm and interest in the breed at that time.

The World Show provides a good opportunity of seeing top-class specimens of the breed.

Photo: Anne-Marie Class.

Frau L. Denger owned a large and very active kennel at Legau and made her imported Enea di Ponzano the hub of her well thought out breeding programme. Enea became an International Champion in 1978. He was a quality, unexaggerated, typical Mastino with a calm temperament which he seemed to pass on to many of his progeny at a time when some temperaments in the breed where somewhat difficult. Frau Denger is now living in Northern Italy and still breeding Neapolitans but not on the same scale.

Herr Walt Weisse of Eiening was for many years the guiding light of the German Molosser Club and he owned, bred and exhibited some very typical specimens of the breed. A pair of bitches from Herr Weisse were the foundation of the Delmast establishment in the UK. Herr Lindemann of Duisburg is still an active exhibitor; and, although her kennel has not been particularly large, Frau Ursula Süss of Wilnsdorf has owned and exhibited some typical and useful specimens of the breed.

Perhaps, in this short survey, you have got the impression that interest in the breed in Germany has flickered to an untimely death. This is not true. There are good Neapolitan Mastiffs in Germany and, we hope, more to come in the future.

THE FCI STANDARD

Scientific Classification: Dog of the Molossoid group (according to Pierre Mégnin's classification). Upright breed with smooth coat, according to Déchambre's classification.
Classification according to use: Guard and defence dog, police and tracking dog.
Origins: Italian, and precisely Neapolitan.

CHARACTERISTICS
(General appearance, conformation, harmony and disposition)
The Neapolitan Mastiff is the guard and defence dog par excellence, of great size, powerful and strongly built, of tough yet majestic appearance, sturdy and courageous, of intelligent expression, endowed with correct mental balance and docile character, non-aggressive, indefatigable defender of person and property.

The general conformation is that of a heavy brachymorph, whose trunk is longer than the height at the withers, harmonious as regards size (heterometry) and profile (alloidism).

Skin not adhering to the underlying tissue but abundant, with slack connective tissue over all parts of the body and especially on the head where it forms wrinkles and folds, and at the neck where it forms the dewlap.

HEAD Brachycephalous – massive, skull broad at the cheek-bones, short. The total length of the head reaches about three tenths of the height at the withers, the length of the muzzle must be one third of the total length of the head.

Neapolitans pictured at the von der Ortelsburg kennel in Germany.

The Neapolitan Mastiff is the guard and defence dog par excellence.

Photo: Sanchez. Courtesy: Vos Chiens Magazine.

In a dog of 70 cm height at the withers, the skull must be 14 cm long and the muzzle 7 cm. The total length of the head 21 cm.

The bizygomatic width of the skull is greater than half of the total length of the head and is all but equal to its length. The total cephalic index has a relationship of about 66.

The directions of the upper longitudinal axis of the skull and muzzle are between their parallel.

Abundant skin with wrinkles and folds, a typical one of which departs from the external palpebral angle and descends with posterior convexity down to the homologous labial angle.

NOSE-TIP Rectilinear. As for the width, measured to half of its length, it must reach about 20 per cent of the total length of the head and about 50 per cent of the length of the nasal shaft.

LIPS AND MUZZLE The lips are of thick tissue, abundant and heavy. The upper lips, seen from the front, define their lower margin precisely up to the conjunction in the shape of a V upside-down, they are abundant and therefore the anterior side of the nose is well developed in height and equally well developed in width.

In addition, given the parallelism of the lateral sides of the nose, the front of the nose must be flat and therefore gives the square of the muzzle.

The lower lateral profile of the nose rises from the lips and the lowest point is not from the lips, but from the labial commisure (junction). The labial commisure is accentuated. In other words its mucosa in the eyelet is formed by the fold of the lower lip with the upper being visible.

The antero-inferior lateral profile of the muzzle presents a fairly closed semicircle.

The length of the mouth is such that the maxillary junction of the lips must meet the perpendicular traced down from the external angle of the eye.

JAWS Strong, well developed and with dental arches meeting perfectly. That is, the inner face of the upper incisors lightly brush the anterior face of the incisors of the mandible (scissors bite) or the terminal surfaces of the upper incisors meet perfectly those of the lower incisors (pincer bite).

The branchiae of the mandible or lower jaw spread out to present a curved profile, especially in the posterior portion. The main section of the mandible should be well developed towards the front and should never recede. It forms a support for the lower lips at the point where they join.

White teeth, regularly aligned, complete in development and number.

FRONT-NASAL DEPRESSION The naso-frontal depression, or Stop, is formed by the meeting of the frontal bones with the aboral line of the two nasal bones and with the upper line of the two upper maxillary bones.

It should present an angle of about 90° when looked at sino-nasally and from 120° to 130° when measured naso-frontally.

SKULL Its length should be equal to two-thirds of the total length of the head and its bizygomatic width should reach its own length.

The cheek bones (zygomatic arches) are

A 17-month-old male showing the typical massive skull with abundant skin and wrinkle.

Photo: Sheila Atter.

prominent, they extend considerably outwards, offering a good insertion for the masticatory and temporal muscles.

Spheroid in shape when seen from the front; in profile it is roughly similar except in its upper aboral part, i.e. between the ears where it is flat. The frontal sinuses are very developed. The mid-frontal suture is well-marked. The occipital crest is pronounced.

EARS Small in relationship to the dog's dimensions, triangular in shape, set well above the cheek bone (zygomatic arch). If left uncut, they hang down flat, close to the cheek and to the parotidea region. In length, they should not extend below the edge of the throat. Where they join the head, the ears rise slightly and then drop abruptly. If the ears are clipped, they are cut almost completely away but point-shaped so as to almost form an equilateral triangle.

EYES The eyelids should normally adhere to the eyeball (neither ectropic, nor entropic). The eyes, situated sub-frontally, are well distanced from one another. The eyelid (palpebral) slit tends to be round, but because of abundant eyebrow skin, it appears to be oval. The eyeball is slightly sunken. Pigmentation on the eyelid edge is black, blue or brown according to the colour of the coat. The colour of the iris blends with darkest colour of the coat.

NECK Short, thickset, very muscular, its length measured from the nape (nuchal crest) to the edge of the skull at the withers it is about 2.8:10 of the height at the withers. Its circumference, measured halfway along its length, is about eight-tenths of the height at the withers. The lower edge of the neck has a great deal of loose skin which forms the dewlap. This should not be too abundant and, most importantly, should not be undivided. The dewlap starts at the branchia of the mandible and ends about half-way down the neck. The upper edge of the neck is slightly convex.

TRUNK The length of the trunk is one tenth longer than the height at the withers when measured from the forward point of the shoulder to the backward point of the buttocks.

CHEST OR THORAX Broad, very open, with very developed pectoral muscles. Its width should be 40-45 per cent of the height at the withers. The manubrium of the sternum should be level with the point of the shoulder.

RIBCAGE Full, descending to the level of the elbow or slightly below. Well convex halfway down its height – its transverse diameter diminishes slightly towards the sternum but without forming a keel. The ribs are long, nicely rounded, oblique, intercostal spaces are well extended, the last false ribs are long, oblique and widely spaced.

The circumference of the ribcage should be about a quarter greater than the height at the withers; measured to the costal arches is about 10 cm less; its transverse diameter should be at least 32 per cent of the height at the withers, the depth should measure 50 - 55 per cent of the height. The thorax index should not be greater than 8, if less than that so much the better.

The sternal region is long and its profile ascends slightly towards the abdomen almost in a straight line.

The body is longer than the height at the withers.

Photo: Sheila Atter.

BACK The upper profile of the back is straight and only the withers rising somewhat above the line. The back is broad and its length is about 32 per cent of the height at the withers.

LOIN AND KIDNEYS Their upper profiles well-merged with the line of the back, slightly convex and well developed musculature in width. The length is a little less than one fifth of the height at the withers; their width approximates to their length as 14.5 to 16.

ABDOMEN AND FLANKS The lower profile of the abdomen is almost horizontal. The flanks must be almost equal in length to the lumbar region. The abdomen appears bulky and the hollow in the flanks should be as small as possible.

HINDQUARTERS The rump, which extends the convex line of the lumbar backwards, should be broad, strong and muscular; hence the transverse diameter between the two hips should be in the ratio of 1.5 to 10 of the height at the withers. The height reaches the upper line of the lumbar. The length should be three-tenths of the height at the withers. The rump slopes down backwards and the slant of the line which joins the external anterior angle of the hipbone to the ischiatic protuberance is about 30° from the horizontal.

SEXUAL ORGANS Perfect, complete, and with an equal development of the two testicles which should be contained in the scrotum.

TAIL The tail is connected to the hindquarters with a wide base; substantial at the root, it tapers slightly towards the tip. When the dog is in repose the carriage of the tail should be scimitar-like , i.e. hanging for the first two thirds and then slightly curved in the lower third. It should never be carried perpendicularly, nor rolled over the back, but horizontal or little higher than the back when the dog is in motion. Its length equals or exceeds by a fraction the articulation of the fetlock. The tail is cut off at about two-thirds of its length.

SHOULDERS The shoulder should be long, slightly sloping and furnished with long muscles which should be well developed and distinctly separated from one another. They should be free in movement. Their length is about three-tenths of the height at the withers. The inclination is 50°-60° to the horizontal. With respect to the mid-plane of the body the points of the scapulae should not be too close and should tend to the vertical.

ARM The arm should be nicely joined to the trunk by its upper three quarters and like the shoulder should have neat, well-developed and strong muscles. Its slant is 55°-60° from the horizontal and its length is about 30 per cent of the height at the withers. Its direction is almost parallel to the median plane of the body.

FOREARMS It presents a vertical straight line and is big boned in structure. Its length roughly equal to the length of the arm. The carpo-cubital groove should be evident. The height of the anterior limb to the elbow is 5.2 to 10 of the height at the withers. The elbows are covered with abundant, slack skin and must lie on a parallel plane to the median plane of the body – and therefore the elbows should not be too tight to the wall of the ribcage and hence eliminating the hollow of the armpit (so-called "closed elbows") nor deviate outwardly ("open elbows"). The point of the elbow should lie on a line descending perpendicularly from the rear point of the scapula.

CARPUS JOINT This lies on the vertical line through the forearm; broad, smooth, dry and free from visible bony reliefs except on its posterior edge where the pisiform bone juts out.

METACARPUS (PASTERN) The metacarpus should be flat from the front to the back viewed from the front and should follow the vertical line of the forearm. Seen in profile, the metacarpus should be fairly spread, about 70-75 degrees. The length should not be less than one sixth of the length of the whole limb to the elbow.

FOOT Round and voluminous in shape with well joined and arched toes, the soles dry and hard, pigmented. Strong nails curved and pigmented.

POSTERIOR LIMBS
THIGH Long and broad, covered with substantial, conspicuous muscles but clearly divided one from the other, the posterior edge tends to be upright. The length of the thigh should not be less than a third of the height at the withers and should be at an angle of about 60°; from the back to the front it almost forms an upright angle with the coaxal. With respect to the vertical, this must be parallel to the median plane of the body.

LEGS With strong bone structure and musculature clearly evident. Length is slightly less than that of the thigh and its inclination from the front to the

back is about 50°-55°; the femoro-rotuleo-tibial angle is about 110°-115°. The grooving in the leg well marked and evident.

HOCK The wider the front the better. Because of the inclination of the tibia, its anterior angle is open. The distance from the sole of the foot to the point of the hock is about a quarter of the height at the withers. Seen from behind, the posterior line descending from the point of the hock to ground should be vertical and an extension of the line of the buttocks. The anterior or tibio-metatarsal angle is between 140°-145° as previously stated.

METATARSUS Robust and lean, nearly cylindrical; its length is about one quarter of the height at the withers; seen from behind, as in profile, it should be vertical, i.e. in perfect plumb. Any single or double spurs which might develop should be removed.

FEET As the forefeet though smaller and with all the attributes of the former.

COAT The hair should be thick, same length all over, uniformly smooth, fine, silky and short with a maximum length of one and a half centimetres; there should not be a hint of a fringe whether on the trunk, limbs or tail. Hair texture is glossy.

COLOUR OF THE COAT The preferred colours are black, lead, grey, and at times with small white flecks on the chest and on the tips of the toes, mahogany, sand or brindle, fawn. All coats may be streaked.

The chest is broad and well-muscled. The ribcage should reach at least to the elbow.

Photo: Sheila Atter.

The forelegs should be strong and straight, and the elbows should not be too close to the body.
Photo: Sheila Atter.

SKIN Abundant all over the body and particularly on the head where it forms numerous folds and wrinkles and at the lower edge of the neck where it forms the dewlap. The pigmentation of the mucosa and the scleroses should be black or brown according to the darker flecks of the coat. The pigmentation of the nails, digital pads and plantars must be dark.

HEIGHT TO THE WITHERS In males from 65 to 75 cm – in females from 60 to 68 cm – with a tolerance of some two cm either way.

WEIGHT From 50 to 70 kgs.

GAIT The gait is one of the typical features of the breed. It is a slow ponderous and loose-jointed lope – like a bear. The trot is slow, with long strides covering a lot of ground. The Neapolitan mastiff rarely gallops.

FAULTS OF TYPE AND CONFORMATION

GENERAL CHARACTERISTICS, APPEARANCE, SYMMETRY A very common fault is a flimsy, bony or spongy structure, lacking in symmetry.

HEAD Upper cranio-facial axle diverging or converging (very serious fault).

NOSE Lower or higher than the line of the nasal bone; protruding from the vertical line of the anterior face of the muzzle – with traces of depigmentation – nostrils not well open, small, with deficient pigmentation.

NASAL SHAFT Long or too short, narrow, lateral lines converging, upper profile not straight.

LIPS AND MUZZLE Muzzle too short or long, lips not sufficiently developed or over-developed and falling below the labial junction, flaccid; folds of the junction too accentuated, dropping too much, turned out too much or lacking. Receding outer edge of the lip. Convergence to the front of the muzzle's lateral walls, i.e. pointed muzzle, and consequently the frontal face of the muzzle is not flat. Upper lip forming a semicircle under the muzzle.

JAWS Weak, prognathism (if the outer aspect of the muzzle is deformed), enognathism due to a deficiency in the length in the mandible's grip (this is a disqualification) or due to deviating teeth (fault). Mandible bones curving inwards too much. Teeth not regularly aligned or else deficient in number; erosion along the horizontal plane of the teeth.

SKULL Small, short, round, narrow on the sides, i.e. at the level of the zygomatic arches and parietals – domed; flattened eyebrow arches; masticatory muscles not well developed; absence of the occipital crest or too exaggerated in development; frontal sinuses not well developed. Naso-frontal depression only slightly accentuated or even receding. Direction of the upper longitudinal skull axis not parallel.

EYES Small or prominent, iris (shading) too light in colour in relationship to the coat; eyelids not in subfrontal position, ectropion, entropion; eyes too close – strabism. Partial depigmentation of the eyelids.

EARS Too long or too short – attached too low – apex of the ear narrow and pointed – badly carried; badly trimmed; hair not short.

NECK Slight or weak, long or too short, flat sides, lacking dewlap or dewlap too abundant and undivided. Deficient curvature at the upper edge; not separated from the nape (nuchal crest); not merging nicely into the shoulders.

SHOULDERS Straight, heavy, short; badly developed muscles; stiff and tight and awkward in movement, points of the scapula too close together.

ARM Too oblique or too straight – short, deficient in musculature, weak bone structure.

FOREARM Slight or spongy bone structure – round bone, deviating from the straight vertical; elbow divergent or convergent – armpit cavity too low. Height from ground to elbow less than half of the height at the withers or considerably more than half.

CARPUS (WRIST-JOINT) With evident hypertrophy of the carpian bone – spongy, small; pisiform bone not protruding; "arrembatura".

METACARPUS Short or too long; weak or slight; too spread out or straight; deviating from the plumb.

FEET Oval, wide, flattened; fat; splayed toes; deficient arching of the toes; carried outward or inwards ("stuck-out" or "pigeon-toes") and thus not in plumb; fleshy digital pads; sole with soft, flabby tissue; deficiency of pigment in the nails and sole. Incorrect positioning of the digital pads and plantars; too long.
BODY Diameter equal to the height at the withers; too long.

CHEST Narrow, not adequately descending; deficiency in development of muscles; manubrium of the sternum situated too low down.

RIBCAGE Deficient in height, depth and narrow perimeter or too wide; decidedly keel-shaped; xifoidean appendix curved inwards; short sternal region; rib cage arches not sufficiently open.

RIBS Not circular; narrow intercostal spaces – short or not sufficiently rounded false ribs; not open and too low.

BACK Short – saddle-shaped or sagging (lordosis), "carpback" (kyphosis); the dorsal line broken at the eleventh vertebra; withers not elevated.

LOINS Long, flat, narrow.

ABDOMEN AND FLANKS Retracted abdomen – flanks with marked inward curve or too long.

SEXUAL ORGANS Incomplete development of one or both testicles; one or both not contained in the scrotum (testicular ectopism) – this merits disqualification – monorchidism and cryptorchidism.

HINDQUARTERS (RUMP) Narrow, deficient in length, not valleyed, horizontal.

THIGH Short, deficient muscular development, narrow, too divaricated in the region of the knee; too straight or too oblique.

LEG Of slight bone structure, leg-fluting not nicely evident; short, too straight or too inclined.

HOCK High, not wide, angle of the hock too open or closed because of forward deviation of the metatarsus; not vertical.

METATARSUS Long, slight, out of plumb; dew-claw.

FEET As for the front feet.

TAIL Too long or too short. Congenital anurism or brachyurism – inserted too low or too high – not sufficiently broad at the root – carried higher than the line of the kidneys – like a trumpet over the back; straight out like a candle – lateral deviation – flaccid, dangling, mouse tail.

HAIR Not short nor hard.

COLOUR OF THE COAT Partially white.

SKIN Adherent to the body in every area; not sufficiently abundant; lack of folds on the head; lack of dewlap.

HEIGHT AT THE WITHERS Deficient or exaggerated.

CHARACTER DEFECTS Timidity, indocility, biting, ferocious (disqualification).

POINTS FOR DISQUALIFICATION

HEAD Accentuated divergence or convergence of the longitudinal, upper skull-facial axis.
NOSE Total depigmentation.
NASAL SHAFT Decidedly "montonina" (sheep-like) – concave.
EYES Magpie like – total bilateral depigmentation of the eyelid – bilateral strabism.
JAW Accentuated prognathism – enognathism.
NECK Deprived of dewlap.
SEXUAL ORGANS Monorchidism – cryptorchidism.
TAIL Anurism, congenital brachyurism, carried like a trumpet over the back.
COAT COLOUR White flecks: partially or completely white.
HEIGHT TO THE WITHERS About 75 cm to the withers, less than 3 cm from the minimum required height.

SCALE OF POINTS	
General conformation and stature	30
Skull and muzzle	20
Eyes and ears	10
Chest	15
Loins and hindquarters	10
Anterior and posterior limbs and feet	20
Tail	10
Fur and colour of coat	15
Expression, presence and character	20
Total points	150

TITLE OR RATINGS	
Excellent	140 points or over
Very Good	130 points or over
Good	110 points or over
Quite good	100 points or over

© *Fédération Cynologique Internationale.*

INTERIM BRITISH STANDARD

GENERAL APPEARANCE
Well boned, large, strongly built, vigorous, alert and muscular. Of majestic bearing, with intelligent expression.

CHARACTERISTICS
A degree of loose-fitting skin over body and head, with some dewlap, is a feature, not to be excessive.

TEMPERAMENT
Devoted and loyal guard of owner and property.

HEAD AND SKULL
Head large, broad short skull. Broad across cheeks. Head proportion: skull length 2:3 to muzzle 1:3. Top of skull parallel to topline of muzzle. Well pronounced, definite stop, nose should not protrude beyond vertical line of muzzle. Nose large with well opened nostrils, lips full and heavy. Upper lip resembles inverted V. Muzzle deep, sides flat and vertical, showing flews. Head deep and spherical.

EYES
Set forward, well apart, rather rounded. Set fairly deep. Rim pigmentation to tone with nose colour.

EARS
Small for size of head, set forward, high and well apart. Triangular, hanging flat towards cheeks, but not reaching beyond line of throat.

MOUTH
Teeth white and regular. Strong, well developed jaws, with scissor bite, but level tolerated. Scissor bite, i.e. upper teeth closely overlapping lower teeth and set square to the jaws.

NECK
Short, stocky, very muscular, dewlap from lower jaw reaching mid-point of neck.

FOREQUARTERS
Shoulder long, slightly sloping with well developed and definite muscle. Elbows not too close to body to allow very free action. Pasterns slightly sloping, legs vertical when viewed from front.

BODY
Longer than height at withers. Broad, well muscled chest, ribcage reaching at least to elbow. Ribs long and well sprung. Topline straight, slightly lower than withers, line of belly parallel to topline.

HINDQUARTERS
Broad loin, well let into backline, slightly rounded with well developed muscle. Croup broad, muscular, with slight slope. Thighs long, broad, moderate stifle, powerful hocks. Dewclaws (single or double) removed.

FEET
Oval; close, arched toes. Pads thick, hard and dark-coloured. Nails curved, strong and dark. Hindfeet slightly smaller than front.

TAIL
Thick at root, set-on slightly lower than topline. Tapering towards tip. Customarily docked by one-third length. Never carried up or over back, but may be carried level with topline when moving.

GAIT/MOVEMENT
Slow, free, bear-like. Slow trot, long steps covering ground well. Rarely gallops.

COAT
Short, dense, even, fine, hard texture, with good sheen. No fringe.

COLOUR
Preferred black, blue, all shades of grey, brown varying from fawn to red. Brindling on either of the latter colours. Small star on chest and white on toes permissible. Pigmentation to tone with coat colours.

SIZE
Height: 65-75 cm (26-29 in).
Weight: 50-70 kg (110-154 lb). Some tolerance allowed. Bitches somewhat less.

FAULTS
Any departure from the foregoing points should be considered a fault and the seriousness with which the fault should be regarded should be in exact proportion to its degree.

NOTE
Males animals should have two apparently normal testicles fully descended into the scrotum.

Reproduced by kind permission of The Kennel Club.

INTERPRETING THE BREED STANDARDS
Whether your interest in the Breed Standard is that of a breeder or of a judge, there is a guiding principle which should be clear at the outset. The Neapolitan Mastiff must not be judged on the same lines as the Mastiff (so often, and quite erroneously, referred to as the Old English Mastiff). In many respects the Neapolitan Mastiff is both physically and mentally unique. Much of the lengthy FCI Standard is self-explanatory and needs no extra comment, but there are some aspects which English-speaking owners do not always understand and they would, therefore, benefit from a few simple explanations.

GENERAL APPEARANCE
"Massive, powerfully built, strong and of majestic appearance with body longer than height at the withers, of heavy substance, and proportionate."

It will be noted that the Standard is not asking for a tall dog or one of light substance. The specification is for good body length and massive build. The Standard also requires the animal to be robust, courageous, not aggressive, and "an unsurpassed defender of persons and property".

As a working guard breed, any exaggeration likely to diminish its abilities to act satisfactorily in the capacity for which it was developed is to be deplored. One should particularly note the word "proportionate" under general appearance.

We must all have seen specimens with heavy bodies hanging with loose skin, and disproportionately short legs which may have massive bone but so often carry deeply wrinkled skin, looking as if the animal was

Fruit D'Amour Felicita, bred and owned by Andrew Spiriev: The Neapolitan's build is both massive and majestic.

wearing "loose stockings". Because of these disproportions, the movement can only be described as a waddle. At the other extreme, one has the "Dane" type – tall, narrow, lacking in rib and body-depth and without the requisite amount of loose skin to be typical.

One sees both of these extreme types being awarded prizes, yet the Breed Standard is quite clear on what is required, and both the extremes are incorrect. One is aware that the FCI Standard, with its multiplicity of percentages and geometric angles, is not the type of document with which British or American breeders and judges are normally acquainted, but it is a comprehensive description of the type for which we should aim, both as breeders and judges.

The specific requirement that "the skin is not adherent to the underlying tissue, but is copious, with lax connective tissue all over the body, especially on the head where it forms wrinkles and folds, and a dewlap on the neck" is important.

In almost any other breed such features would be penalised and considered coarse and untypical. This requirement of loose skin makes the Neapolitan a distinct breed. One

should be able to pick up handfuls of loose skin on either side of the neck. The reason for this goes back to the breed's history as a fighting dog. When fighting, an adversary would grab a mouthful of skin at the neck instead of getting at the vital windpipe or jugular.

HEAD

The somewhat precise geometrical requirements need deep study and almost require geometrical drawing instruments to correctly measure the requisite angles. The most important requirement which makes the Neapolitan head quite distinct, is the statement in the Standard which specifies that "the longitudinal axis of the top of the skull, and the top of the muzzle, are parallel." In the Mastiff this axis is quite curved. In the Neapolitan, the top of the skull between the insertion of the ears should be quite flat. In many of the modern dogs one sees a definite curve where there should be flatness.

The muzzle/skull proportions are that the muzzle should be one-third of the total length of the head. The muzzle is quite distinctive. When viewed from the front, the side faces of the muzzle are parallel and the front face is deep, as well as wide, thus giving the requisite overall squareness.

The lips should be thick, copious, and heavy. If viewed from the front, the upper part of the lips join to form an inverted V; this is important. The line of the top of the nose should be a continuation of the line of the muzzle. The nose should be large, with large, well-open nostrils, black in black dogs, dark in all other colours except mahogany, where it must be brown. The FCI Standard speaks of the "labial commisure" of the lips. This is the lowest point of the head profile, where the upper and lower lips join in a fold. The mucosa (in layman's terms the inner surface of the point of the juncture) should be visible. The frontal lower profile of the

The top of the skull, between the two ears should be quite flat.

muzzle is shaped almost as in a closed semicircle.

JAWS

Two types of bite are permitted, scissors or pincer. An overshot or undershot lower jaw is considered a fault.

EARS

"Small in comparison with the size of dog." Before the law prohibited the cropping of ears, ear size was unimportant as, after removal or cropping, the evidence of ear size was removed. It is strongly rumoured that in the reconstruction period, a dash of Bloodhound was introduced, chiefly to assist in giving the necessary loose skin on the head. There is no proof that this actually happened, but it would account for the breed's considerable scenting abilities. In my experience, the breed uses its nose far more effectively than its eyes. There are still some houndy ears on some otherwise good Neapolitans, and one sometimes senses something of the hound in their tail carriage and facial expression.

EYES

"Not showing entropion or ectropion." One sees the occasional case of entropion (in-turning of the eyelid) but the condition is rare as compared to the number showing ectropion (sagging of the lower eyelid). Again, if there was an introduction of Bloodhound at some stage, it is not surprising that descendants show "haw" (ectropion). What I have found is that, where a dog shows slight ectropion and the animal is unwell, or in a stressful situation, the amount of haw greatly increases. Too much haw spoils the intensity of the true Neapolitan expression.

The Standard calls for heavy hanging skin on the eyebrows (almost as if the animal is wearing spectacles). Most owners of the breed would agree that, while the long sight of these dogs is good, their close sight is suspect in many specimens. This could be due to their overhanging brow which gives the appearance of the eye being only half-open. You will note that the breed frequently gives a slight backward tilt to the head when looking for something in close range, rather in the manner which we humans do when wearing bifocal spectacles. It may also be the reason why many Neapolitans use their powers of scenting, as they find this quicker than focusing their sight. This is a personal theory based on watching the breed over the years. As far as I am aware, it has never been scientifically investigated.

NECK

"Short and stocky, muscular, with the lower line of the neck having much loose skin to form a dewlap which must be divided into right and left sides."

It is not often that a Breed Standard does not ask for a long, clean neckline. In most breeds a neck as specified by the Mastino Standard would be considered to be a bad fault. I have known judges condemn it as

Sp. Ch. Hatrim de Los Azores: The neck should be short and stocky, with loose skin forming a dewlap.

three-quarters of its length, and endowed with strong, well developed muscles. Its angle is 55 to 60 degrees from the horizontal, and its length thirty per cent of height at the withers. Its direction is almost parallel to the median plane of the body.

FOREARM
Very heavily boned, straight and vertical to the ground.

ELBOWS
It is here that there are again differences from the accepted norm. The elbows must not be too close to the ribcage, but must also not be too far out. The point of the elbow to be in a line drawn from the caudal (bottom) edge of the scapula (shoulder blade) perpendicular to the ground.

MOVEMENT
Because of the overall "looseness" of construction, the breed has a characteristic movement which is rarely understood. It has been described as like that of a bear.

A correctly constructed Mastino has the walking style of a stalking tiger with a precise, long and ponderous stride. Because of the length of stride, while the legs appear to be moving very slowly, the distance

"coarse" and penalise the exhibit for what is an essential feature. To some it may appear coarse, but it is a requirement of the Standard and must be appraised as such.

The FCI Standard is quite clear about the body, chest and ribcage and these are the standard requirements for any of the Molosser group, but there is a special requirement for the abdomen. The bottom line of the abdomen should be practically horizontal, i.e. there should be no (or very little) tuck-up of the flank, which is the usual feature of most breeds.

SHOULDERS
"Long, slightly sloping, with long, well developed muscles, which should be clearly divided from one another." It should move freely. The scapulae (shoulder blades) should be fairly well separated from one another and tend toward the vertical, to the plane of the body.

UPPER ARM
Well adherent to the body for the upper

Do not make the mistake of judging the Neapolitan by the criteria used when assessing a Mastiff.

covered with very little effort is great. The same applies to the breed's characteristic steady trot. It rarely gallops. They sometimes "pace", which is not considered to be a fault under most of the experienced judges.

I would conclude this brief survey by emphasising that one cannot assess the quality of the Neapolitan Mastiff by judging it on "normal" principles. One must study this highly individualistic breed by its own standard, and not attempt to apply inappropriate criteria.

Man-work in France: The Neapolitan still retains the characteristics of an exceptional guard.   *Photo: Sanchez.*

CHARACTER OF THE NEAPOLITAN MASTIFF

The breed is unique, both physically and mentally. There is an aura of ancient mysticism in their inscrutable expression and few can overlook their compelling presence. Loyalty and companionship to those that it loves are its passwords. Not only is it deeply affectionate but, when the very necessary degree of rapport has been established between dog and owner, the breed is so perceptive that it frequently seems to be able to read the thoughts of the person to whom it has become attached. This attachment to one person is a breed characteristic. It needs close contact and the ability to share its deep affection with its owner. It is when starved of affection that the temperament can become unreliable. To strangers there is usually a degree of controlled intolerance. Visiting friends are accepted with a calm indifference.

Its role as a guard and battle dog has not been lost in the mists of time, but today, in a more civilised environment, such urges are cunningly controlled.

It may not be the ideal large breed for the complete novice, but you can make of Neapolitans what you will. If you own it, train it, and offer companionship but, at the same time, insist on the necessary degree of control, you will be rewarded by owning a breed which has few peers. If you neglect it,

fail to understand and to control it, or encourage it to be vicious, you will create a liability both to yourself and anyone with whom the dog comes in contact.

Every owner or prospective owner should realise that it is extremely unlikely that you can safely run two adult males together after they are about 14 months old. An interesting characteristic of Neapolitans is that the male will usually tolerate a bitch's attempt to exercise her authority over him, but no male will accept such behaviour from another male in the same house or kennel. I emphasise this because I have known unsuspecting purchasers to have been persuaded by a breeder to purchase two eight-week-old male puppies on the grounds that they will be company for one another. This may be so, until the first skirmish occurs. Neapolitans have exceptionally long memories. Once the first test happens, there will be no truce. From then on the dogs will have to be housed and exercised separately.

I am not denigrating a breed to which I am deeply attached, or painting it as an unreliable renegade. I just do not consider it to be a suitable breed for someone unfamiliar with dogs of this size, temperament and ability. All too often I get distress calls from Mastino owners asking for advice on how to control some antisocial habit which should

It is unwise to attempt to keep two males together once they are both fully mature.
Photo: Sanchez. Courtesy: Vos Chiens Magazine.

never have been allowed to occur in the first place.

Mastini, by their nature and their inherent instincts, are natural guards. They need no stimulation to encourage them to carry out their centuries-old duties. By encouraging aggression you are creating a time-bomb which will do extensive damage if it is allowed to explode.

If you own a Mastino from a puppy, and rear it sensibly, just calmly controlling any wayward tendencies, problems should be non-existent or, at the worst, fairly petty.

One of the reasons why I do not recommend people taking on a rescue dog is that, all too often, such dogs have been badly treated or badly trained and the loving, but controlling human hand, has not been applied. Very specialised knowledge and treatment is required. This is not a task for an amateur when dealing with a determined animal of Mastino strength and capability.

Rogues occur in most animals – and in humans – but the rogue or maladjusted Mastino is a reflection not so much of the dog or its ancestors, but of the inability of its owner to develop and channel the natural sagacity of the animal and to capitalise on its inherent desire to love and be loved.

All too frequently the general public imagine that a guard dog is uncontrollably vicious, jumping six feet into the air behind his fence in an attempt to break out and attack. This is not Mastino style. I have emphasised the breed's intelligence, but it also has a degree of cunning which has, undoubtedly, been the reason for its survival over the centuries. In most circumstances, and away from their home they appear to be quite disinterested in making war. At the first show of the Societa Amorati del Napoletana Mastino which I attended, I was most impressed with the calmness and good nature of most of the exhibits. These were dogs which it would be most unwise to trifle with, but there was a sense of mutual respect, provided that there was no undue familiarity. This attitude runs through the breed. My own housedog is not completely reliable if strangers attempt to touch her, but she is fine once she has scrutinised them and decided that they are suitable. She will then allow herself to be patted and will become quite a gracious hostess.

Some years ago I was staying in Florence and called into a trattoria. I noticed that one table in a prime position had a reserved noticed on it. Then a very well-dressed and obviously wealthy lady arrived – preceded by a black Mastino male dog, who went ahead

The well-reared Neapolitan is quite capable of adapting to family life.

The tough exterior belies a more gentle side to the Mastino temperament.

of her to the table, and then settled himself beneath it in the typical alert Mastino pose, with his head on his paws and all his senses active. They were effusively welcomed by the waiter. I saw this happen in several occasions and finally asked the waiter about it.

I was informed that she was the wife of a wealthy but elderly Count who did not wish to keep her in a gilded cage but did require her to have some protection when she went out alone. He had given her the Mastino, called Benno as her bodyguard. I said that I thought it was remarkable that Benno never showed any sign of aggression. The waiter looked at me in amazement. "Benno would kill anyone who attempted to do her harm. He loves her more than the Count. He looks angelic when all is good, but if anything is wrong he is the very devil."

I have mentioned previously my Rosemaund Netta. When I collected her she had never before been in a car and, having unwillingly clambered in, she spent the whole of the journey trying to go through the back windscreen to apprehend any car driver who, in her opinion was coming too close behind us. On her first night with me she tore off the door of a nearly new kennel, climbed over a six foot chain link fence and, at two in the morning was yelling as only Mastini can at my front door. I had to bestir myself and go down as I thought, to shut her back in her kennel – until I saw the state of the kennel! She therefore followed me back into the house, up the stairs and, with a typical loud Mastino sigh, flopped down on my bed. She slept there for the next eight years.

CHOOSING A PUPPY

If you decide on Neapolitan Mastiff ownership, start with a puppy of eight to ten weeks of age. Rescued animals may tug at the heartstrings – but are you sufficiently experienced to take the risks involved?

A Neapolitan Mastiff puppy differs in

A litter of six-week-old puppies at the kennel of Mr B. Oloterbridge.

construction from the other Mastiff breeds described in this book. Because of the overall looseness of construction some special requirements should be observed in rearing. As with all large breeds, puppies should not be sold under the age of eight weeks and should have been treated for intestinal worms before being sold.

Always buy from a reputable source, and view any advertisements with the utmost suspicion. Good-quality puppies are not a quick-selling commodity and always available, like some merchandise on a supermarket shelf. If you choose to buy from a reliable source you may have to wait for a while before puppies become available – but this is, in many ways, advantageous. While waiting, you can be gathering information on the breed and, if possible, attending a few shows where the Neapolitan is scheduled.

REARING A MASTINO

Once you have taken possession of the puppy, its future health and development will, to a major extent, depend on your feeding, exercising and training. Neapolitan puppies are normally quite greedy feeders. Once you have decided on the diet and feeding times, these should be adhered to, as any violent change can upset a youngster's metabolism.

Feeding should ensure that the necessary proteins, vitamins, minerals and trace elements are in the correct proportion. If a correctly balanced diet is being fed, supplements are quite unnecessary – in fact they can cause the balanced diet to become completely unbalanced!

From the age of eight weeks, exercise is important but long treks are to be avoided. Mastino puppies have heavy bone in the limbs and feet which look disproportionately

If you are planning to show your Neapolitan, the breeder will help you to assess its potential.

Left: Introductions to the family should be closely supervised.

Below: By eight months of age, the Neapolitan is already a very substantial animal.

Right: Fruit D'Amour Notabile: Junior World Champion 1998: Firm co-operative handling will result in a dog that will accept the authority imposed by his owner.

large and heavy. As the whole body is somewhat lax, to be taken for long walks at this stage can cause undue stress to the vulnerable joints and ligaments. The ideal situation is a large fenced play area, plus somewhere dry to sleep when tired. Even better would be access to the play area via a patio door of the house so that the dog does not feel isolated. House-training in this breed is quite easy.

It is a mistake to overfeed the puppy and get it too heavy. As a very rough guide I recommend that you should be able to feel the ribs in a growing puppy but should not be able to see them. As Neapolitans tend to develop up to the age of at least three to four years, a nutritious diet is necessary to maintain growth, but overweight is not helpful. Raw large marrow bones are a boon to the puppy. Quite apart from keeping it happy and occupied, the gnawing is good for the teeth and for the development of the jaw and jaw muscles. A not-so-obvious advantage is the exercise to the feet and toes which occurs as the bone is held down and turned for gnawing.

As growth progresses, there is a need for some firm, but co-operative handling, especially in the male youngster. Show affection, but always make it quite clear that you, the owner, are head of the pack. Bitches are more biddable than dogs and do not seem to experience the aggressive phase which many male youngsters seem to go through at about 14 months of age. Aggressive behaviour in a puppy or young adult must be dealt with promptly. In a very young puppy the surest method of correction is to lift the puppy up by the scruff of the neck, shake it and at the same time scold it in a growling type of voice. Neapolitans are intelligent animals and learn quickly. However, that same intelligence can be used by the dog to try out his strength and possible dominance. Corporal punishment should not be necessary. A reprimanding tone of voice is normally sufficient, as basically this breed does not intentionally wish to incur the owner's displeasure, provided that the essential owner/dog rapport has been established.

Most owners will want to play with the puppy, which is quite understandable, and, to some extent, desirable, but too much rough play with Neapolitans is unwise. Playing wrestling games with a growing youngster, especially if it is male, can develop into an unwanted test of strength when the animal is adult. The dog is more than likely to be the winner in such a contest, with unfortunate consequences should it occur. Why sow the seeds which may allow it to happen?

8 THE SPANISH MASTIFF

By Carlos Salas Melero

Spain's history is based on its grazing animals. Over the last thousand years bulls, pigs, goats, horses, asses and sheep have provided an important source of general wealth and the basic subsistence for the great majority of the population.

Because of the climatic characteristics of the Peninsula – extremely cold in winter and very hot in summer – livestock migration took place on a grand scale. In summer the sheep were pastured in the high mountainous areas of the North; then, when the winter arrived, the flocks were moved to the flat areas of the South which had a more benign climate. Sometimes they travelled hundreds of miles. This form of seasonal migration, with thousands of sheep always using the same tracks, was called the Transhumancia. The economic, social and political importance of these displacements was such that in 1273 King Alfonso X the Sage, regulated all the laws relating to them by means of the "Honrado Consejo de la Mesta y Pastos de Castilla". Some of these laws refer to the "Mastiffs" that protected the flocks, determining their right to a portion of daily food, who should be responsible for them and the form of litigation in the event of their loss through theft or death. The abundance of predators such as the bear, the lynx and, mainly, the wolf, was a source of constant concern, as much during the migration times as when the herds were in the grass areas. Spain is still, today, one of the few places in Europe where wolves maintain a large enough population to worry the cattlemen and shepherds and only the use of guard dogs has been effective against these predators, from time immemorial. The Transhumancia, the wolves and the Spanish Mastiffs comprise an inseparable trilogy in the pastoral culture of the Iberian Peninsula.

The feeling for the Spanish Mastiff in his own country is very deep; the seductive power of this breed cannot be explained by means of simple clues, and its fascination works even with people who know nothing about dogs or dog breeds. It can be said that there are cultural and mythical roots that make everybody feel truly involved with this breed.

The whole of Spanish geography is filled with legendary old cattle paths, tracks and gorges through which the herds have moved for centuries; the Spanish Mastiff has always been deeply involved in the ancestral habit of transhumance. In other words, the Spanish Mastiff has meant, and still means, a lot more to shepherds than any other dog because it is like a protective totem, the personification of Goodness against Evil (the Evil would of course be the wolf), a real symbol, appreciated and worshipped as a minor god.

The physical and psychological

Ciro: The physical and psychological characteristics of this massive dog are adapted to its own peculiar lifestyle.   *Photo: Carlos Salas.*

characteristics of this massive dog are completely adapted to a very peculiar lifestyle: in transhumance, speed, for instance, is not so important because it is the slow motion of the cattle, or the sheep, which dictates the rhythm, and time is measured in terms of seasons, not hours. The enemy, the real enemy – apart from the wolf – the daily enemy, is the climate and the rather scanty means of fighting its severity. Therefore the Spanish Mastiff must be well coated, with a sturdy, resistant texture – the kind of coat that will preserve it against all sorts of climatic extremes when it is guarding the herds and lying near them. These dogs are very sure of themselves, of their strength, and of their deep, raucous and harsh bark that they know is enough of a deterrent against any possible enemy. Nevertheless, whenever required, the Spanish Mastiff will defend his herd and master with surprising courage and energy, although the fieriness needed in decisive moments is always compatible with the extremely noble and sweet personality characteristic of this huge, pleasant and yet powerful nomad.

THE ORIGIN OF THE SPANISH MASTIFF

Spain is undoubtedly a country of Mastiffs; the use of these dogs as herd-guardians is historic and legendary and the first documented references come from as far back as the Roman authors Virgil, Apuleius and Columella, all of whom specifically referred to the courage, vigour and strength of the Mastiffs found at the Iberian Peninsula; but it can be deduced from their works that these dogs existed in the pre-Roman era, when the Celts and Iberians were already using them to support their herding activities. Nevertheless, it is quite impossible nowadays fully to detail the morphological characteristics of those Mastiffs, and we absolutely have to reject the theory, which is so often repeated, of the "purity of the race". According to such a theory, there was a time when "pure" Mastiffs existed, with all the virtues and the attributes and with no faults, when they were as homogeneous and beautiful as no other, without a single drop of undesired crossbred blood running through their veins. Later on,

145

lack of attention to breeding, inadequate crosses and indifference resulted in the loss of beauty and type.

Unfortunately, the idea that the "purebred Spanish Mastiff" was a divine gift, and that the racial prototype couple was saved for posterity in Noah's Ark, is believed by too many people. The reality is rather different; the Peninsular Mastiff population is, and has been, very heterogeneous, not only in terms of aspect, size, colour, coat, character, etc., but also with regard to its genetic code – and it could not have been otherwise because the Spanish Mastiff is the result of longterm selection, bred for utility, and evolved throughout centuries by cattlemen, who used different individuals and different lineages too.

In the formation of the Spanish Mastiff breeds, "Molossers" of diverse origins have been introduced throughout the centuries. One of the most identifiable types is similar to the modern Turkish dog, the Anatolian Karabash, that was very possibly introduced into Spain during the centuries of Muslim dominance of the Iberian Peninsula. Similar types to these dogs frequently occur in our current breeding and are somewhat pale yellow in colour, with a black mask. Also in Turkey, as formerly happened in Spain, the owners usually crop the ears of the dogs that work with the sheep and they use protective collars with iron spikes, called carlancas, on the dogs.

A second breed that has influenced the formation of the Spanish Mastiff was the Old Spanish Presa, a bulldog "molosoides" which had rounded ribs, a wide chest, a rectangular construction and was frequently brindle in colour. These features have been incorporated in good measure in the prototype selected at the moment as the modern Spanish Mastiff.

Lastly, there is also certainly the influence of dogs coming from the strain of "Montana", which are mixed-race molosoides

found in the Tibetan mountains, the Caucasus, the Alps, the Pyrenees etc.

Selection and adaptation to the special conditions of the Spanish Transhumancia forged in all these breeds a stock of Molossers with the appearance and temperment of the modern Spanish Mastiff.

Many breeds of big, powerful dogs would be able to face wolves in a fight. But they do not all possess the qualities and aptitude

Verdugo: A typical Spanish Mastiff of the seventies, with the famous cattleman Trota.
Photo: Carlos Salas.

required to carry out the task of guarding livestock. Confrontations between dog and wolf are not very frequent because the wolves avoid them as much as possible. The good guard dog should be able to follow the flock, walking with the sheep without scaring them or bothering them, and possessing a sure and independent nature, with "sleeping aggressiveness" that is only revealed when the occasion really requires it. The independent spirit is important, because during the night the dog has to carry out its guard work without man's presence or orders. The protective instinct means that, without the necessity of having to learn it, the Mastiffs know how to work the whole flock, some going as an advance party before the flock, while others are located either side of it and others are next to the shepherds in the rear guard. They do not waste energy rushing about, and, in this way, they can maintain their strong bodies with small quantities of food. The sheep are, for them, a real treasure to protect. They never show aggression to them and in no circumstance would they eat their meat. There are multiple examples of Mastiffs that remained for several days, without being able to eat or drink, guarding a wounded sheep until the shepherd's arrival, and then still not eating the sheep should it die.

EVOLUTION OF THE BREED

The Spanish Mastiff has been part of the Spanish organised "cinofilia" since its birth at the beginning of the century. In Volume 1 of the LOE (Stud book of the year 1912), the Mastiff "Machaco" was inscribed with the number 11. But unfortunately the inscription in the LOE was exceptional, although numerous families of the aristocracy possessed immense flocks, with thousands of Spanish Mastiffs guarding them. It was an old tradition to use a Spanish Mastiff for each 200 sheep and, from the sixteenth to the

Giron: A working dog of the sixties.
Photo: Carlos Salas.

nincteenth century approximately 5,000,000 sheep did the transhumancia every year in Spain. The impressive number of 25,000 Mastiffs of different types worked as protective dogs with the shepherds during those times.

When the Spanish Civil War ended in 1939 the number of wolves increased in an alarming way and forced the shepherds to make an effort to select the Mastiffs in order to get more weight, strength and courage. The best Mastiffs, which were also known as good reproducers, gained fame among the shepherd transhumantes and they mated a multitude of females from different bloodlines. This caused a quick improvement in a large part of the Mastiff population and also a homogeneity of the characteristics that are today considered typical. For many veteran fans, the fifties can be considered as the "golden age" of the breed.

Dog shows began to peak in Spain in the 1970s and the Spanish Mastiff acquired an influential leader and enthusiast in Luis Esquiro Bolanos, who carried out an exhaustive study of the bloodlines of the breed which the cattlemen owned. At the same time the affix El Pinotar was exerting a predominant influence, chiefly by the

Higueros de Quinta Durea with the typical iron collar, for protection against the wolves.

Photo: Carlos Salas.

progeny of Alejandre and Leon. With these dogs an upgrading began and exemplary and notable specimens were taken to Madrid. These breed improvements were carried out by such breeders as Manuel Diaz Navarro under the El Aviador affix. The food company Visan became interested. The brother and sister partnership of Jaime and Alvaro Garcia Andrade, with the Colmenares affix, was established, as was the Sayanes of Teresa Noguera.

Breeding in the modern sense began in the following decade. In 1980 the "Asociacion Espanola del Perro Mastin Espanol" (AEPME) was formed. This breed club registers new affixes, searches for top-quality dogs in the field to take to the shows and to incorporate into breeding plans – and, most importantly, to introduce shepherds to this modern project, registering litters and

tattooing Mastiffs that are carrying out their traditional work. The Breed Standard has been modernised so that it reflects the ideal sought for by all, following the description outlined by the Federacion Cinologica International (FCI). In 1981 the first Exposicion Monografica (the yearly Exhibition of Breeding) took place in the city of Trujillo.

Many new affixes were incorporated into a methodical structure with very defined objectives – "Enderika", "Campollano", "Quinta Aurea", "Los Lirones", "Molorgaz", "Montejaena", "Espinillo" and, especially, "Transhumancia" of the pioneer Luis Esquiro who, after unstinting work in the field, found the right conditions to develop a breeding plan. Numerous working Mastiffs are bought in by these breeders, presented in shows and employed with success in breeding

programmes. Their names are legends today for those devotees of the breed, because they are the ancestors of the Mastiffs of the present time: "Navarro", "Compromiso", "Turko", "Moro", "Linda", "Lobata" and particularly "Tigre", the Spanish Mastiff par excellence during recent times.

THE AMAZING TIGRE

Tigre (Tiger) was a unique dog with an incredibly seductive aura. With his impressive size and his noble bearing, he moved over the grass like a phantom. He was conscious of his mythical status and he imposed a slow and unreal rhythm around himself. He was a field dog, selected, using utility critera, by the Extremadura shepherds from among the transhumantes Mastiffs. When Verdugo and Navarra, his parents, were mated, no-one was looking for a show dog; they wanted to obtain a clever Mastiff, powerful and intrepid, capable of fighting against the wolves, defending his merino sheep and, at the same time, giving pride to his masters for his magnificent appearance.

His bloodline was not written in any paper but it was very good news for all the shepherd world. Among his ancestors there are names of legendary Transhumantes Mastiffs, like Oliveros, Belga, Leon – names never written in a pedigree but with very accurate details about their conformation, character and deeds known in the oral traditions of the shepherd world, which are unfortunately disappearing in the modern world.

"Tigre" was much more than a dog. His presence had the power to evoke the endless silences of the pastures in Extremadura, where he was born on June 20th 1977.

In Madrid, so far from the ambience in which he grew up, he co-existed with other magnificent Mastiffs from different areas of Spain. Some were taller, longer, better movers, fiercer, but none expressed the grandeur and nobility of their ancestors as Tigre did.

Lying down he looked like a sphinx and, whether getting soaked by sun or rain, he had the gift of harmonising with the wild scenery. He looked as if he had been there for ever. His calm figure was, however, deceptive. When it was necessary, he used all the energy accumulated in his superb body. He was not quarrelsome but I still remember being shocked the few times that I saw him going to a fight. He was fast and without hesitation, with surprising vigour and courage. I have not seen many dogs so serious in those dramatic moments. However, his natural attitude was so gentle, it was much easier to imagine him caring for the sheep than fighting against the wolf.

The glamour of the dog shows really

Compromiso II: A famous Champion of the 80s, he also worked sheep in the Leon country. He was exported to Switzerland.

Photo: Carlos Salas.

required the other side of his nature from his eternal free and wild life. He never liked the show world and, for him, it was a punishment to be caught and handled with the lead. The World Show in 1983 was a hard show for all of us. However, "Tigre" got rid of all his energy and had the capacity for sacrifice that is inherent in his breed. Mysteriously he understood that it was the most important moment of his life. He was representing the thousands of Mastiffs who live in the far sierras. He was a worthy ambassador and he won the Best in Show at the World Show 1983.

EXPORTING MASTIFFS
In the current decade of the nineties, the number of puppies inscribed in the LOE has stabilised annually to about 500. This is an important figure if we keep in mind that they no longer register dogs not of controlled genealogy. It is obligatory to tattoo all dogs, and before being allowed to reproduce, all the dogs must have to undergo an examination at the start the year with a specialist judge.

The selective effort developed during the 15 years of controlled breeding has given very positive results, mainly regarding the homogeneity of type.

Breeding groups exist in several countries of Europe, in Latin America and Russia.

However, the Spanish Mastiff breed is practically unknown in Great Britain, the USA and Canada.

Unfortunately the exports have not been of the first order of quality and there have been few dogs of true quality that have left Spain, which hinders the popularisation and the knowledge of the breed at international level.

But the health of the breed in Spain is now highly satisfactory. The last National Speciality Show (Cantabria, April 1998), which I judged, had an all-time record entry, with 133 Spanish Mastiffs, most with maximum qualifications and a very high level of quality.

MASTÍN ESPANOL (SPANISH MASTIFF) STANDARD

ORIGIN: Spain.
USE: Guarding and defence of herds, farms, people and property.
FCI QUALIFICATION: Second Group, Section 2, Molossers.

SHORT HISTORY OF THE BREED
These dogs have for long been related to herding and transhumance, defending cattle and shepherds from the wolf and other predators.

GENERAL APPEARANCE
It is a large dog, well proportioned and muscled, with compact skeleton, a huge head and a half long coat.

150

Trabuco (named Jorgito) was Best in Show in 1988 Spanish National Speciality. He was considered the model for the breed in his time.

Photo: Carlos Salas.

IMPORTANT PROPORTIONS

Length of body to be larger than height to withers. Length of muzzle/length of skull = 4/6: minimum brisket perimeter – height to the withers plus 1/3. Skull = equal to or higher than its total length.

BEHAVIOUR AND CHARACTER

Meek and docile with people, it becomes extraordinarily aggressive with strangers and beasts, especially when defending cattle or properties. Its bark is deep, intense and can be heard from a considerable distance. It is a very intelligent, good-looking dog. It can be easily seen from its behaviour what it proposes to do. Any animal that is excessively shy, cowardly or unreliable ought to be disregarded for breeding.

HEAD

Large, strong and broad at the base, with a rather soft stop. The width of the skull should be equal or superior to the length. Occiput crest well marked. Seen in profile the muzzle should look moderately rectangular, slightly diminishing towards the nose; the muzzle never to look snipy or pointed.
Eyes: Small in size if related to the skull, preferably dark or hazel, showing aggression when looking at strangers and yet sweet to friends. The lower eyelid shows some haw. Both eyelids to be black.
Ears: Medium sized, V-shaped and plain, inserted well over the eyeline; when alert they should be separated from the face and partially lifted. Shall never be cropped.
Mouth: Scissor bite; with rather small incisors compared with the size of canines and the strength of the molars. Must have premolar teeth.

NECK

Wide, strong, muscled and flexible, with a double and well developed dewlap.

BODY

Rectangular, strong and showing great power, although agile and flexible at the same time. Straight dorsal line, even movement and well defined withers; deep, wide chest with a well marked breastbone, rounded brisket and well separated ribs. The back will narrow to the hips.

FOREQUARTERS

Straight and parallel when viewed from the front; with well muscled sloping shoulders. The elbows will be tight to the brisket. The forearm will triple in length to the pastern.

HINDQUARTERS

Adequate rear angulations, strong and muscled, heavily boned with well defined hocks; clearly showing the tendon, with no deviations.

FEET

Cat feet; may show single or double dewclaws, that can be amputated if desired.

TAIL

Strong at the root and medium set, strong, flexible and showing longer hair than in the rest of the body. Reaches the hocks, when in rest; while moving or whenever excited, the tail will be carried as a sabre, but never totally curled nor resting over the hips.

COAT

Half long, thick and lying flat to the body; shorter on the legs and longer on the tail.

COLOUR

Undetermined, although plain colours are favoured; yellowish, red, black, etc. Also brindles are appreciated.

GAIT

Trot is preferred and it will be powerful with a sense of purpose and straight, never plaiting.

WEIGHT AND SIZE

There are no limits to the maximum height and those well-proportioned animals that are taller will be more appreciated. Minimum height at shoulder for dogs 77 cms, for bitches 72 cms, but it will be preferred that males reach a minimum of 80 cms and bitches of 75 cms. Weight will depend on height.

FAULTS

Sheep-like head and face profile; the absence of any premolar teeth, level bite; weak backline or sagging or not rigid during movement; poor bone and shyness.

SERIOUS FAULTS

(which will exclude exhibit from the "excellent" qualification)
Overshot lower jaw; lack of several premolar or canine teeth; snipy muzzle; roach back; lateral swinging of hips when moving; long, undulating or curly coat; tail or ears cropped; entropion or ectropion whenever excessive; lethargic type; tail resting over loins.

ELIMINATING FAULTS

Broken nose; any degree of undershot lower jaw; unpigmented nose or mucosa with light eyes; monorchid (unilateral cryptorchid) or cryptorchid specimens.

SPANISH MASTIFF TYPE

The Standard of a breed refers to the ideal dog that a group of breeders is trying to produce in a joint effort to improve quality. In order to ensure that such a task can be continued and will never depend only on the personal ideal of each individual, it is absolutely necessary to accept the Standard as the ultimate reference in order to be able to make the difference between what are to be

Espartero: Best in Show in 1991 Spanish National Speciality.

Photo: Carlos Salas.

Gaspar de Transhumancia: A star of the breed, winning Best in Show at the Spanish National Speciality 1998 at 22 months old, judged by Carlos Salas.

considered virtues and what are faults. Therefore, fidelity is essential on the part of breeders and judges, who should conform to what they read in the Standard, to ensure the future of any breed, of course, but particularly the future of one whose roots come from such a varied and heterogeneous population as the Spanish Mastiff.

As there are so many different kinds of Spanish Mastiffs around the country it is even more important to outline which type is to be selected – type taken for the characteristics that should be aimed to be transmitted to further generations, and type that will make the complete difference between this particular breed and any other whatsoever. The Standard, any Standard, always needs to be synthesised when put into words but, at the same time, it also needs to be amplified whenever necessary with further details on any specific matter that may arise, especially when it has to do with type.

In this study we shall consider some of the transhumant Spanish Mastiff characteristics that have been fixed since the 1981 Spanish Mastiff new Standard.

GENERAL APPEARANCE
In the first place, a Spanish Mastiff will always have to be a powerful, large-sized dog, with height well over 77 cms for males and 72 cms for bitches; with strong bone and a deep wide chest, like a real Molosser; and it is always stressed in the Standard that the animal shall be in proportion, with a powerful gait at all times.

More than anything else, the first impression of a Spanish Mastiff will be that of a grandiose, majestic animal, well-built and sure of himself. This, of course, is a good Standard and is absolutely essential, but it would not be complete unless other aspects are taken into consideration; here below I will define those characteristics that I find essential in a real Spanish transhumant Mastiff.

THE HEAD
The head is very important and will surely determine the essential breed differences between the Spanish Mastiff and other kindred breeds such as the St Bernard, the Tibetan Mastiff, the Old English Mastiff, the Anatolian Shepherd Dog, etc. It has to be large but in perfect harmony with the rest of the body, with soft lines, showing no major sharp edges. The stop is not particularly accentuated either; the muzzle is strong and the skull wide. It is also necessary, in order to give the Spanish Mastiff the proper expression, that the skin forms a loose wrinkle outside the eye. The ideal proportion between skull and muzzle will be 6 to 4 (that is to say that for every 6 cms of skull, from the point of the occiput to the eyeline, there should be another 4 cms of muzzle, from the eyeline to the point of the nose. On the other hand, the skull-facial lines are slightly divergent.

THE COAT AND SKIN
The skin should always be thick and loose to give the impression of volume around the neck, the chest and the bottom line – very much like that of fighting bulls. This characteristic is most important.

Coat is a very important matter for type; it must be thick and flat, with mid-long cover coat and woolly, dense undercoat to protect the animal from the cold winter. The length measured in the area of the withers should not surpass 6 cms.

BODY
The body should be rectangular, never square, and with rounded ribs. The trunk should give a impression of great strength. The loins should also be wide and powerful, the same as the croup. The stomach should not be too tucked up, which means that the underline of the trunk will be almost parallel to the top line.

FEET
Cat feet are a real virtue, usually associated with solid ligaments; the feet should have tight toes with high, well-curved nails.

COLOUR
As far as colour is concerned, although all the colours are admitted, traditionally the uniform colours have been more appreciated, or those with small white areas. The most common colours in the breed are yellow, brindle and black. The 'yellow' colour is in different tones, from almost white to almost red.

9 THE PYRENEAN MASTIFF
(El Mastín del Pirineo)
By Rafael Malo Alcrudo

Where there are cattle or sheep there are predators – and then there are the guardians of the cattle, the Mastiffs, the descendants of the Molosser.

During the Middle Ages the Christians in the north of the Iberian Peninsula and the Moslems in the south fought against each other for almost seven hundred years for control of the land that would one day become known as Spain. In the Christian kingdoms, lamb's wool was the basic trade of the people.

At that time two hegemonic kingdoms existed in the yet unborn Spain – Castilla and Aragon. Each one had its particular way of life, and each gave birth to different breeds of dogs which were used to guard their flocks. Wise and solid Castilla, under the very detailed rules of the 'Honrado Consejo de la Mesta', produced the Spanish Mastiff. Heterogeneous Aragon possessed a different law in each valley, and was the home of the Pyrenean Mastiff.

EARLY HISTORY
The history of the Pyrenean Mastiff is deeply connected to the Aragonese nomadic sheep-herding tradition. For a long time sheep were a very important part of the economy in the old Kingdom of Aragon. Wolves and bears were not unusual in the Pyrenean mountains, so it was necessary to have a guard dog which

would guarantee that both men and animals would be able to come back home safe and sound. That dog was the Pyrenean Mastiff, "o Mostín", as it was known in the old Aragonese language.

The origins of the Pyrenean Mastiff breed are the same as those of the Molosser shepherd breeds which were developed in the southern part of Europe, from the Black Sea to the Atlantic Ocean, and which have been traditionally dedicated to guarding sheep or cattle.

Those breeds were selected in order to adapt them, both physically and psychologically, to the ecological, social, economic and working circumstances of the different countries in which they were needed. All of them were shepherd Molosser, that is to say, they came from the lines known as "canis familiaris inostranzewi" and "canis familiaris metris optimae", after the classifications used by the zoologists from the eighteenth century. The genetic contribution of the Molosser was essential in order to give to those breeds the physical power to be able to take on, and to beat, their natural opponents. But it was also necessary to include the genetic inheritance of the sheepdog, to guarantee that these guard dogs also had that special quality needed in a dog which must live peacefully with the flock and protect it as it would protect something of its own.

The Pyrenean Mastiff: Guardian of sheep and cattle. Quinta Tajadera Del Tio Roy – an Italian Champion.

Did those dogs come from the legendary Tibetan Mastiff, from the Molosser of Assyria or Epirus? Were they brought by the successive migrations of the Aryan people or by the Phoenicians? There is no definite evidence that any of these theories are true. We only know for sure that all those shepherd Molosser breeds existed for many centuries, from the Caucasus to the Alentejo and from Leon to Istanbul, living, killing and dying beside the flocks and the property of the people of the Tatra Mountains, the Abruzzi and the Pyrenees.

The dog we know as the Mastín del Pirineo, or the Pyrenean Mastiff, is, no doubt, the most impressive of all those shepherd Molosser dogs and, together with the Mastín Espanol, the largest one.

This powerful Molosser breed is the traditional guardian of the sheep flocks in the Old Kingdom of Aragon, in today's North-East Spain. Of course, there is a connection between the Pyrenean Mountain Dog and the Pyrenean Mastiff, as well as the Spanish Mastiff.

It is clear that today's concept of the breed is not the same as that of two hundred years ago. The Pyrenean Mastiff had its own habitat which was different from that of the other two breeds, with its natural borders being the Southern Pyrenees and the river Ebro. It was more rustic and Molossoid than the French Pyrenean Mountain dog, and very different from the Mastín Espanol. This was because in the seasonal migrations of the people of Castilla and Leon were much longer compared with those of Aragon and Navarra. The Mastín del Pirineo had its historical crisis when the bears and wolves disappeared from the Pyrenees. This fact

Vesc De L'Estany: A Spanish Champion wearing the traditional carlanca.

marked, almost definitively, the breed's decline, and indeed almost finished it forever. The Spanish Civil War had just ended and the economy was in decline. We can easily imagine how difficult it was to keep those big dogs with their huge appetites and no work to do.

Those old good times, when the Pyrenean Mastiffs walked proudly ahead or beside the flock, their throats protected by their imposing carlancas, the special collars made generally of iron, with sharp protruding spikes, were definitely over. It was only thanks to a few cattle raisers and some farmers who, mainly because of tradition, retained some dogs to guard their farms and houses, hat the breed survived at all. The

blood of the Aragonese Molosser remained in these dogs and so the breed was in a "stand by" situation that would go on for more than thirty years.

DEVELOPMENT OF THE BREED
In the mid-seventies, a small group of passionate devotees began the task of restoring the old Pyrenean Molosser. Travelling across the Pyrenees, they were responsible for giving the Pyrenean Mastiff a new start. Their work, at that time, was to find dogs of the right type and to convince their owners, who were usually farmers, that they possessed a real treasure, of both historical and zoological interest.

In 1977, I founded the Club del Mastín del

Rafael Malo Alcrudo judging the breed in Finland.

Photo courtesy: Anne-Marie Class.

Sp. Ch. Xesta Del Raitan: In the 1970s, a group of enthusiasts set about re-establishing the breed.

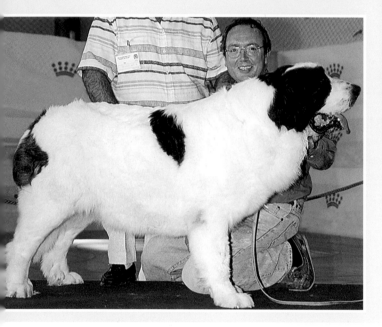

Above: Sp. Ch. Yu De L'Estany: The Pyrenean Mastiff should appear large, well-proportioned and well-muscled.

Left: Sp. Ch. Walaulor Tajadera Del Tio Roy with her breeder, Rafael Malo Alcrudo, the author of this chapter.

Pirineo de Espana (Spanish Pyrenean Mastiff Club), the first Club to be dedicated to any Spanish dog breed, and from that moment it became the real instrument of the Pyrenean Mastiff's revival. Step by step, new people who were interested in the breed started to join the Club and, in 1981, we celebrated the first Pyrenean Mastiff Club Show, with an entry of 24 dogs and bitches. Since then our Club Show has been the main yearly event for the Pyrenean Mastiff breeders and fanciers, and today this is the occasion where the best dogs can be seen, not only the Spanish ones but also many foreign ones as well.

The task of resuscitating the breed was not easy, of course. In the beginning the most important objective was to select dogs with the more traditional characteristics of the breed that we could see in old pictures, many of which were provided by members of our Club, who had known the old Pyrenean Mastiff in its times of splendour. I also remembered the dogs that I had seen in my childhood, when I went to my uncle's farm in a little cattle town near the Pyrenees. I remember very clearly, from that time, every place I visited during my search, every shepherd with whom I shared a dish of "migas", a glass of wine and a long talk about the "Mostín". It was a time of such a special kind of romantic enthusiasm, looking forward to saving the dog of my childhood dreams!

In the beginning, of course, we chose from every litter the puppies that looked, in body, size and character, more like the traditional dogs. A few years later, more than thirty breeders were dedicating time, enthusiasm and money to the Pyrenean Mastiff, most of them to the exclusion of any other breed. A solid human group was built around the Club with just one idea – saving the old "Mostín".

A little later, the first foreigners started to take an interest in the breed, and Pyrenean Mastiffs were exported abroad. First was Sweden, then Finland (where today it is the second biggest Molosser breed, behind the Bullmastiff), Norway, Denmark, Germany, Italy, France, Portugal, Hungary, then the whole of Europe. More recently our breed has travelled to the Americas, first to Brazil, Santo Domingo, Peru, Mexico and, a while later, to the USA.

Sometimes we wonder how this breed, in such a short time, has conquered the hearts of so many people around the world. The secret, as everyone tells us, is the particular temperament of the Pyrenean Mastiff, a dog with a sound mind and an impressive and powerful Molosser appearance.

THE PYRENEAN MASTIFF STANDARD

NAME OF THE BREED
Mastín del Pirineo/Pyrenean Mastiff.
Synonyms: Mostín d'Aragon; Mostín dell'Arago.

ORIGINS
Aragonese and Navarre Pyrenees; Aran Valley.

FCI QUALIFICATION
Second Group, Section 2, Molossers.

GENERAL APPEARANCE
It is a large-sized dog, well proportioned and muscled, with a compact skeleton and never cumbersome or lethargic.

CHARACTER AND BEHAVIOUR
Affectionate, docile and particularly intelligent, it is, at the same time, brave and fierce with strangers. In its relations with other dogs it shows extreme benevolence, knowing its own strength. Should the occasion arise, it is skilled at fighting, remembering its acquired behaviour after centuries of fights with wolves. Its bark is low and deep and it has a bright expression.

SIZE
There is not a maximum size for the breed, though in the same proportions, the bigger specimens are always more valuable. The minimum height limits are 77 cm. for the male and 72 cm. for the bitch.

CONFORMATION
Rectangular structure. Longitudinal diameter

Sp. Ch. Haritzeder de Monte Gorbea: The head is large, strong, and moderately long.

slightly longer than height at the withers. Harmonic and proportioned in all circumstance.

USE

Mainly as a defender of cattle and as a guardian of people and property. Excessively shy dogs, cowards or specimens with bad conformation should not be bred from. In the past this dog was used as a defender against wolves and bears. Actually it is an excellent watchdog, having a natural receptiveness to training.

HEAD

Large, strong and moderately long. The relationship between the length of the skull and muzzle is 5 to 4. The axis of skull and foreface will be very moderately divergent with a slight tendency to parallelism. The skull will look uniform and showing no specific difference in width when seen from above. From the side it will look deep, not wolf-like.

SKULL REGION

Wide skull, strong, with subconvex profile. The width of the skull will be equal or slightly superior to its length and the occiput crest will be well marked.

FACE REGION

Straight profile. Seen from above, the foreface will look somewhat triangular, large and slightly diminishing towards the nose, but never looking snipy.

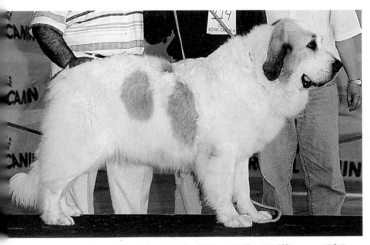

Sp. Ch. Big Michel De Wella Brillante: The body should give an impression of great power.

NOSE

Black, wet, big and wide.

LIPS

Upper lip covering the underlip, but not hanging excessively. Under lip bag well marked. Black in colour.

TEETH

White, strong and healthy. Big and long canine teeth. Very powerful molars. Rather small inscisors. Scissors bite. Complete teeth.

EYES

Small, almond shape, preferably dark. Attentive, noble, nice and intelligent look. Stern expression in front of any adversary. The eyelids will be black and preferably close to the eye when the dog is being attentive; when resting, the lower eyelid may show slight haw.

EARS

Medium-sized. Triangular-shaped, plain and inserted over the eye-line level. When alert they should be separated from the face and partially lifted. Should never be cropped.

NECK

Wide, strong, muscular and flexible. Thick skin. Double dewlap well defined but not excessively exaggerated.

BODY

Rectangular, wide, strong and showing great power. Wide and deep chest with a well-marked breastbone. The proportion between the height at withers and the girth of chest will be approximately 7 to 10. Rounded ribs and well separated ribs. Well-marked withers. Straight topline. Long, wide and powerful loin. Wide and strong croup; its inclination is about 45 degrees in relation with the topline and the floor. Descended flanks.

FOREQUARTERS

Straight and parallel when viewed from the front, showing muscles and tendons; with well-muscled and sloping shoulders, longer than forearms. The elbows are tight to the brisket. The forearms will triple the pastern in size. Strong bones. Cat feet, toes well arched.

HINDQUARTERS

Adequate angulations. Powerful and muscular, heavily boned, with well-defined hocks, showing the tendon and with no deviations. Must be able easily to propel the dog, with strength and elegance. Cat feet, slightly oval, may show single or double dewclaws, that can be removed if desired, although when choosing two similar dogs, the one showing double dewclaws will be preferred.

TAIL

Strong at the root and medium-set. Strong, flexible and showing an important degree of feathering. Reaching the hocks when resting and while moving it will be held as a sabre, rather curled at the bottom but not totally curved and never resting over the croup.

GAIT

Trot is preferred and it will be harmonic, powerful and elegant. Straight, never plaiting. Without any pacing.

COAT

Half-long, thick and dense. The ideal length at the topline will be about 6 to 9 cms. being longer at shoulders, neck, lower abdomen and behind forearms and hindlegs, as well as at the underpart of the tail. The texture of coat never to be woolly.

COLOUR

Basically white and always with a well-defined mask; marks similar in colour to that of the mask spread over the body, with irregular but well-defined shape. Ears always marked. Totally white or tricolored animals are undesirable. The most popular colours are snow white with medium grey marks, deep gold yellow, dusk, black, silver grey, light tan, sand or brindle. Red markings or yellowish white for the whole base colour not desirable.

SLIGHT FAULTS

Sheep-faced profile. Lack of a premolar; pincer bite. Slight distortion of the top line when moving. Very slight shyness. Slightly curly coat or a coat more than 9 cm. long.

Randa De Moralet: A top-quality bitch showing the typical proud, yet sweet expression.

SERIOUS FAULTS

Snipy or excessively rounded muzzle. Weak bone. Incorrect laying of the quarters. Moderate undershot jaw. The absence of several premolar or canine teeth if the cause is other than an accident. Saddle-backed. Croup much taller than withers. Very curly coat, or a coat less than 6 cms. or over 11 cms in length. Unpigmented ears. Ears or tail cropped. Exaggerated ectropion or entropion. Tail carried over the back, with no feathering or not curved at the end. Unhealthy and lethargic appearance. Unstable character.

ELIMINATING FAULTS

Excessive overshot or undershot lower jaw. Lack of pigmentation at the nose and mucosa. The absence of white coat. No white markings at the quarters and toes. Completely white specimens. Absence of mask. Coat shorter than 4 cms or longer than 13 cms. Monorchid or cryptorchid animals. Any marks that are not clearly defined and could mean mixed breed blood.

UNDERSTANDING THE STANDARD

So, we have been able to read the official Standard, but a Standard is just like a song. It has words and music. Everybody can read the words or even learn the song from memory, but you must really know the breed in order

to be able to "listen to the music" and to judge correctly. This is particularly true in the Molosser breeds.

The first thing to consider, when judging the Pyrenean Mastiff, is type. Is the dog a typical specimen or is it not? If it is, let us continue. If it is not, why should we judge it?

But what is type? In my opinion type means all the characteristics, some of them almost imperceptible ones, which are particular to the breed. A typical Pyrenean Mastiff must be, above all, healthy in body as well as in mind. Soundness and a balanced character are the first things we must look for. Fortunately, it seems that judges are now considering the dog as a whole and not looking at specific features. A dog is always a compromise striving to attain the practically unreachable ideal model described in the official Standard.

Because of this, sometimes a slight fault may be overlooked for the benefit of the whole dog, but this does not mean that mediocrity should be valued. Just the opposite. A good judge always appreciates the dog's positive values, and never begins with assessing its faults. But, at the same time, a judge must be intransigent about faults which concern type and health, both in body and mind.

A Pyrenean Mastiff must be powerful, proud and bold, but also sweet and beautiful, with a special sympathetic expression.

This is a rectangular dog, with a moderately thick and long coat, which should never be silky. Its head must be impressive – both big and wide. We should never forget that we are looking at a Molosser breed, so the head must never be light; it will always be desirable to have a slightly heavier-type than a head lacking volume and massiveness. It is very important that the proportion between skull and muzzle of 5 to 4 is adhered to. The skull is slightly rounded, broad and convex, with a prominent occiput and wide, deep muzzle, with the upper lip covering the lower lip. Thin noses are strongly penalised. Sometimes there are excellent specimens that have a foreface with a slightly "Roman" profile. This is not a major fault. In fact several breeders like this characteristic, which comes from Yogui, who was a legendary stud dog at the beginning of the breed's revival. The ears should not be too heavy and they must be set very slightly above the eye line. If the ear-set is too high,

Sp. Ch. Yoni Bi Gud Tajadera Del Tio Roy: An impressive male illustrating the size and power of the Pyrenean Mastiff.

Javier Demetrio Tajadera Del Tio Roy: A Spanish, European and Club Champion.

Niudo Taco Machaco De Raco Vedat: A Spanish, Italian and Club Champion.

it can sometimes change the whole appearance of the head and even alter the expression itself. The stop must be defined but not exaggerated and the eyes dark, giving a sweet, not too hard, an expression.

In blonde and white dogs a lighter iris pigmentation is tolerated but, in spite of that, dark eyes are preferred; they are always bigger than those of the Pyrenean Mountain Dog and with a totally different expression. If we say that the Pyrenean Mountain Dog has a "dreamy" expression, we should say that the Pyrenean Mastiff has a "sweet and expressive" look.

The neck is strong and not too short, with a developed dewlap being one of the most important characteristics of the breed. The chest must be wide and powerful. The shoulders are well-placed and the scapula and humerus well-inclined to each other and showing strong musculature. Flat ribs are incorrect. A strong and "sound Molossoid topline", is universally desirable.

The croup has to be strong, wide and rather long, without an excessive inclination of the pelvis. The tail, of medium set, must reach the hocks, being slightly curved, but never carried over the croup. The gait must be powerful, wide and sound, without any sign of weakness or unsound construction.

And then there is the colour. Black and white, white and grey, white and blonde, white and brown, white and gold, even white and brindle, are typical colours. The mask should be as symmetrical as possible; the colour will be lighter around the eyes but must be evident on both ears. These are the only markings for the Pyrenean Mastiff breed. It is desirable that at least two-thirds of the dog is white. Large markings that cover the dog from the shoulders to the beginning of the tail should be severly penalised.

A Pyrenean Mastiff must be a beautiful giant, healthy and functional, full of the joy of life, balanced and vigorous. That is the Pyrenean Mastiff that we want.

CHOOSING A PUPPY

The first thing we need to consider when thinking about having a dog is whether we really can give it enough care, in the widest sense of that word. In the case of a Molosser dog, that includes living in a big place, giving plenty of exercise, providing a lot of food and having a special understanding of the behaviour of Molosser breeds. You need to be more a friend than a boss to your dog, but without forgetting that the dog is a hierarchical animal, and it is important that the rules of mutual friendliness and respect are recognised on both sides.

The Pyrenean Mastiff puppy looks most appealing – but bear in mind how big it will be when mature.
Photo courtesy: Anne-Marie Class.

163

After the decision to own a Pyrenean Mastiff has been taken, contact the national club of the breed. In the case of the Spanish Pyrenean Mastiff Club, every person asking about puppies is given the address and telephone number of all the breeders, so they can contact every one of them if they so wish. One of the best places to contact the breeders is, of course, at the Club Show which we hold every year in a different Spanish region. That is the most important show, and there you will find the majority of breeders.

You can see a variety of different dogs and bitches and make up your own mind about which are the ones you like most. You can then contact the breeders which you wish to see, and arrange to visit them to view their kennel, their dogs, and their puppies if they have any. Probably this is the best way of finding your Pyrenean Mastiff puppy. Remember that all these breeders are real lovers of the breed, and it is a passion that costs them a lot of time, work and money. Any one of them will be happy to give you information about their dogs' bloodlines and when their bitches will have puppies.

But please, do not rush it. Getting a dog is not the same as buying a pair of trousers, and sometimes we spend less time choosing our live four-legged companion than buying an inanimate and trivial object. Check that all the puppies look happy and healthy and, if you can, go with somebody who knows as much as possible about dogs in general or Molossers in particular.

Then there is the question of whether to choose a male or a female. Males are bigger and stronger and that is why many people chose them.

Generally, bitches are closer to their season human owners (but not in all cases – there are always some exceptions), and it is not difficult to take care of them when they are in season, which is just a couple of times a year. You could say that males are in season 365 days a year, particularly when all the bitches of all the neighbours are in season.

I have had both males and bitches that I will never forget, including, of course, some sweet "gentlemen" dogs and some authoritarian, trouble-making bitches. But I have loved them all. Luckily dogs are not machines – every one of them is different, with its own personality and its own characteristics. All of them have given me all their love and broadened my experience. I will always keep that in my memory and in my heart.

The male is bigger and stronger than the female – and is often a first choice.
Photo courtesy: Anne-Marie Class.

The female tends to have a closer relationship with her human owner.
Photo courtesy: Anne-Marie Class.

10 THE TIBETAN MASTIFF

By Pamela Jeans-Brown

There has been an enormous amount of hyperbole about the origins of this splendid breed, reputed to be one of the oldest pure-bred dogs, originating from the Tibetan plateau.

In common with a great many of the other Molosser breeds, characteristics of the breed can be seen in the famous Assyrian bas-reliefs, but whether this really means that Tibetan Mastiffs *per se* were thriving in the palace of Nimrod in 640 BC is open to speculation. What is more specific to the Tibetan Mastiff is the fact that rock carvings found in the Himalayan kingdom of Zanskar, said to be at least 3000 years old, and possible older, show Tibetan Mastiff-type dogs in a human community.

In Chinese writings, in a record of 1121 BC, it is stated that the people of Lim, a land situated west of China, sent to the Emperor Wou-Wang a great dog of the Tibetan kind. Mastiff-type skulls have been found in the area dating from the Stone and Bronze ages.

PURITY THROUGH ISOLATION

There is no doubt that the Tibetan Mastiff is an ancient breed and it has remained relatively pure bred due to its geographical situation in a country which virtually closed its doors to the outside world for many centuries.

Tibet, the land of snows, is also a land of high plateaux and green valleys, with an area of over a half million square miles, located on the northern slopes of the Himalayan mountains in Central Asia, north of Nepal and India. It is isolated by the high snow-covered mountain ranges to the south and by the almost uninhabited desert to the north.

Tibet became a Buddhist country in the seventh century AD, controlled by Buddhist monasteries with the Dalai Lama as their spiritual head. It remained a very powerful country until overrun by the Mongols in 1279 under the inspired leadership of Kublai Khan, grandson of Genghis Khan, who was the first Mongol Emperor of China and Tibet. Kublai Khan became a convert to Buddhism in its Lamaithc form and gave the sovereignty of Tibet to the high priest of the Tibetan monastery at Sakya, and thus began the rule of the priest kings, bringing more power and stability to the region.

The main trade route from the Mediterranean to the Far East lay through Tibet and across the Gobi Desert to Northern China. Camel trains brought merchants to China to seek silks, and they brought their own guard dogs with them. The population of Chinese and Tibetan dogs became mixed with these Western strains, but those dogs living high in the mountains, well away from the trade routes, remained uncontaminated by other breeding lines.

*The Tibetan Mastiff: A companion watch dog, of solemn but kindly appearance.
This is Qassaba Ausables Rakpa Of Chokola, an influential sire in the development of the breed.*

Photo: Russell Fine Art.

DEVELOPING A ROLE

The monasteries and settlements all had their guarding dogs; the shepherds and herdsmen needed dogs to guard as well as to herd; the nomads also had their canine guards and companions, so there were dogs in Tibet fulfilling three similar but different roles.

None of these dogs were cosy fireside companions; they all had to be able to withstand the rigours of the climate and lifestyle, and only the strongest survived. A dog in these conditions had to be strong – with good bone, a strong frame and physique, the ability to move soundly over rugged terrain, a thick coat and an even thicker undercoat, a strong temperament and a cast-iron constitution – any weakness would be found out by the punishing conditions. Genetically strong and healthy dogs thrived for generations – nature did the culling and the bloodlines were pure. Any inbreeding in very isolated areas where gene pools were

small may have produced some defective specimens, but they would not have survived to reproduce their faults.

There are various nomenclatures for the various types of large dog found in Tibet, in many tongues and spellings, but the basic categories are these:

• The Dzi-Kyi or guarding dog, "the size of a fat sheep, with a long muzzle and a short coat, usually black in colour", who was never tied up but allowed to roam free.
• The Naj Khji, or cattle dog, bigger than the Dzi Khyi, and only loosed at night. These two were kept to protect the flocks of yak and other livestock.
• The Sang Khyi, Do Khyi or Sgo Khyi, the door dog, bigger than the other two, also black and tan, chained beside the main gate or door to the house or monastery. "His bark resembles the sound of a copper gong."

The size of these dogs has also been a source of hyperbole – but then we have all heard stories from fishermen about the one that got away. All travellers exaggerate their adventures, and even Chaucer wasn't adverse to a little exaggeration in order to enhance a good tale!

Marco Polo's account of dogs as big as donkeys in Nepal is less amazing if one remembers that the size of the donkey in Nepal is not the same as his Mediterranean cousin; in fact he measures about 1-1m.20 in height.

ARRIVAL IN THE WEST

Rumours had reached the West about these impressive dogs, but the inaccessibility of their natural environment proved a great disincentive and it was not until the 19th century, when exploration really took hold among enthusiastic wealthy individuals as well as commercial companies, that the Tibetan Mastiff became known again in Europe.

In 1897 Queen Victoria was sent a specimen from India. In 1874 Edward VII, when Prince of Wales, brought back two large dogs from Tibet who were exhibited at the Alexandra Palace dog show in December 1875. In 1895 Mr Borak's D. Samu was being exhibited, followed in 1906 by another dog imported by Edward VII. These dogs were impressive but not the stuff of legends, and not all of them had temperaments suited to life in the Home Counties – hardly surprising, really.

In 1929 Col. and the Hon. Mrs Bailey imported two dogs and two bitches to the UK, who, between them, produced eight litters. However, the gene pool was still too small and eventually the breeding programme had to stop. Tibet was invaded by the Chinese in 1951 and many dogs were destroyed. A few intrepid souls managed to escape with their canine companions, and word again spread to the west about this remarkable breed.

ESTABLISHING THE BREED

There was little importation of Tibetan Mastiffs until the early 1980s and it was only in 1983, after an absence of about fifty years, that Crufts saw a Tibetan Mastiff again, when Mrs Leeton's Ausables Tudorhill Dalai won a first and third in the two classes he entered. He had come from the USA, where Tibetan Mastiffs had been imported since 1969 and where Jumla's Halu of Jumla was the first documented Tibetan Mastiff imported from Nepal. He became the foundation stud dog of the West Coast. The doyenne of the breed on the West Coast was Ann Rohrer who worked unceasingly to develop the breed and to educate the public about them. On the East Coast, Steve Nash of the Ausables

Ku-Kyanvd Krekelberg Of Millbone (Cesar's Tagtru Rambo – Daila): Imported from Holland by M and R. Fletcher.
Photo: Eileen Haynes (Riches).

Chortens Ben Sharbaz (Altan De La Tour Chandos At Rarewood – Delviento Than-Che): Crufts BOB winner 1992, and now Fr. Int. World Champion – the only Tibetan Mastiff to have won all these titles.
Bred by Messrs. Reed-Jones and Holliday.
                    Photo: Eileen Haynes (Riches).

Chokola Ku-She (Qassaba Ausables Rakpa Of Chokola – Conrikyi Ku-Ke Of Chokola). Crufts BOB winner in 1991, 1994 and 1996.
Bred and owned by K. Giles and T. Emms.
              Photo: Eileen Haynes (Riches).

Rockanoar's Night Vigilante (Akbar De La Tour Chanos Of Conrikyi – Farnemoor Kie-Rani Of Rockanoar): Crufts BOB 1993.
Bred and owned by Eileen Haynes (Riches).
              Photo: Eileen Haynes (Riches).

Farnemoor The Sultan (Jastone Rockanoar Khan Of Farnmoor – Assam De La Tour Chandos Of Rockanoar): BOB Crufts 1995, and again in 1997 when he was aged nine. In the same year he also sired his first litter.
Bred by J. Hall.   Photo: Eileen Haynes (Riches).

kennels was also devoting his energies to the breed.

Since these small beginnings in the seventies, the breed has flourished, with the East Coast now importing from Europe while the West Coast seem to be going to Taiwan to find dogs exported from Tibet.

In Europe, one male arrived in Switzerland in 1972, four dogs in Holland in 1976, and one famous dog in Germany in 1979 – the great Tubo. The first European litter was Swiss-born in 1978. Holland now has some excellent Tibetan Mastiffs with the Reusens' Ni A Soechavati kennels producing consistently good stock including several World Champions as well as European and International winners. The breed has thrived in Finland since its recent introduction – climate may play a part here – while in the Republic of Czeckia and in Hungary the breed also is doing well.

Gone, however, are the dogs of the pure-bred Tibetan dogs in the high mountains. The Tibetan Mastiff seen around the world now has taken on local characteristics with great variations of size and type.

In England, the country responsible for the international Standard of the breed, the type has been relatively consistent but often without the real substance and bone that the breed demands. Mrs Pauline Brigden had imported two Tibetan Mastiffs in 1981, but they died in quarantine. In 1982, from the Nash's Ausables kennels, she brought in two bitches in whelp who produced between them thirteen healthy puppies, before returning to the USA.

Iris Feddon, Secretary of the Tibetan Mastiff Club of Great Britain, remembers seeing these puppies on the TV show *Blue Peter* and falling in love with the breed there and then. One of these dogs was Mrs Karen Giles' famous Qassaba Ausables Rakpa – Rio to his friends – who did so much as an ambassador for the breed in the UK. Since then, dogs have been imported from France, Holland and the USA. In 1991 Tibetan Mastiffs were awarded their first classes at Crufts, a real milestone in the breed.

THE BREED STANDARD (INTERIM)

GENERAL APPEARANCE
Powerful, heavy, well built, with good bone. Impressive; of solemn but kindly appearance.

CHARACTERISTICS
A companion, watch and guard dog, slow to mature, only reaching its best at 2-3 years in females and at least 4 years in males.

TEMPERAMENT
Aloof and protective.

HEAD AND SKULL
Fairly broad, heavy and strong. Skull massive, with strongly defined occiput and stop. Proportions from occiput to stop and stop to end of nose equal, but nose may be a little shorter. Muzzle fairly

Jomolunga Juppie Ni A Soechavati, a two-year-old male. The head should be broad and heavy, with a strongly defined occiput and stop.

Photo: Reusen.

Ie Phuntso Ni A Soechavati, a three-year-old female. The muzzle should be broad, well-filled and square.

Photo: Reusen.

Dzjong Ni A Soechavati, a three-year-old male. The nose should be well pigmented, and the lips well developed with moderate flews.

Photo: Reusen.

broad, well filled and square, viewed from all sides. Broad nose, well pigmented, well opened nostrils. Lips well developed with moderate flews. Some wrinkling, in maturity, on head, extends from above eyes, down to corner of mouth.

EYES
Very expressive, medium size, any shade of brown. Set well apart, oval and slightly slanting.

EARS
Medium size, triangular, pendant, carried low, dropping forward and hanging close to head. Raised when alert. Ear leathers covered with soft hair.

MOUTH
Scissor bite – jaws strong, with perfect, regular and complete scissor bite, i.e. upper teeth closely overlapping lower teeth and set square to the jaws. Level acceptable. Essential that dentition fits tightly, to maintain square form of muzzle.

NECK
Strong, well muscled, arched. Not too much dewlap. Shrouded by thick upstanding mane.

FOREQUARTERS
Well laid shoulders, muscular, strong boned. Straight legs strong, slightly sloping pasterns, well covered all over with strong hair.

BODY
Strong, with straight back, muscular, almost imperceptible croup. Chest rather deep of moderate breadth, with reasonable spring of rib, to give heart-shaped ribcage. Brisket reaching to below elbows. Body slightly longer than height at withers.

HINDQUARTERS
Powerful, muscular, with good angulation from well bent stifle and strong low-set hocks. Hindlegs, seen from behind, parallel. Removal of dewclaws (single or double) optional.

FEET
Fairly large strong, compact. Cat-feet having good feathering between toes.

Rich black: Qassaba Ausables Kara Of Rockanoar.
Owned by Eileen Haynes (Riches).
Photo: Eileen Haynes (Riches).

Black and tan: Rin-Chen Pino Ni A Soechavati.
Photo: Reusen.

Gold: Qassaba Ausables Rakpa Of Chokola.
Owned by K. Giles.   Photo: Eileen Haynes (Riches).

Grey and tan: Rockanoar's Blue Bijou.
Photo: Eileen Haynes (Riches).

TAIL
Medium to long, but not reaching below hock joint. Set high on line with top of back. Curled over back to one side. Well feathered.

GAIT/MOVEMENT
Powerful, free, always light and elastic. At speed will tend to single-track. When walking appears slow and very deliberate.

COAT
Males carry noticeably more than females. Quality of greater importance than quantity. Mainly fairly long, thick, with heavy undercoat in cold weather which becomes rather sparse in warmer months. Hair fine but hard, straight and stand-off. Never silky, curly or wavy. Heavy undercoat, when present, rather woolly. Neck and shoulders heavily coated, giving mane-like appearance. Tail bushy, densely coated, hindlegs feathered on upper rear.

COLOUR

Rich black, black and tan, brown, various shades of gold, grey and blue, grey and blue tan. Tan ranges from a very rich shade, through to a lighter colour. White star on breast permissible. Minimal white markings on feet acceptable. Tan markings appear above eyes, on chest, lower part of legs and underside of tail. Tan markings on muzzle; spectacle markings around eyes.

SIZE

Height; dogs: 66cm (26in) minimum; bitches: 61cm (24in).

FAULTS

Any departure from the foregoing points should be considered a fault and the seriousness with which the fault should be regarded should be in exact proportion to its degree.

NOTE

Male animals should have two apparently normal testicles fully descended into the scrotum.

Reproduced by kind permission of The Kennel Club.

UNDERSTANDING THE BREED STANDARD

The most important thing to note about the Breed Standard is that it emphasises the size and power of the Tibetan Mastiff. This is not a slight, dainty breed. It should have good bone and substance and be an impressive guardian when fully mature. It should have a broad skull, a broad muzzle, well-filled and square, and a broad nose. Obviously we are not looking at a square head like a Bullmastiff, but we do not want a weak, narrow head or a snipy muzzle. Ear-carriage is important to give the head its correct balance. Ears should not be set too low and when the dog is alert the ears should be raised, giving a straight line across the skull – not an exaggerated curve as happens when the ears are too low set.

The neck should be strong and well-arched – a neck which is too short can make a dog look unbalanced and rather stuffy. The

Rockanoar's Night Vigilante showing a large, broad skull, a deep, well-cushioned muzzle, and excellent overall breed type.
Photo: Eileen Haynes (Riches).

forequarters are strong and muscular, with straight legs and strong but slightly sloping pasterns. The body should be strong and slightly longer than the height at the withers, with a deep, well let down, chest and a reasonable spring of rib.

The hindquarters should be powerful and muscular with good angulation. The Tibetan Mastiff should have fairly large compact cat feet, with feathering between the toes as a protection against snow. Some Tibetan Mastiffs have strong webbing between their toes, again as a help when moving about in snow.

The tail should be well-feathered (except in a time of moult), and should be carried curled over the back when the dog is alert and on the move. This is a breed that should move powerfully without appearing ponderous. It should cover the ground in a purposeful manner, looking as if it is always moving well within itself, as if it could go on at a steady pace for hours. It does tend to single track when moving at speed. Nimble and light-footed, the breed's size does not prevent it from being extremely agile – and something of an escape artist.

The Tibetan Mastiff male has a heavier coat than his female equivalent. It should be fairly long and thick with hard, straight hairs – never silky, curly or wavy. The undercoat is heavy and woolly. The neck and shoulders are heavily coated, looking like a mane, originally providing extra protection if attacked by predators. The hindquarters have extra feathering.

There is a variety of colours allowed – black, black and tan, various shades of gold, and even grey with gold markings. A white star on the chest is allowed, as are minimal white markings on the feet. The wonderful sleeping eye markings of tan or gold above the eyes are seen in the black and tan.

THE TIBETAN MASTIFF CHARACTER

The Tibetan Mastiff is still considered a primitive animal, which is not surprising when you consider that only about forty years ago the breed was still relatively unknown except as a guardian in the Himalayas. That it has adapted in such a short time to life in the West, and is now a recognised part of the show scene, says a great deal about its powers of survival.

One clear reminder of its recent advent into Western society is the fact that the bitches usually only come into season once a year, normally about the end of autumn. This seems to be triggered by the shortening of the days and by the accompanying drop in temperature. The phenomenon makes perfect sense, bearing in mind that nomadic tribes pitch camp during the most inhospitable months, and so pups could be carried and reared during a static time. They would then be ready to fend for themselves once the flocks moved on to fresh pastures in the Spring.

The character of the Tibetan Mastiff is one of its greatest charms, but it does reflect its centuries of guarding duties. It is wary of strangers and is certainly not a cuddly teddy bear. It is not the ferocious creature described by ancient travellers, but it does not give its favours freely and it is not an ideal breed for a completely novice owner. Like all the Molossers, it will take over if it does not perceive a very clear hierarchy with its own role clearly defined. What appears a bundle of fluff at eight weeks is quite a different prospect when it flexes its muscles at eight months and, if unchecked, could become a liability at eighteen months.

Like the other Molossers, the Tibetan Mastiff is a people-orientated dog but it will defend its territory and its people against all comers. This is what it has been bred for over the past several thousand years, and any owner needs to be aware of this characteristic.

Dignified and sometimes aloof, the Tibetan Mastiff is also calm, even-tempered and affectionate.   Photo: Eileen Haynes (Riches).

Qassaba Ausables Rakpa Of Chokola (Rio): Top Tibetan Mastiff in the UK in 1987 and 1988 in serious show pose.

Rio relaxing at home.

SOUND EFFECTS

One side effect of its guarding instinct which can cause problems in our over-crowded communities is the Tibetan Mastiff's propensity for nocturnal communication. Tibetan Mastiffs which are left outside at night make their presence felt by this wondrous booming bark "like a well-tempered copper gong" – a sound which may echo magnificently through the mountains in Tibet but which can cause insomnia for fellow town-dwellers. Snow leopards and other potential predators may have been deterred by such sounds, and I am sure contemporary burglars would think twice before investigating the source of the bark – but it can cause friction between neighbours.

Another aspect of behaviour which can cause anxiety to Tibetan Mastiff owners, even if they have bred and owned many other breeds, is the fact that a Tibetan Mastiff bitch is quite likely to shout her head off while being mated. This is not because she is suffering, more likely she is warning any further suitors not to waste their time as she is no longer available. This behaviour may not seem very modest, but it is no more forward that the behaviour of urban vixens who have been known to position themselves under street lights in London and then scream loudly to alert males in the area to the fact that they are seeking a mate!

PUPPY POWER

The Tibetan Mastiff needs careful handling as a puppy – patience allied with firmness, determination armed with affection. It can be taught the basic stages of obedience which make life together so much more pleasant. Sit, Down, Stay, Come, Give are well within its range – but like all Molossers, the Tibetan Mastiff is a thinking dog and there are times when it will query the intelligence of the command. If you throw a stick, any self-respecting Molosser will fetch it for you –

Azziz at six months.

Azziz, fully mature, at three years of age.

once. If you repeat the exercise, the dog will make it very clear that it has humoured you on this one occasion, but if you persevere in this aberrant type of behaviour you are on your own!

Puppies, especially males, often rebel at about eight months, just like adolescent humans. It is better to remain firm on essentials, but to allow a little flexibility. Try to avoid confrontations as they only lead to a hardening of attitudes and a lot of frustration.

Knowing the bounds of their territory is very important because young Tibetan Mastiffs could revert to their natural instincts and begin to guard the whole village if they are allowed to roam.

The Tibetan Mastiff has one secret vice, which many owners discover to their cost. It adores wood and will eat its way through furniture, trees and doors, without making any distinction between a rough piece of four-by-two or a precious Louis XV table-leg. Left alone in a house, a Tibetan Mastiff has been known to eat its way through the front door and be waiting for its owners in the front garden. One solution is to give it its very own log, or to invest in a steel kennel and mesh run.

THE FAMILY DOG

You may be wondering why anyone in their right mind would want to own a Tibetan Mastiff after this catalogue of potential problems. However, the advantages far outweigh these petty difficulties. The Tibetan Mastiff, as a family member, is even-tempered, calm and discreet, even docile, full of charm and affection, seeking the companionship of its people and happy to be with them.

It is particularly good with children, provided, of course, that the children behave in a civilised fashion towards it – a proviso for all dog/child relationships. It can set aside its aloofness and its dignity, and play like a puppy. This rapport with children may be a throwback to the days in the Tibetan villages when these great guard dogs were looked after by children rather than by adults.

Like all dogs it will defend its own young humans, and great care should be taken if young friends come to play. Children's squabbles and games may not be understood by a canine observer, who may think his own human is in danger. This is a situation which adult humans should be present to control, whether they are dealing with a Molosser or a Toy breed.

The Tibetan Mastiff is affectionate but rather reserved – the French describe it as *très zen* – it watches and thinks, and this impression of a thoughtful observer of human foibles is underlined by the presence of those wonderful 'sleeping eyes', the flashes of tan or gold above the eyes which give it the appearance of watchfulness even when asleep. It is seen by its aficionados as being very intuitive, able to sense mood changes in its human companions. This human understanding has been developed over centuries of close relationship with man, working as a guardian and protector.

Like all Molossers, it can be very stubborn and it will seek to maintain its independence within a loving relationship, even though it wants to please.

A publication on this splendid breed, issued by the Tibetan Mastiff Club of Great Britain, sums up the character thus:

"A disposition and temperament of controlled strength, spirit, initiative and fearlessness, tempered by patience, loyalty, gentleness, and a very strong desire to meet with approval. He is a playful, fun-loving dog and exuberant in showing his affection. His loyalty is with his master, but he can think like a wild dog, if the need arises."

If it is provoked or threatened or confronted by intruders it can become a terrifying sight. Its hackles go up and its coat seems to double in bulk, it stiffens and grows in height, it bares its teeth and its eyes glow red – a formidable adversary and not one with whom to trifle.

CHOOSING A PUPPY

A Tibetan Mastiff bitch can produce a litter of anything from two to thirteen puppies although six to eight is probably the average. Some bitches will reject the modern advantages of a whelping box and infra red lights and will seek the nearest equivalent to a cave. One breeder got over this problem by covering the table with a bedspread and the Tibetan Mastiff has accepted this compromise with good grace, bringing up her litter in this safe haven. Most bitches are very good mothers, and are relatively relaxed about visitors.

When selecting a puppy from a litter, if the breeder does not guide you, look for signs of sociability and confidence. Do not choose the little one all alone in the corner which may be too introverted or nervous and subsequently difficult to socialise. Go instead for the big, bossy one which may need to be kept in its place in your hierarchy but which

These puppies show the typical kind but solemn expression of the breed. The skull is fairly broad and strong, the occiput and stop are well-defined, and the muzzle is well-filled and square.

Strong, with a straight back and a rather deep chest. The brisket should reach below the elbows.

The movement is free, light and elastic. The tail-set is high, on a line with the top of the back, and curled over to one side.

177

will be even-tempered and outgoing.

Tibetan Mastiff puppies look very different from their adult relatives. They are covered in a very teddy-bear-like fluff which gradually becomes the thick coat and dense undercoat which characterises the adult dog. Like all the big breeds, the youngsters need very little exercise while growing. They should not be allowed to play too roughly with siblings or other canine companions, since too much rough play can result in shoulder injuries.

By the same token, a Tibetan Mastiff puppy should not be taken on long walks until at least twelve months old, when the bone has developed; too much exercise too young, when bones and joints are still soft, can lead to terrible problems later. It is very tempting to think a six-month-old puppy is big and therefore ready to walk and walk, but I have seen too many adult dogs in pain and discomfort from injuries incurred while still in a period of growth, and, consequently, I am rigorous in my exercise plans. Puppies need a great deal of rest interspersed with short periods of play or exercise, and, if

necessary, this rest should be strictly regimented by allowing the pup its own place which no-one else invades.

A puppy should grow big but not fat – it should not be overfed just as it should not be over-exercised. You are not paying good money for good food to produce an obese animal. You want to produce good bone and a healthy puppy, not a small unsteady barrel. Tibetan Mastiff puppies do not always want to eat – they are good at judging their own needs and will stop when they have had enough. This may well be a throwback to earlier days when food was not regularly presented to them or even readily available.

Adult dogs and bitches will often regurgitate food for puppies, and, given half a chance, will go hunting for them. I have been told by one breeder of an interesting power struggle between father and son, once son became adolescent. Father brought home a rabbit and instead of giving it to son, sat guarding it, refusing to allow son to eat it. This stand-off lasted all night, and, in the morning, father graciously allowed his son to

Muscular, strong-boned forequarters with well laid shoulders.

Adult males are surprisingly tolerant with puppies.

THE SUMMER COAT

Photos: Eileen Haynes (Riches).

Conrikyi Kong.

Rockanoar's Night Vigilante.

eat, having made the point very graphically that he was still in charge.

Grooming a Tibetan Mastiff is a relatively simple task. Dogs normally shed their undercoat once a year, in the Spring, just as the show season starts! It is sometimes hard to believe that one dog can shed so much without becoming totally bald, and one can understand why the Tibetan nomads spin all this hair into clothing for themselves. The undercoat comes out in large tufts and the moult can be helped by regular vigorous brushing. The winter coat is then replaced by a sleeker summer coat which usually sheds very little.

The Tibetan Mastiff has no doggy smell and requires little or no bathing, old hair and skin being shed at the time of the winter moult. People who are allergic to dog hair often find that Tibetan Mastiffs do not affect them at all, such is the quality of their coat. If they are brought up in the house they are affected by the central heating and this can change their coat development.

One last point about Tibetan Mastiff behaviour – when cross or when losing an argument, they will puff out their cheeks and huff and puff in a very disapproving fashion, blowing out through their whiskers. It is a very effective way of showing displeasure!

11 THE FILA BRASILEIRO

By Jaime Pérez Marhuenda

Since 1500, the year in which the Portuguese Pedro Alves Cabral discovered Brazil, the Fila Brasileiro has been recognised and developed as a separate breed, adapting to the requirements of the people of the New World. In 1550 the process of colonisation was hastened as a result of the administrative reforms of King João III of Portugal, who replaced the Captaincy system in operation in those days by a Colonial Government. This was the start of a new era, with Brazil becoming home to people from a variety of backgrounds, religions and cultures, ranging from the Jesuits, who tried to evangelise the Indians, to slave traders whose main goal was financial gain.

It was in the light of this situation that some of the native dogs were discovered to be of great value. Not only could they be used to subdue the Indians who were trying to resist capture, but they could also pursue them if they tried to escape. To carry out this task, they needed animals who were so fierce and courageous that they would seize people who were fighting for their lives. The dogs also needed a well-developed sense of smell and the skill and determination to track across hostile terrain.

Although the Jesuits played a large part in stopping the enslavement of native Indians, the slave traders were not deterred. They looked towards the African coast, and again, their dogs proved of considerable value. In 1630 the East Indies Company, attracted by the cotton trade, sent a fleet to Brazil which conquered Pernambuco. The Dutch Sovereignty lasted until 1654 and, during that time, the trade of goods, people and animals flourished between the two continents.

During this period, organised gangs of people appeared from São Paulo in search of slaves and gold – they were known as 'bandeirantes' Once again, native dogs proved essential partners, with the attributes of ferocity and good sense being most highly prized. It was not until the 17th century that the bandeirantes eventually discovered gold in the mountains of the Brazilian Central Plateau. This resulted in mass emigration to the area known as Minas Gerais, accompanied by slaves to work the land and to mine the gold, and aggressive guard dogs.

The European immigrants who arrived in Brazil brought many different breeds or types of dogs, and it is very likely that they mated without any control. The two types most highly favoured were the Mastiff type, prized for its tenacity and strength, and the Bloodhound because of its keen nose. It is fair to assume that, from this time onwards, nature selected those animals who were better adapted to the environment and to the task they had to perform.

Lendo Do Amparo, owned by Jaime Pérez Marhuenda. Mastiff, Bloodhound, and Bulldog are components in the make-up of the Fila Brasileiro.

As the population increased, cattle ranching developed to meet the growing demand for food. This led to dogs such as the Bulldog being imported, as they were used to bait the cattle. The dog's task was to take charge of the cattle as they were herded from place to place, and to protect them against the Brazilian jaguar as well as cattle thieves. At their destination, the dog helped his owner to herd the cattle into the pens. One of the most used routes was along the bank of the River San Francisco, which connected the interior of Minas Gerais to the coast.

THE DEVELOPMENT OF THE FILA BRASILEIRO

The Fila Brasileiro, as it is known today, has evolved from the breeds, or types of dog, mentioned previously. It is impossible to know the individual influence of any one breed because of the lack of written evidence.

In Stonehenge's *The Dog in Health and Disease*, written in 1859, it is stated: "The Mastiff was crossed lots of times with the Bulldog." Some modern bloodlines are full of it, which is characterised by little semi-erect ears, snub noses and general structure. There is no objection to a little infusion of this

181

Nega Do Engenho Velho, bred and owned by Iliano Pinto. Great physical stamina and a good sense of smell are essentials in the breed.

blood that mixes very well with Mastiff's; however, the cross with Bloodhound has to be emphatically avoided, due to the fierce temperament that that breed transmits." However, this advice came too late, or it was simply unknown.

The result of these accidental crosses was a dog with the following characteristics:

• Large, with a somewhat coarse coat.
• Great physical endurance, due to the lack of attention from his owner, so that the dog had to acquire his own food once his work was finished. Those that could not withstand these conditions simply died.
• A good sense of smell, needed to detect the presence of the jaguar or any other enemy, before he himself was detected. For that, a good-length muzzle was necessary, and the mixture of Bloodhound in him helped towards this, giving the muzzle and skull the proportions of 1:1, different from the rest of the Molosser breeds.
• Powerful bite, with teeth not large enough to break – leaving the dog defenceless – but,

at the same time, broad at the root with sharp edges enabling rapid entry into the flesh.
• Broad and deep muzzle to accommodate its powerful jaws.
• The ability to make very rapid changes of direction, necessary for his work with cattle. The dog also needs to be loose-jointed, allowing him to attack his aggressor even though he has been bitten or pinned down during the attack. The energy-saving gait (pacing), needed for long days working was also typical.
• Thick and loose skin to prevent cuts, caused by the rough undergrowth, becoming deep and infected. The loose skin also protected him when attacked by the jaguar, who would tear at the plentiful skin, but fail to penetrate to the vital organs.
• High fertility rates resulted in numerous large litters, which guaranteed at least a minimum number of survivors.
• Affectionate with his owner and family, but aggressive towards strangers. This was a dog who remained loyal to his master despite

the minimal care given to him. He also guarded, with his life, the property of his owner whether this was land, slaves or cattle.

A NEW ROLE

Slavery was abolished in 1888, and so the Fila was used as a cattle herder, a hunter, and a guard dog ('fazendas'). These animals worked during the day with the cattle and at night they were stationed in their owner's property defending it from strangers. When his aptitude as a guard dog became more widely known, the Fila was brought to the cities on the coast.

During the 1940s the lawyer, Paulo Santos Cruz, needing protection for his collection of birds and having heard about the excellent qualities of the fazendeiro's dog, he started to visit fazendas to acquire puppies. Fascinated by the Fila's behaviour, he started breeding using the affix 'Cadyz y Cadyz' and later the world-famous 'Parnapu·n'. He also wrote the Standard of the breed, which was recognised by the FCI in 1946. Known all over the world as the 'father of the breed', Paulo Santos Cruz was widely respected for his huge knowledge of the Fila, and he was largely responsible for the establishment and development of the breed today.

FIGHTING FOR SURVIVAL

In the 1970s, unscrupulous breeders crossed the Fila with the Mastiff, the Great Dane and the Neapolitan Mastiff. This, together with the fact that the Brazilian Kennel Club (BKC) closed the 'initial register' of the Fila Brasileiro, resulted in near extinction for the breed.

On March 19th 1978 the Comissão de Aprimoramento do Fila Brasileiro (CAFIB) was created, its main task being to fight against cross-breeding. In August of 1979 the Committee decided to separate from the BKC and set up as an independent club. Thanks to its work, the pure Fila Brasileiro, without cross-breeding characteristics and with the typical temperament, has been successfully re-established.

Trevo Da Boa Sorte, bred and owned by Marilia Barroso Pentagna. The Fila is now well established in many parts of Europe.

THE FILA BRASILEIRO IN EUROPE

The Fila Brasileiro reached Europe in 1954 when the German Prince, Albrecht von Bayern, imported the male Dunga do Parnapu·n. He fell in love with the breed, and made a special trip to Brazil in search of more dogs. He bought Garoa and Hera do Parnapu·n, and he also travelled around the interior of Minas Gerais with Dr Paulo Santos Cruz looking for more Filas.

It was in Germany where the breed developed most quickly, thanks, to a great extent, to these early imports which were soon followed by more. By 1979 there was a group of 70 dogs in Germany. However, not all of the imports contributed to the breed's improvement, and Christofer Habig, executive of the German Molosser Club, protested officially against the import of two untypical dogs: a dappled-coat female (crossed with a Great Dane) and a male with undeniable Mastiff characteristics.

It is a fact that the initial breeding stock in Europe was formed both with pure and with crossbred dogs, causing the same situation as occurred in Brazil. This made for considerable problems with registrations, which have eventually been resolved. Today, Spain is the centre of reference in the breeding of the Fila Brasileiro, not only in Europe but also in the world (obviously excepting Brazil).

There is a large population of Filas in the south of Europe, mainly in the Czech Republic, though unfortunately the quality is not as good as it might be. The breed's presence in central Europe is relatively modest, although there are some breeders who are working hard to establish it. The problem for the breed is its inclusion in legislation relating to dangerous dogs (its import is banned in the UK, for example), although there is no documented evidence to justify such severe restrictions.

SHOWING THE FILA BRASILEIRO

It is easy to see that the glamorous environment of a conformation dog show is not the ideal place for the Fila. However, it should not be an unattainable goal, as long as the judge assumes that it is not necessary to touch the dog in order to assess him, and the handler has complete control over his dog.

Cross-breeding is the reason for finding too many Filas in Europe with faulty temperaments – it is not unusual to see apathetic or even fearful dogs at a show. Paradoxically, dog shows are responsible, to a great extent, for this situation. The reason is that, until recently, judges faulted dogs that

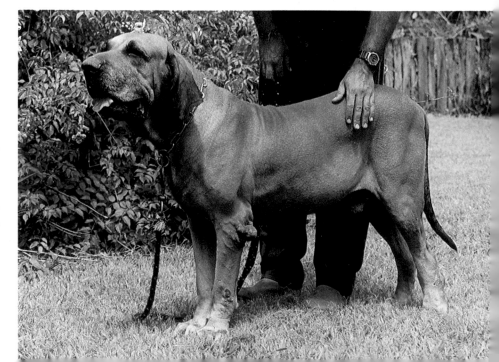

Nagan Do Amparo, bred and owned by Carlos Do Amaral Cintra Filho. This six-year-old male shows the correct proportions for the breed.

Timbo Do Itapua, bred by Giovani Eder, owned by Jaime Pérez Marhuenda. Note the typical head and expression of calm self-assurance.

showed aggression, and rewarded dogs with faulty, untypical temperaments. Consequently these winning dogs were used for breeding, and the faults were perpetuated.

It is vital to remember that at FCI shows, dogs are judged according to their Breed Standard. In the Standard for the Fila there is a complete paragraph concerning temperament, and an obligatory temperament test if the dog is to become a Champion.

THE FCI STANDARD

GENERAL CONFORMATION: Typically molossoid breed. Powerful bones, rectangular structure, compact but harmonious and in proportion. Added to his massiveness a great agility is easy to be seen. Bitches must show a well-defined femininity, which differs them from males.

CHARACTER & TEMPERAMENT: Courage, determination and outstanding braveness are part of his characteristics. He is docile to his owners and family and extremely tolerant with children. His faithfulness became a Brazilian proverb. He is always looking for the company of his master. One of his characteristics is his distrust of strangers. He shows a calm disposition, self-assurance and self-confidence, not being disturbed by strange noises or when facing a new environment. An unsurpassed guardian of property, he was also bred to hunt big game and to herd cattle.

MOVEMENT: The Fila should have a long reach and elastic gait. His smooth stride reminds you of the big cat's movements. His main characteristic is the PACE – a two beat lateral gait in which the legs of each side move back and forth exactly as a pair causing a rolling or rocking motion of the dog's body (called the camel's pace), accentuated all along the top line to the tail. During the walk he carries the head lower than the back region. He shows a smooth, free and effortless trot with a powerful stride. His gallop is powerful with surprising speed for such a large and heavy dog. Due to his loose jointedness, typical of molossers, the Fila's movements give the impression, and in fact it is so, of being capable of instant and very rapid changes of direction.

EXPRESSION: In repose it is calm, noble and full of self-assurance. Never discloses a bored or absent expression. When at attention his expression reflects

Raruska Do Engenho Velho: Excellent stop and protruding occiput.

Madonna Da Boa Sorte: A young bitch with excellent ear-set, and with the correct muzzle/skull proportions.

determination and alertness with a firm look in the eyes.

HEAD: The Fila head is big, heavy, massive, and always in proportion to the whole body. From a top view it resembles a trapezoid figure in which the head is inserted in a pear form shape. From side view, muzzle and skull should have approximately the proportion of 1:1 (one per one) with the muzzle slightly shorter than the skull.

SKULL: The profile of the skull shows a smooth curve from the stop to the occiput, which is protuberant, especially in puppies. From a front view it is large, broad with the upper line slightly curved. Lateral lines come down almost vertical, in a curve narrowing towards the muzzle. Never shows a stop.

STOP: FRONTAL DEPRESSION: From a front view it is practically non-existent. The medium furrow is slight and runs up smoothly. Looking sideways the stop is low, sloped and formed only by the well-developed eyebrows.

MUZZLE: Strong, broad and deep, always in harmony with the skull. From a top view, it is full under the eyes slightly narrowing toward the middle of the muzzle, and, again, broadening slightly to the front line. From a side view, the nose is straight or has a Roman line, but is never turned up. The front line of the muzzle is close to a perpendicular line with a depression right under the nose and forming a perfect curve with the upper lips which are thick, pendulous and drooping over the lower lips, giving shape to the inferior line of the muzzle which is almost parallel to the upper line. The labial rim is always apparent. The lower lips are close and firm up to the fangs and from there on they are loose with dented borders. The muzzle has a great depth at the root but without surpassing the size of the length. Edges of the lips form an inverted "U".

NOSE: Well-developed, broad nostrils not occupying entirely the maxillar width. Colour: Black.

EYES: From medium to large size, almond shaped, spaced well apart, medium to deep set. Permissible

Vulca Do Amparo: Typical nose with a Roman line.

colours: from dark brown to yellow, always in accordance to the colour of the coat. Due to the profusion of loose skin many individuals present drooping lower eyelids, which is not considered as fault as such a detail increases the melancholic expression, which is typical of the breed.

EARS: Pendant, large, thick, V-Shaped. Broad at the base and tapering to the ends. Rounded tips. Inserted at the posterior part of the skull in line with the eyes when in repose. When roused the ears are above the original position. The root is oblique with the front border higher than the back border. Drooping at the cheeks or folded back allowing its interior to be seen.

TEETH: Wider than longer, strong and white. Upper incisors are broad at their root and sharp at the edges. Canines or fangs are powerful, well set and well apart. The ideal bite is a scissor bite, but a level bite is acceptable.

NECK: Extraordinarily strong and muscled giving the impression of a short neck. Slightly curved at

Odin Da Boa Sorte: This dog has an excellent head, showing a deep, strong, well-defined muzzle and a strong, well-muscled neck.

Piata Da Caramona: The legs should be straight and strong, and the body should be broad and deep, covered by loose skin.

the upper side and well detached from the skull. Dewlaps at the throat.

TOPLINE: Withers in a sloping line, are set well apart from each other due to the distance between the scapulas. Withers are set in a lower level from the croup. After the withers, the upper line changes direction ascending smoothly to the croup. Back line shows no tendency to sway or roach back.

CROUP: Broad, long, with an approximately 30 degrees angulation from the horizontal line showing a smooth curve. The croup is set a little higher than the withers. From a back view the croup is ample approximately as wide as the thorax, being permitted to be broader at bitches.

BODY: Strong, broad and deep, covered by thick and loose skin. The thorax is longer than the abdomen. The length of the body is the same as the height plus 10 per cent when measured from the point of the shoulder to the point of the buttocks.

THORAX: Well-sprung ribs though not interfering with the position of shoulder. Deep and large chest going down to the level of the elbows. Well pronounced brisket.

LOINS: Shorter and not so deep as the thorax showing well a separation of the two component parts. In bitches the lower part of loins are more developed. From an upper view the loins are narrower than the thorax and croup but should not form a waistline.

LOWER LINE: A long chest and parallel to the ground in all its extension. Tuck up slightly in ascension but never whippety.

FORELEGS: The shoulder structure should be composed by two bones of equal length (scapula and humerus) being the first one at 45 degrees from the horizontal line and the last one 90 degrees from the first one. The articulation scapula-humerus forms the point of shoulder, which is situated at the level of the prosternum but a little behind it. In the ideal position, the point of shoulder should be halfway from elbow to withers. An imaginary perpendicular line coming down from the withers should cut the elbow and reach the foot.

LEGS: Strong bones, legs parallel and straight to the pasterns. Metacarpus short, strong apparent carpus slightly sloping. Length of the leg from ground to elbow should be 50 per cent of the length from ground to withers.

FEET: Strong and well arched toes not too close together. Pads thick, broad and deep. The ideal position of feet is pointing to the front. Strong dark nails, white nails permissible when this is the colour of the feet and toes.

HINDLEGS: Less heavy boned than forelegs but never light as a whole. Upper thigh with curved borders shaped by strong muscles coming from the ilium and ischium which design the borders of the rear, and, for this reason, the ischium must have a good length.
Hindlegs are parallel, with strong tarsus, metatarsus slightly bent, higher than the metacarpus. Moderate angled stifle and metatarsus.

Xango Do Engenho Velho: A young male with an excellent topline.

HIND FEET: A little more oval than the forefeet but the same goes for the whole description. Should not have dewclaws (the fifth toe).

TAIL: Very wide at the root, medium set, tapering rapidly when reaching to the hocks level. When the dog is alert the tail is raised high and the curve at the extremity is more accentuated. Should not be carried curled over the back.

.

HEIGHT: Males: From 27 ins to 29.52 ins. (75 cms) at the shoulder. Females: From 24 ins (60 cms) to 27.56 ins at the shoulder.

WEIGHT:
Males: Minimum: 100 lbs (45 kgs)
Females: Minimum: 90 lbs (40 kgs)

COLOUR: All solid colours are permitted except the disqualifying ones (white and mouse-grey) (patched dogs or dapple coat). Brindles with a solid coat may have stripes of less intensity or very strong dark stripes. A black mask may or may not be present. In all permitted colours, white marks are allowed on the feet, chest and tip of tail. Not desirable at any other part of the coat. White markings exceeding one fourth of the total body must be penalised.

SKIN: One of the most important breed characteristics is the thick, loose skin over the whole body, chiefly at the neck, forming pronounced dewlaps and often it can be seen at the brisket and abdomen. Some individuals present a fold at the sides of the head, also at the withers running down to the shoulders. If the dog is in repose the head is free of wrinkle. When alert, the contraction of the skin at the skull forms small wrinkles running in a longitudinal line on the skull.

COAT: Short, smooth, dense and tight to the body.

TEST OF TEMPERAMENT
This is compulsory to all individuals (after 12 months) in order to obtain a registered Championship title. All Champions must have a

---

DISQUALIFICATIONS

1. Aggressiveness to his owner.
2. Cowardice.
3. Pink nose.
4. Overshot teeth.
5. Undershot teeth showing the teeth when the mouth is shut.
6. Lack of 1 (one) canine or 1 (one) molar, except the 3rd one.
7. Blue eyes (porcelain like).
8. Cropped ears or docked tail.
9. A croup lower than the withers.
10. All white dogs, mouse-gray, patched dogs or dapple coat (merle).
11. Under minimum height (65 cms for males, 60 cms for bitches).
12. Lack of loose skin.
13. Lack of the typical pace (camel's pace).

Arua Da Barra: A top-quality brindle.

VERY SERIOUS FAULTS

1. Small head.
2. Tight upper lips (without flews).
3. A pronounced stop from a front view.
4. Protruding eyes.
5. Lack of 2 (two) teeth, except the PI.
6. Lack of dewlaps.
7. Apathetic or timid.
8. Negative sensitivity to shooting.
9. Roach back.
10. Level back line (not ascending towards the croup).
11. Excessive tuck up.
12. Cow hocks.
13. Lack of angulation at the hindquarters (straight hocks).
14. Light bones.
15. Lack of substance (shelly).
16. Over the maximum height (75 cms males, 70 cms bitches).
17. White markings exceeding l/4 (one fourth) of the body.
18. Lack of pigmentation at the eye-rims.
19. Round eyes.
20. Square figure.

SERIOUS FAULTS

1. Short muzzle.
2. Small ears.
3. Highly set ears.
4. Excessively light coloured eyes.
5. Wrinkles at the skull when the animal is in repose.
6. Undershot.
7. Lack of 2 (two) teeth.
8. Folded skin under the throat that is not a dewlap (horizontal folds).
9. Sway back.
10. Narrow croup.
11. Curled tail carried over the back.
12. Chest lacking depth.
13. Any deviation of carpus or metatarsus.
14. Over angulated hindquarters (sickle hocks).
15. Short steps (poor reach).

certificate of approval at the temperament test. This sort of test is made at all speciality shows. It is optional at general shows, up to the judge's will, provided it is public and takes place outside the show ring.

The trial includes:

1. Attack with a stick. The dog is supposed to attack in front of the handler, without being coached, and the exhibitor or handler will remain in his position. It is forbidden to touch or to beat the animal.

2. Shooting test. Blanks will be fired at a distance of 5 metres from the dog. The dog should express attention, show self-confidence and self-assurance.

3. During all performance in the ring the judge will analyse the behaviour and temperament of the specimen, paying attention to his expression. During the temperament test the following should be observed:

Jaime Pérez Marhuenda with his dog Timbo Do Itapua. The Fila is a fierce protector of his owner and his owner's property.

a) The dislike of the animal to strangers
b) The self-assurance, courage, determination and braveness of each individual.

FAULTS - GENERAL: Cryptorchids, or monorchids, use of artificial ways to produce certain effects, albinism, lack of type, etc.

MINOR FAULTS
Anything in disagreement with the Standard.
NOTE: Male animals should have two apparently normal testicles fully descended into the scrotum.
Copyright: The Fédération Cynologique Internationale.

THE FILA CHARACTER

Temperament is, beyond any doubt, the factor that characterises and differentiates the Fila Brasileiro from any other breed. Likewise, it is his typical behaviour that gains the Fila his human fans.

The Fila has an ongoing love/hate attitude to life: he loves everything he considers his own, e.g. his owner, family, and property – and hates all the rest. Everything outside his territory is considered an aggressor and he acts with the aggression he thinks they deserve.

Zulu Do Engenho Velho: An intense dislike of strangers is an inherent characteristic.

Starting from puppyhood, the Fila shows a very distinctive trait, quite unlike any other breed. Youngsters are not inclined to be playful with strangers, however much the stranger tries to engage their attention. From the age of four months, the Fila puppy starts to be suspicious towards people, avoiding contact and withdrawing ungraciously. As he grows older, fear and suspicion turn to deep hatred and his aggressive patterns towards strangers also increase, coinciding with increasing aggressiveness and his physical development.

For the first nine months, the Fila may show inconsistency in his reactions. But these changes in behaviour are absolutely normal, as it would be for a developing child. However, typical behaviour starts to appear, and it is only a matter of time before all strangers will receive a hostile response.

A dog raised in the correct environment must appear aggressive by the time he reaches 12 months of age. This is part of his strong guarding instinct, and it is our duty to keep it this way. The Fila does not need any training to guard adequately – in fact, if he needs to be trained he has a serious fault in temperament. In the Breed Standard, the "apathetic or timid" dog is classed as among 'very serious faults' which would be penalised more severely than some faulty point of conformation such as high ear-set.

However, the Fila should be trained in basic obedience, although *never* by a stranger. Training is, in fact, an easy task for the owner, as the dog's main interest is to please his master. Therefore it should not be difficult to establish control, and for the Fila to live and socialise in the most civilised way.

LIVING WITH FILAS
The belief that a Fila Brasileiro will make a good guard if he is left alone in a kennel all day, only seeing his master when he is fed, is a total misconception. From puppyhood, and throughout his physical and mental development, he needs contact with his family, love (above all things), and to be cared for. The Fila needs support from his owner in order to carry out his guarding duties, and this should not arise from fear, but from loyalty.

How about Filas and children? This is a question that is often asked. I have to say that, in my experience, there is no problem, and with correct handling a sound relationship

The correctly reared Fila will accept the rules of his family, but he should always be kennelled if strangers come to the home.

will develop between dog and child. Docility with his family and tolerance of children are typical characteristics, and they are part of the Breed Standard. But do not expect the Fila to accept children outside the immediate family – they are strangers and will be treated as such. For this reason, the Fila should always remain kennelled when strangers – young or old – are on the premises.

There are those who seek to modify the natural instincts of the Fila through training in order to make it more socially acceptable. Those breeders who have worked to keep the breed pure see this as total sacrilege. The temperament and character of the Fila Brasileiro is its most striking characteristic, and it is what differentiates it from all others. In fact, the Fila that has been correctly reared is perfectly well adapted within a family group, that is, his own social unit. He will attack an intruder, without encouragement from his owner, and, the next second, he will allow the youngest of the family to pull his ears in the most undignified manner.

Those who are not prepared to accept and respect these very particular characteristics, should look for another breed.

CHOOSING A PUPPY

I will assume that the reader knows the basic criteria needed to select a good puppy, such as a knowledge of the pedigree, an evaluation of the immediate family members, and an assessment of the lines involved in this or previous crosses. I will therefore confine myself to the qualities needed to select a good Fila.

AGE

It is generally assumed that the Fila's aversion to strangers, a basic trait of the breed, is, to a great extent, acquired by imitation as well as being genetically transmitted. Therefore, it is of the utmost importance that the puppy should remain with the mother at least until two months of age. During this period he should be able to observe and learn the aggressive reactions of the mother towards strangers.

SEX

As a general rule, it is advisable to select a female as a first choice. They are normally more affectionate and devoted to their owners, and they are also more watchful and

Fila puppies must stay with their dam until they are two months of age.

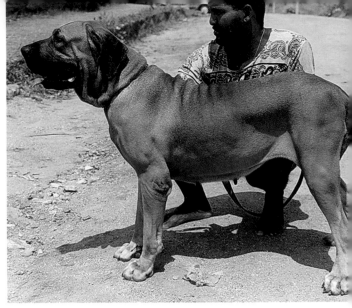

Large ears, a pronounced occiput and plentiful loose skin are essential breed points to look for when choosing a puppy.

Morena II Do Ibituruna, bred and owned by Paulo Angotti. If you cannot cope with the unique character of the Fila, you should find another breed.

alert. The reason for this is that males tend to be more self-assured, making them more relaxed. The insecurity in the female makes her a superior guard.

TYPE
The puppy should be selected among those of average size, ignoring the smaller and bigger individuals. The points to look for are:
• Large ears, positioned at the posterior part of the skull in line with the eyes.
• Pronounced occiput.
• Loose and plentiful skin, two well-defined folds of longitudinal thick skin in the neck.

These characteristics should be evident from an early age. It is important to avoid the puppy that looks like a miniature adult Fila; this type may well suffer from growing problems. So, you are looking for the puppy that looks ungainly and may appear big and clumsy. Ideally, the skull should show a slight curve, because the bigger the gap, the wider the skull will be in the future.

COLOUR
Obviously this is a very personal matter, and is only of aesthetic value. The only precaution to take is in the case of brindle puppies where the stripes should be perfectly defined over a solid background. The Fila with undefined brindle, as in the Bullmastiff, shows a clear cross-breeding in his ancestry, and often there will be some other fault confirming the existence of foreign blood.

Black colour has brought controversy among Fila breeders. Some believe that it is the result of cross-breeding with Great Danes and Neapolitan Mastiffs – it has been proved that about four per cent of puppies are born with this colour. The truth remains that there were no black puppies registered between 1956 and the 1970s, and then, coinciding with the cross-breeding development, black puppies were registered with the Brazilian Kennel Club.

12 THE DOGUE DE BORDEAUX

By Anne-Marie Class

The Dogue de Bordeaux is probably one of the most ancient French breeds, though it only became known by this name in the second part of the nineteenth century. Gaston Phébus, the Count of Foix, whose book about gun dogs is famous, wrote in the 14th century about the "alans vautres" which were the ancestors of the Dogues de Bordeaux.

HISTORY OF THE BREED

Somewhat disappointingly, few historical details about the Dogue de Bordeaux exist before 1863. In earlier days, this dog was called a Dogue or a Mâtin. This latter name comes from the same root as the word 'Mastiff' which is why the Dogue de Bordeaux is sometimes called a French Mastiff. The first reference by name appeared in a French show catalogue in that year, when one specimen of the breed was exhibited. The purpose of this show was more to exhibit different breeds than to judge dogs against their Standard. By the end of the century, the name Dogue de Bordeaux was better established.

In the old days, Dogues de Bordeaux were kept for all sorts of jobs: hunting, fighting, guarding, pulling loads. Butchers used them to prevent steers getting away and to keep them in their place and also for pulling loads of meat from the slaughterhouse to their shops. During the First World War, some Dogues de Bordeaux helped to drag injured people to safety. Another task given to them was hunting animals such as boars. Unfortunately, Dogues were also involved in deplorable dog-baiting spectacles where they were made to fight with other dogs, or even bears or bulls, simply for man's entertainment. It is sad to say that not only Dogues de Bordeaux were thus treated – many Molossers went through this cruel ordeal.

In Britain, the Dogue was only officially recognised by the Kennel Club in November 1997, but the breed was known and appreciated by fanciers in England at the end of the nineteenth century and at the beginning of the twentieth. As far back as 1893 the Kennel Club Gazette mentions judges' reports about exhibitions where Dogues de Bordeaux were shown in Britain. The *New Book of the Dog*, written by Robert Leighton and published in 1910, describes the dog and mentions that "the Dogue de Bordeaux has often been seen on this side of the Channel, but in 1895 efforts were made by two or three well-known Bulldog men to establish the breed in England." A certain Sam Wodiwiss even presided over the Dogue de Bordeaux Club founded in 1897. The *Kennel Club Gazette* of November 1897 relates the report of Mr Krehl who judged

Hercule des Molosses D'Aquitaine.
The Dogue de Bordeaux: An ancient fighting dog of great courage.

Photo: Anne-Marie Class.

Breed specialist Raymond Triquet with stuffed specimens (c. end 19th century) displayed in the Bordeaux Science Museum.
Photo: Anne-Marie Class.

the Club Show. In December of the same year, the *Kennel Club Gazette* wrote of 14 Dogues de Bordeaux entered at a show, and in the November 1898 issue it is possible to read about the judging of Dogues de Bordeaux at the Kennel Club Crystal Palace Show.

Meanwhile, what was happening on the other side of the Channel? It is interesting to note that documentary evidence uncovered by Raymond Triquet proves that English-bred Bullmastiffs were sold in France in the Bordeaux area in the late nineteenth century. What are the chances that Dogues de Bordeaux and Bullmastiffs from both France and Britain were crossed from time to time? Do not forget that at that time a dog's utility was its most important feature and breeders used to cross different breeds without referring to any Kennel Club or breed Club for advice, in order to obtain certain qualities or improvements.

THREE DIFFERENT TYPES

Around that time, there were three types of Dogues, the "Parisien" (from the Paris area), the "Toulousain" (from the Toulouse area), and the Bordelais (from the Bordeaux area). There was also the Doguin which was a kind of miniature Dogue (said to be a cross between a Bulldog and a Dogue de Bordeaux).

According to Triquet, the Parisien was born in the Paris area, had little undershot and poor stop and was often of mixed appearance. The Toulousain had a large strong head with less stop, and a slightly down-facing longer muzzle. Caporal, one of the earliest and most famous Dogues, was of the Toulousain type. The Bordelais was very much like the dog as described in today's Standard. In the Bordeaux Science Museum there are two stuffed specimens of the breed; the male is a Toulousain type, the bitch is a Bordelais, very similar to bitches of contemporary type.

MEN OF INFLUENCE

Three men have been influential in the history of the Dogue de Bordeaux. Firstly, there was Pierre Mégnin, a vet and editor of the French Magazine *Eleveur* (the Breeder), who published a study describing the Dogue de Bordeaux in 1896. This study led to the publication of the very first description of the Dogue de Bordeaux in *L'Annuaire Richard*. Mégnin preferred the brown mask to the black one, claiming that the latter was the result of cross-breeding with English Mastiffs.

Secondly, there was Professor Kunstler who taught at the Bordeaux Natural History Museum. He wrote the first Standard in 1910. Unlike Mégnin, Kunstler preferred the black mask (Raymond Triquet, *La Saga du Dogue de Bordeaux*). Kunstler was very critical about the type differences in the breed and spoke out about them most strongly. According to Raymond Triquet, "Kunstler created the modern Dogue de Bordeaux."

Third is Professor Raymond Triquet who wrote the 1971 Standard with the help of a great dog expert, Doctor Luquet, and who reformulated this Standard in 1995. Raymond Triquet says that he took a leaf out of Kunstler's and Mégnin's books, when he wrote the 1971 Standard. Several years of work in the most important French and foreign libraries led Raymond Triquet to recount the history of Molossers and the Dogue de Bordeaux in the book *La Saga du Dogue de Bordeaux* published in 1997.

Marius de Tropez (left) a typical black mask, belonging to Bruno Cazalis, and Navarre de la Seigneurie des Chartrons, a brown mask.

Photo: Bruno Cazalis.

Ulcha de l'Aube Rouge. Until the 19th century, the breed was almost unheard of outside Bordeaux.

Photo: Anne-Marie Class.

DIFFERING STANDARDS

So almost a century separates the first Standard from today's. What can be said about the breed during that period? Until the nineteenth century, the Dogue de Bordeaux (as it was later to be named) was virtually unheard of outside the Bordeaux area. At the beginning, few Dogues de Bordeaux were shown and it is extremely difficult to get a clear picture of the animal at that time. Opinions differed as to the perfect and genuine Dogue de Bordeaux and most breeders sought greater utility rather than adherence to Standard. Even the three types mentioned previousley were not strictly and particularly defined. Fanciers and specialists of the breed disagreed about mouths or masks. Mégnin was for a level mouth, Kunstler for an undershot mouth.

Another influential person was Barès, a Bordeaux printer, who founded a club in 1926 and bred between the two World Wars. His breeding and widespread influence left their mark on the history of the breed. The Dogue greatly suffered during the first World War, and Barès created a club in 1924 which helped to build up the breed again. A Standard was published in 1926, admitting both mask colours and giving two possible heights and weights (referring to the Doguin as being smaller and lighter), and requiring an undershot of at least 1 cm. Faults to be avoided and a points scale were later added to this Standard, which remained in effect until 1971.

After the Second World War, there were very few specimens left in France, as was the case with the Mastiff in England. Even though Barès was still present and keen, the situation for the Dogue was not very good and was not to improve until the 1970s.

DEVELOPMENT OF THE BREED

In France, in the 1970s the breed flourished.

Influential breeders pictured outside the Bordeaux Science Museum: Mr Coiffard, Professor Triquet, Mr Daniaux and Philippe Serouil.

Lucciano de Rauchebruy, with Mr Daniaux pictured at the 1997 French Breeding Show, Jonzac.

Helsinki 1998 World Championship Show: Best of Breed She Comes From Russia.
Photo: Anne-Marie Class.

At the end of the fifties, Raymond Triquet had come across a Dogue de Bordeaux, César de la Croix Coupée and fallen in love with the breed. Ever since that moment, he has worked to develop the breed, to build up the Club, and to promote the breed in France and abroad. He used to breed under the kennel name De La Maison des Arbres. His undertaking has been successful. So, rather oddly, a man from the North has given a new lease of life and added vigour to the Southern-born Dogue de Bordeaux. Author of several dictionaries and many publications, university lecturer, Doctor of Linguistics and polyglot, Raymond Triquet is also honorary member of the British Legion. He has judged all over the world and wherever he has spoken he has spread the word about what a good Dogue de Bordeaux should be like. His charisma and instructiveness have done a great deal to promote the breed. Sixty-six puppies were born in France in

A group of Dogues de Bordeaux from Anna-Lisa Sirkia's kennel in Finland. Diva vom Hessenbleck (aged eight) pictured with four of her offspring (three of them are seven-year-olds).

Photo: Anne-Marie Class.

In the USA, Bonnie Gordon, USBC secretary with Mugsie de Merignac (aged seven), Big House Bordeaux Sassy (22 months), and Big House Bordeaux Indiana (eight months). Bonnie has registered more than 3000 Dogues de Bordeaux in the registry established by Peter Curley in the USA. Photo: Gordon.

1970, one hundred and forty-three in 1976, two hundred and three in 1979, two hundred and fifty in 1980 and four hundred and eleven in 1997.

What about the situation outside France? The Dogue has been bred and appreciated in Germany since the beginning of the twentieth Century. I particularly remember a very nice German Dogue de Bordeaux, Beau Vom Hessenbleck, who was my Best Male at the Molosser Show in 1995 at the age of seven. In the Netherlands, the breed has been very popular. Surprisingly, more Dogues de Bordeaux were born in the Netherlands between 1995 and 1998 than in France. The first Dutch breed specimens were registered at the beginning of the twentieth century. A lovely Dogue, Belmondo the Red Powerpack,

which was born in Germany and lived in the Netherlands, was sold for a very high price to a Russian fancier. Belgium has also been an excellent breeding ground for the Dogue, as has Spain more recently. The first Dogue de Bordeaux in Belgium was registered shortly before the turn of the century.

Some Dogues from these countries have been very successful at the French Championship Shows and the French breeding shows. Though as yet not recognised by the American Kennel Club, the Dogue de Bordeaux is quite popular in the USA. The breed is exhibited in Specialty Shows organised by breed clubs or in exhibitions organised by the Rare Breeds Association. Amusingly, a Dogue de Bordeaux, Fidelle de Fenelon, was registered in America in 1959 as a Mastiff and bred from! There are fanciers in Finland, Russia, Italy, Switzerland and nice specimens of the breed in those countries. There are Dogues de Bordeaux in most other countries including Australia, Austria, Finland, Japan and Brazil. In Great Britain, even before official recognition of the breed by the Kennel Club, some people have started breeding programmes and working for the breed.

FCI STANDARD

GENERAL APPEARANCE Typical concave lined brachycephalic molossoid. The Dogue de Bordeaux is a very powerful dog, with a very muscular body yet retaining a harmonious general outline. He is built rather close to the ground, the distance from sternum to ground being slightly less than the depth of the chest. Stocky, athletic, imposing, he has a very dissuasive aspect.

IMPORTANT PROPORTIONS The length of the body, measured from the point of the shoulder to the point of the buttock, is superior to the height at the withers, in the proportion of 11/10. The depth of the chest is more than half the height at the withers. The maximum length of the muzzle is equal to one third of the length of the head. The

Zeus, owned by Bruno Ettore: The correct, balanced proportions for a Dogue de Bordeaux.

Photo: Bruno Ettore.

minimum length of the muzzle is equal to one quarter of the length of the head. In the male, the perimeter of the skull corresponds more or less to the height at the withers.

BEHAVIOUR AND TEMPERAMENT An ancient fighting dog, the Dogue de Bordeaux is gifted at guarding, which he does with vigilance and great courage but without aggressiveness. A good companion, very attached to his master and very affectionate. Calm, balanced with a high stimulus threshold. The male normally has a dominant character.

HEAD Voluminous, angular, broad, rather short, trapezoid when viewed from above and in front.

CRANIAL REGION In the male the perimeter of the skull measured at the level of its greatest width corresponds roughly to the height at the withers. In bitches it may be slightly less. Its volume and shape are the consequences of the very important development of the temporals, supra-orbital arches, zygomatic arches and the spacing of the branches of

the lower jaw. The upper region of the skull is slightly convex from one side to the other. Fronto-nasal depression or stop is very pronounced, almost forming a right angle with the muzzle (95° to 100°). The frontal groove is deep, diminishing towards the posterior end of the head. The forehead dominates the face. However, it is still wider than high. The head is furrowed with symmetrical wrinkles, each side of the median groove. These deep ropes of wrinkle are mobile depending on whether the dog is attentive or not.

FACIAL REGION
Nose: Broad, well opened nostrils, well pigmented according to the mask. Upturned nose (snubbed) permissible but not if it is set back towards the face.
Muzzle: Powerful, broad, thick, but not fleshy below the eyes, rather short, upper profile very slightly concave, with moderately obvious folds. Its width hardly decreasing towards the tip of the muzzle, when viewed from above it has the general shape of a square. In relation to the upper region of the skull, the line of the muzzle forms a very obtuse angle upwards. When the head is held horizontally the tip of the muzzle, truncated, thick and broad at the base, is in front of a vertical tangent to the anterior face of the nose. Its perimeter is almost two thirds of that of the head. Its length varies between one-third and one-quarter of the total length of the head, from the nose to the occipital crest. The limits stated (maximum one third and minimum one quarter of the total length of the

Rano de l'Aube Rouge, bred and owned by Mr Vandermynsbruggen-Hustin: A typical head, showing correctly placed oval eyes, and a broad jaw.

The underlip is described as an upside-down V.
Photo: Anne-Marie Class.

Excellent expression with the ideal colour for a red mask. *Photo: Anne-Marie Class.*

Incorrect: In this case, the underlip is curved like a U.
Photo: Gordon.

This head has good expression, but the eye colour is too light. *Photo: Gordon.*

head) are permissible but not sought after, the ideal length of the muzzle being between these two extremes.

Jaws: Very powerful, broad. Undershot (the undershot condition being a characteristic of the breed). The back of the lower incisors is in front of and not in contact with the front face of the upper incisors. The lower jaw curves upwards. The chin is well marked and must neither overlap the upper lip exaggeratedly nor be covered by it.

Teeth: Strong, particularly the canines. Lower canines set wide apart and slightly curved. Incisors well aligned especially in the lower jaw where they form an apparently straight line.

Upper lip: Thick, moderately pendulous, retractile. When viewed in profile it shows a rounded lower line. It covers the lower jaw on the sides. In front the edge of the upper lip is in contact with the lower lip, then drops on either side thus forming a reversed wide V.

Cheeks: Prominent, due to the very strong development of the muscles.

Eyes: Oval, set wide apart. The space between the two inner angles of the eyelids is equal to about twice the length of the eye (eye opening). Frank expression. The haw must not be visible. Colour: hazel to dark brown for a dog with a black mask, lighter colour tolerated but not sought after in dogs

Odin de l'Aube Rouge: The chest is powerful and deep, and is let down lower than the elbows.

Photo: Vandermynsbruggen.

with either a brown mask or without a mask.
Ears: Relatively small, of a slightly darker colour than the coat. At its set-on the front of the base of the ear is slightly raised. The ears must fall back, but not hang limply, the front edge being close to the cheek when the dog is attentive. The tip of the ear is slightly rounded; it must not reach beyond the eye. Set rather high, at the level of the upper line of the skull, thus appearing to accentuate its width even more.
Neck: Very strong, muscular, almost cylindrical. The skin is supple, ample and loose. The average circumference almost equals that of the head. It is separated from the head by a slightly accentuated transversal furrow, slightly curved. Its upper edge is slightly convex. The well defined dewlap starts at the level of the throat forming folds down to the chest, without hanging exaggeratedly. The neck, very broad at its base, merges smoothly with the shoulders.

BODY
Topline: Solid with a broad and muscular back, withers well marked, broad loin, rather short and solid.
Croup: Moderately sloping down to the root of the tail.
Chest: Powerful, long, deep, broad, let down lower than the elbows. Broad and powerful breast whose lower line (inter-axillae) is convex towards the bottom. Ribs well let down and well sprung but not barrel-shaped. The circumference of the chest must be between 0.25 to 0.30 m greater than the height at the withers.
Underline: Curved, from the deep brisket to the rather tucked up, firm abdomen, being neither pendulous nor whippety.
Tail: Very thick at the base. Its tip preferably reaching the hock and not below. Carried low, it is neither broken nor kinked but supple. Hanging

when the dog is in repose, generally rising by 90° to 120° from that position when the dog is in action, without curving over the back or being curled.

LIMBS
Forequarters: Strong bone structure, legs very muscular.
Shoulders: Powerful, prominent muscles. Slant of shoulder-blade medium (about 45° to the horizontal), angle of the scapular-humeral articulation a little more than 90°.
Arms: Very muscular.
Elbows: In the axis of the body, neither too close to the thoracic wall nor turned out.
Forearms: Viewed from the front, straight or inclining slightly inwards thus getting closer to the median plane, especially in dogs with a very broad chest. Viewed in profile, vertical.
Metacarpal region: Powerful. Viewed in profile, slightly sloping. Viewed from the front sometimes slightly outwards, thus compensating for the slight inclination of the forearm inwards.
Feet: Strong. Toes tight, nails curved and strong, pads well-developed and supple: the dogue is well up on his toes despite his weight.
Hindquarters: Robust legs with strong bone structure; well angulated. When viewed from behind the hindquarters are parallel and vertical thus giving an impression of power even though the hindquarters are not quite as broad as the forequarters.
Thigh: Very developed and thick with visible muscles.
Stifle: In a parallel plane to the median plane or slightly out.
Second Thigh: Relatively short, muscled, descending low.
Hock: Short, sinewy, angle of the hock joint moderately open.

The shoulder angulation allows for far-reaching movement. Photo: Anne-Marie Class.

Powerful drive comes from the strong, well-muscled hindquarters. Photo: Anne-Marie Class.

Metatarsus: Robust, no dewclaws.
Hindfeet: Slightly longer than the front feet, toes tight.

MOVEMENT Quite supple for a molossoid. When walking the movement is free, supple, close to the ground. Good drive from the hindquarters, good extension of the forelegs, especially when trotting, which is the preferred gait. When the trot quickens, the head tends to drop, the topline inclines towards the front, and the front feet get closer to the median plane while striding out with a long reaching movement of the front legs. Short gallop with vertical movement rather important. Capable

of great speed over short distances by bolting along close to the ground.

SKIN Thick and sufficiently loose fitting.

COAT
Hair: Fine, short and soft to the touch.
Colour: Self-coloured, in all shades of fawn, from mahogany to isabella. A good pigmentation is desirable. Limited white patches are permissible on the chest and the extremities of the limbs.

MASK
1. Black mask: the mask is often only slightly spread out and must not invade the cranial region. There may be slight black shading on the skull, ears, neck and top of body. The nose is then black.
2. Brown mask (used to be called red or bistre): the nose is then brown; the eye-rims are also brown.
3. No mask: the coat is fawn; the skin appears red (also formerly called "red mask"). The nose is then reddish or pink.

SIZE Height should more or less correspond to the perimeter of the skull.
Dogs: 60-68 cm at the withers. Bitches: 58-66 cm at the withers.
1 cm under and 2 cm over will be tolerated.
Weight: Dogs: at least 50 kg. Bitches: at least 45 kg.
Bitches: Identical characteristics but less prominent.

FAULTS Any departure from the foregoing points should be considered a fault and the seriousness with which the fault should be regarded should be in exact proportion to its degree.
Serious faults:
Hyper-aggressive, timid.
Head short and round with protruding eyes.
Hypertypical bulldoggy: flat skull, muzzle measuring less than a quarter of the total length of the head.
Important lateral deviation of the lower jaw.
Incisors constantly visible when the mouth is closed.
Arched back.
Fused but not deviated vertebrae of the tail.
Forefeet turning inwards (even slightly).
Forefeet turning outwards too much.
Flat thighs.

Angle of hock too open (straight angulation).
Angle of the hock too closed, dog standing under himself behind.
Cow hocks or barrel hocks.
Stilted movement or serious rolling of rear.
Excessive shortness of breath, rasping.
White on tip of tail or on the front part of the forelegs, above the carpus and the tarsus.
Disqualifying faults:
Long, narrow head with insufficiently pronounced stop, with a muzzle measuring more than a third of the total length of the head (lack of type in head).
Muzzle parallel to the top line of the skull or downfaced, Roman nose.
Twisted jaw.
Mouth not undershot.
Canines constantly visible when the mouth is closed.
Tongue constantly hanging out when the mouth is closed.
Tail knotted and laterally deviated or twisted (screw tail, kink tail).
Atrophied tail.
Fiddle front with splay feet.
Angle of the hock open towards the rear (tarsal deviated towards the front).
White on the head or body, any other colour of the coat than fawn.
Identifiable disabling defect.

NB: Male animals should have two apparently normal testicles fully descended into the scrotum.
© *Fédération Cynologique Internationale.*

Reformulated in 1995 by Raymond Triquet with the help of Philippe Serouil and the SADB Committee and translated into English by Raymond Triquet and Tim Taylor.

COMMENTS ON THE STANDARD

When writing the 1995 Standard, Raymond Triquet was careful to allow a certain leeway in his description. Accordingly he allows some differences to exist (for instance muzzle length, which may vary from a third to a quarter of the total length of the head, the ideal size being somewhere between the two extremes), in order to keep genetic diversity in the breed – for he thinks that a breed must be able to evolve if necessary.

The 1995 Standard is sufficiently clear as to require very little comment. It highlights the most important points and how to appraise and judge a Dogue de Bordeaux.

HEAD Eyes and expression: oval shape and a good distance between the eyes contribute to the typical expression of the breed. Profile: the bridge of the nose very slightly concave and the line from the nose to the mouth outwardly curved. A straight bridge as well as an upturned nose are not ideal. Lips: from the front the upperlip describes an upside down V which should not be too acute or too curved like a U. The former would look like a Neapolitan, the latter like a Bulldog. Undershot: the 1995 Standard allows less undershot than the previous one. Having the slightest undershot suffices.

BODY AND BUILD Not only must the Dogue de Bordeaux have a wide front and well-muscled straight forelegs but its hindquarters must also be suitably powerful though narrower. A good reaching movement will be achieved by well-angulated hindquarters which ensure that the dog is propelled forward from the rear rather than pulled along from the front. The Dogue de Bordeaux's hindquarters are more angulated than the Bullmastiff's, but must not be excessively acute. The Dogue de Bordeaux's shoulder is more overloaded than the Bullmastiff's and more angulated.

The feet are less arched than the Bullmastiff's. The ribs should not be flat. Over-wrinkled Dogues or Dogues with too pendulous flews are not desirable. The coat is softer than the Mastiff's and Bullmastiff's. The topline is never perfectly straight. It is often somewhat diving but not in the Bulldog fashion. The Dogue is lower to the ground than the Mastiff and the Bullmastiff. Any Dogue with a disqualifying fault should not breed.

Dogues whose features may appear spectacular but which may not be suitably well-balanced should get less attention than a possibly less impressive but better balanced animal. Raymond Triquet likes to say that in the old days dogs used not to have a Standard but they did have a strong constitution.

BORDEAUX CHARACTER

Faithfulness to its master is one of the Dogue de Bordeaux's main features. It is a very affectionate and gentle dog with its owner. It would be an error to leave it alone to guard property or keep it in a kennel all day long. It is gifted at guarding without aggression. It has an instinct for protecting "its" family and especially the children. It is calm and not easily upset. Its reaction threshold is high, which means it does not easily become aggressive. The Dogue has an intrinsically deterring attitude in its stance and behaviour. However, its natural good character may give way to a strong reaction when it feels it is being provoked or when it feels its master is in danger. It tends only to bark when it has good reason, so when it does, it is better to go and see what is causing the trouble.

Its least pleasant feature is its dominant character over other dogs, especially in the case of males. In general, it is inadvisable to have two males in the same home.

The Dogue de Bordeaux is sociable with people. Problems while judging are extremely unusual, as long as the Dogues are treated with respect.

Dogues have a strong sense of devotion to their master and always like to be nearby. This character trait can be used to obtain an obedient Dogue. Praise it every time it does something which pleases you – lying quietly, coming when called, walking at your heel in the street and so on. Do not be afraid to praise the Dogue too much, it really enjoys making you happy. When giving orders, be absolutely firm, as you should also be when forbidding something.

Give lots of encouragement and express warm approval when you ask it to do something. Wherever you go, take the dog along with you to get it used to as many different everyday situations as possible. While young, it should be given a great deal of contact with other dogs and animals as well as with children and street life. If it seems to be about to get into a fight, act immediately and very firmly so that it understands that fighting is strictly forbidden.

CHOOSING A PUPPY

When choosing a good Dogue de Bordeaux puppy, the first thing to do is to look at the parents – their heads, movement, and temperament. Christian Porries, who is responsible for character testing for the French breed club, points out that the

The Dogue de Bordeaux transmits power through its stance and general behaviour.

Rano de l'Aube Rouge and Tess de l'Aube Rouge: Dogues can live together in harmony, but it is inadvisable to keep two males in close proximity.

Photo: Anne-Marie Class.

Dogue's temperament is constant in certain breed lines. To a certain extent, this is also the case for health and type.

When Claudine Acker, who has been breeding Dogues de Bordeaux for years, chooses a puppy, she looks for the following features: a relatively short dog; the right distance between the eyes; a well-marked stop; as dark a colour as possible; excellent general condition. She adds that it is difficult to choose a good Dogue de Bordeaux puppy at the age of two months, because this breed changes more than other Molossers as the dog grows up.

She gives another piece of advice: do not choose a puppy with too much undershot as it generally becomes excessive with age (puppies are born without undershot). Care must be taken about the tail which must be examined along its whole length (especially when choosing for breeding) in order to pick out any puppy with a knotted tail, as such a dog should be excluded from any future breeding.

Genetically speaking, the red mask is recessive, so a red-masked mother and a red-masked father can never produce black-masked puppies. Bordeaux bitches breed quite easily and are generally excellent mothers. It is important to note that breeders traditionally help during whelping as undershot mouths are said to make cutting the umbilical cord bothersome for the mother. At birth, a Dogue generally weighs between 400 and 800 grams, at one week between 1 and 1.3 kilos, at two weeks between 2 and 2.4 kilos, at ten weeks about 10 kilos and at three months between 13 and 17 kilos.

According to most Bordeaux breeders, the best way to feed them is on a good brand of dried food for dogs of large size. You can, of course, add some cheese or meat cut into slivers, for extra taste. Some Dogues may have a small appetite when they are young and you must make sure that they eat enough. Dry food is generally well-balanced and you should remember that it could be dangerous to add mineral or vitamins without a vet's or the breeder's advice. Too much may be as bad as too little. Dogues should be given two meals a day to prevent gastric torsion and they should be left in peace after feeding.

The Dogue de Bordeaux, like any other dog, is not invulnerable to health problems. The Dogue's life expectancy is comparable with that of other Molossers. It is no frailer than any other Molosser but the following ailments are known to have occurred in the breed.

Heart problems have sometimes been

At fifteen days old, this puppy is already alert and inquisitive.   Photo: Vandermynsbruggen.

recorded, and the French Club has started looking into this. As many dogs as possible will be examined before breeding. This appears to be the most serious problem facing the breed. Some cases of epilepsy have also been found. Even though X-rays reveal that quite a few Dogues de Bordeaux are prone to hip problems, as are many Molossers, this does not turn out to be a serious affliction in most cases. X-raying dogs before mating will help the situation.

Dogs must be kept fit and a balance must be struck between soundness of body and type. Their muscles must be kept in shape by regular activity. The Dogue loves his master so much that he does not like to exercise alone, and even if you have a big garden, walking with it is necessary. Dogues de Bordeaux generally do not like the heat, so they should not be left in a car when the weather is warm, or be exercised when it is too hot.

A FINAL COMMENT

As with all short-faced Molossers, the Dogue de Bordeaux is one of those dogs which has always had close links with man, one of those dogs used by man for guarding and hunting as well as for fighting in wars or against other animals, one of those dogs whose look alone is enough to deter. That this kind of dog may have descended from the prehistoric short-faced Borophagus or Aelurodon rather than a wolf or a jackal is a tempting hypothesis. This unfortunately remains an unproved part of the legend. But it is certain that this kind of dog, unlike many which tend to form packs, turns more readily to man.

As Raymond Triquet puts it, the Dogue de Bordeaux has a sour mug but a golden heart. This, along with an expression of tenderness and sweetness, makes it irresistible.

ACKNOWLEDGEMENTS
Special thanks to Dominic Williams for helping me put this chapter into the English language.

A well-reared puppy ready to take his part in family life.   Photo: Anne-Marie Class

13 THE ANATOLIAN SHEPHERD DOG

By Margaret Mellor

The visitor's acquaintance with Turkey is usually confined to the fringes of the country, where the land meets the sea. The Aegean coast to the west and the Mediterranean towns to the south are famous for their classical history, and bustle with the thriving international trade they have enjoyed for centuries with their neighbours in Europe and the Middle Eastern states. The temperate Black Sea coast, with its links northwards to the Balkans, has its own busy ports and industries. And then, of course, there is Istanbul, sprawling across the Bosphorus where Europe meets Asia: with its domed palaces, its minarets and markets, this cosmopolitan city is the most likely image that non-Turks have of Turkey.

For a western European to venture into the heartland of Asiatic Turkey there would traditionally have to be good archaeological or diplomatic reasons: it is not a place for the casual tourist. The central Anatolian plateau is a vast, inhospitable expanse of mountain and steppe, embracing the modern capital, Ankara, and stretching eastwards – large enough to accommodate the British Isles three times over, penetrated by few modern roads and only sparsely populated. The climate is continental, ranging from 40 degrees C in summer to -30 degrees C in winter, or even lower in the eastern mountains. This is the real Anatolia.

In the dry central plains crops can only be grown in the valleys along the line of rivers which dwindle to a trickle in summer. Grazing is too sparse and the terrain and weather too harsh for cattle, and so the mainstay of the economy and village life is sheep-rearing. Wool plays a vital part in Turkey's textiles industry and is of course the raw material for one of the country's most famous products – carpets.

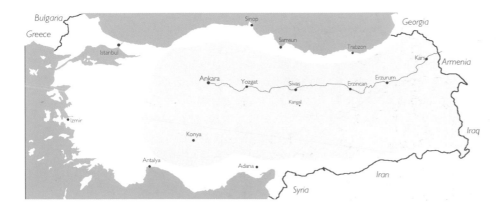

Map of Turkey showing the central Anatolian plateau.

The Anatolian Shepherd Dog: Large and upstanding, with a steady, bold temperament. This is American Rare Breeds Ch. Wiley Creek la Tiffa, bred by Ruth Webb. Photo: Sheila Atter.

It has been estimated that Turkey has over 36 million sheep, and most of them are reared on these vast open plains. The flocks range over huge areas, browsing on the scrubby grass and at nightfall, if the grazing is not too far distant from the shepherd's village, they are brought back to the area around the settlements, where they are less liable to attack by predators. If they are further away, then they have to be guarded overnight on the mountainside. In many regions shepherds employ the ancient system of transhumance, whereby whole flocks, and often most of the population of the village to which they belong, migrate to summer pastures (*yaylalar*) and back with the changing seasons. Life is hard for the Anatolian shepherd, and his livelihood depends to a great extent on one valuable asset – his dog.

THE WORKING DOG

All over Anatolia, large, strong dogs are used by the shepherds to protect their sheep. The dogs' role is to watch for the approach of danger, which can be in the form of predatory wolves, jackals, eagles or even bears and wildcats, and to place themselves between that threat and the flock. The dogs are also used to escort the sheep on their frequent treks to and from water and pasture, a task that an experienced dog will sometimes perform without human supervision.

The Turkish name for any dog that does this work, whatever its shape or size, is *çoban köpegi* – 'shepherd dog' – and type does vary, depending mainly on which part of Turkey the dog comes from. 'Anatolian shepherd dog', therefore, is a job description rather than the name of a 'breed' in the sense that Western dog specialists would understand.

A fair comparison in a Western context would be the use of the term 'Collie' or 'setter' to describe a work-related type of dog rather than a specific breed: a Welsh Collie, for example, is different from a Border Collie; a Gordon Setter is different from an English Setter; yet their working characteristics are similar.

Under this broad heading of *çoban köpegi*, then, are a number of specific types of dog which could reasonably be regarded as breeds, since over the centuries they have developed into uniform populations breeding to type, assisted both by human intervention selecting for particular characteristics, and by geographical isolation limiting genetic resources.

At the same time, it must be acknowledged that there are a great many Turkish shepherd dogs of no particular type, working effectively as livestock guardians – again, just as there are efficient collie-cross dogs working for Western farmers. In the east and south-east of the country in particular, there are still populations of nomadic herdsmen, using dogs (*yürük* or *göcebe köpekleri*) which, although usually tall and strong, are very mixed in type and whose ancestors could have come from, for example, Syria, Georgia or Afghanistan.

For anyone wishing to make a study of Turkish dogs, this rather complex situation is not helped by the fact that Turkey has no official body for the registration of breeds of dog. Until recently there has been no tradition of keeping pets; dogs were, and still are, kept primarily as working animals for hunting or protection. However, as we shall see in the case of the most famous of the breeds of Anatolian shepherd dog, those Turks who use dogs recognize the value of good type and working attributes, and have maintained their own unofficial standards for centuries.

THE KANGAL – TURKEY'S MASTIFF-TYPE SHEPHERD DOG

There can be no doubt about the identity of

Turkey's 'national' dog or the esteem in which it is held. The Kangal or Sivas-Kangal dog is known throughout the country, to city dwellers and country folk alike, as a treasured part of the national heritage, so much so that it has twice featured on Turkish postage stamps, once in 1973 with its generic title of *çoban köpegi* and again in 1996 as *Kangal köpegi*. This is the breed that was introduced into Great Britain in the 1960s under the name *Karabash*; in Turkey dogs of this description are also referred to as *çomar* or *samsun*, both of which translate as 'Mastiff'.

IDENTIFYING A KANGAL

Ask a Turk to describe the shepherd dog of Anatolia and, with great pride and enthusiasm, usually accompanied by accounts of superior strength and prowess against the wolf, his description will be of the Kangal dog.

The name is taken from the small town of Kangal, to the south-east of Sivas in central Turkey, the area where the most typical specimens of the breed are found. The town in turn is named after the Kangal family, for centuries landowners in the region and renowned for the excellence of the horses they bred and the quality of the shepherd dogs they produced and used.

Despite the relative obscurity of its place of origin, it is astonishing to observe both how widespread and how uniform this breed of

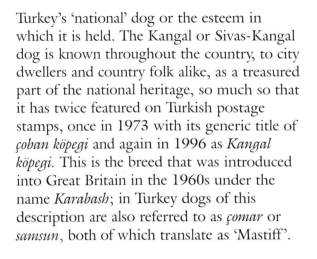

Turkey's 'national' dog depicted on postage stamps.

A good example of a Kangal dog in Turkey.

Photo: Nippers.

A Kangal dog takes his sheep to water, near Sivas.

Photo: Mellor.

dog is throughout central Anatolia. A summer traveller taking the main road from west to east across Turkey (the ancient caravan route which runs through Ankara, Sivas and Erzurum towards Georgia and Iran) will pass countless flocks of sheep escorted by shepherd dogs. From Yozgat to Erzincan, a distance of around 250 miles (450 km) almost every working dog seen will be a Kangal dog. To an onlooker it may at first appear that there is no dog in attendance, but closer inspection will no doubt reveal that what looked at first like a sheep, behind and slightly apart from the rest, is in fact a Kangal dog plodding steadily along in the dust behind his charges.

The Kangal dog is a large, powerfully-built animal with the typical colour pattern of the Mastiff breeds: a whole-coloured coat ranging from cream through dun and fawn to a reddish-gold, with black mask and ears. A characteristic not shared with his cousins in the West is a long, slightly bushy tail, carried high above the back in an open curl when the dog is alert, and low with a slight curl at the tip when relaxed. From a distance, in his

In a typical Anatolian landscape, a Kangal bitch (foreground) with her flock at sunset.

Photo: Rose.

The iron collars used for Turkish shepherd dogs: Some made of articulated spiked links, one (second from right) a solid iron band with welded spikes.

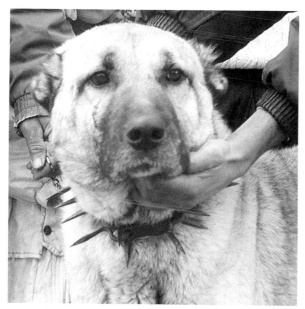

An adult Kangal dog with cropped ears and spiked collar.　　　　*Photo: Carr.*

natural environment, the high tail-carriage is often the only way to tell him apart from the flock as he is quite likely to be standing among his sheep, which are of comparable size and – especially with a good coating of Anatolian dust – similar in colour. The sheep, meanwhile, will be completely unperturbed by his presence.

An adult male stands about 30 inches (75 cm) high at the shoulder and weighs about 130 lb (60 kg); bitches are usually significantly smaller and less heavy in build. Compared with other dogs of Mastiff type, the Kangal is somewhat finer in construction, but this is an advantage for an animal that has to be capable of a good turn of speed in a working situation. These dogs, although content to watch quietly for hours on end, can give chase at speeds of up to 30 miles (50 km) per hour when necessary.

The Kangal has a double coat perfectly suited to the rigours of a working life spent out of doors in all conditions. It is short and close-lying, made up of a very dense soft undercoat covered by smooth, slightly longer and coarser hair that acts as a weatherproof jacket. The woolly under-layer provides insulation not only in the severe Anatolian winter but against the fierce summer sun, although a complete twice-yearly moult modifies the thickness needed for the coming season. The outer layer repels rain or snow, and mud, once dry, simply falls off the short, straight hair.

Like all the Turkish shepherd dogs, a working Kangal will probably have had his ears cropped by the shepherd at the age of a few weeks. This is done for various reasons, not all of them plausible, it must be said. First of all, for appearance: the cropped ears give a fierce, bear-like expression to the animal. Secondly, for protection: in an encounter with a wolf or other predator, ear-flaps are easily bitten or torn, and so could be a site of infection. Associated with this is the wearing of spiked metal collars to protect the throat in an attack; as soon as the young dog begins his working life the shepherd will provide him with an iron collar fitted with very sharp, and sometimes quite long, spikes. The ear-flaps of a Kangal would catch on a collar of this kind.

Finally there is the popular notion that cropping the ears enables the dog to hear better. A rather unpleasant story exists that when the ears are cropped the offcuts are cooked and fed back to the dog to increase his strength. It is certainly true that a cropped Anatolian looks very different from one with the ears intact. When the first imported Anatolian with cropped ears was brought for inspection in Britain, local Anatolian-owners found it difficult to recognize the breed they were familiar with.

THE LIFESTYLE OF THE SHEPHERD DOG

Turkey is almost entirely Muslim. Although Mustafa Kemal Atatürk introduced many measures to 'westernize' the country in the early part of the twentieth century, among them the replacement of Islamic law by a secular, European-style system, many of the religious traditions remain. One is the belief that the dog is an unclean animal that should not be allowed to enter a Turkish house. However, dogs are allowed around human habitations and Kangal dogs are a common sight within the villages of central Anatolia. Some are kept on running chains outside their master's house; others, having learned the boundaries of their access, are allowed to wander about freely.

A Kangal dog in a village near Sivas.
Photo: Mellor.

A village in central Anatolia.   *Photo: Mellor.*

A Kangal dog intervenes between his sheep and the photographer.   *Photo: Vink.*

214

The villages consist of flat-roofed, often whitewashed houses made of clay bricks, sometimes built into the hillside in such a way that it is easy to find oneself accidentally walking on the grassy roof of someone's home, the only tell-tale sign being a small white chimney-stack on the ground! The owner's dog will often dig himself a cave into the hillside near the house, out of the heat of the sun and the winter snow. In the severe winters roads are impassable and most villages completely cut off. Livestock are kept in low, mud-built barns and fodder is stored to quite a depth on the flat rooftops of these barns and of the houses – adding welcome insulation for the comfort of the occupants. Very often a black face will peep out from within a stack of fodder, betraying the fact that 'Karabash' has found a warm billet for the night.

Away from the village, a Kangal on duty out on the mountainside will usually station himself on a high vantage-point overlooking his flock and simply watch and listen. In the full heat of the day he will dig himself a cool hollow in the ground and settle into it, making himself almost invisible to anyone approaching. Many an unwary stranger has been taken by surprise by a great dusty Kangal dog suddenly hauling himself to his feet to bark a warning.

A novice dog will be sent out to accompany an older one and learn his technique by experience; in the process he will also learn where he stands in the hierarchy of dogs. A steady, experienced Kangal is the shepherd's most valuable asset, for the job of training the new generation will largely be done by the dogs themselves.

Very often the dogs will work in pairs, or teams for a larger flock, taking up positions around the sheep and changing shift from time to time. They do not waste energy by running around needlessly and in the daytime are content to lie still and quiet. The night watch, however, is a different matter, for it is then that they actively patrol along a wide perimeter, sounding their presence from time to time as they go.

The behaviour of the dog when his suspicions are aroused is fascinating to watch. First of all he will stand full-square with his tail up and ears erect, listening. Then there will been a quiet 'wuff', just enough to signal to the sheep that something is up, followed by the sharp bark that is the signal to the other dogs and the shepherd to get into position. The sheep, who have learned to trust the dog, will bunch together and – far from moving away, as would a flock used to being driven by a herding dog – gather towards their protector.

The Kangal's first instinct is to place himself between the perceived source of danger and his sheep or master, and he will trot back and forth across the line of approach, gradually coming closer to them. (This is a very powerful instinct and one that can be observed in Kangal dogs that have never seen active service but live in a domestic setting in other countries: faced with a stranger, they will stand *across* their owner's path until assured that all is well.)

With the sheep safely behind him he can then go out to confront the intruder and the bark becomes a full-throated roar, an unmistakable threat. Usually the dog need do no more than chase off the interloper, but a hungry or foolhardy wolf may stand his ground, in which case the Kangal dog will run forward at great speed and, using his substantial forehand weight, hurl a shoulder against the wolf to knock him to the ground. He will then attack the throat and the tendons of the hind legs. The villages and markets of Anatolia frequently display the skin of some unlucky wolf as a trophy or for sale.

215

A good Kangal puppy is a prized possession.
Photo: Rich.

REARING A KANGAL IN ANATOLIA

Working dogs have to be very resourceful to survive. The shepherds feed them a plain barley mash, supplemented with whatever food scraps and bones they have left over. Meat is normally available to dogs only in the form of what they can catch, usually rodents living in the desert or around the village, or the odd bird or hare. Male dogs tend to get preferential treatment and so the females have to learn to live by their wits.

Despite the apparent informality of the village environment, matings are usually planned, in the sense that a shepherd will have his eye on a particular stud dog for the next generation. Bitches tend to come into season only once a year – some would say out of self-preservation – with the alpha bitch in the village giving the lead to the others.

A Kangal bitch will usually do her best to give birth to her puppies underground, out of reach of other dogs and interlopers, so she will most likely dig herself a tunnel under a rock or building, ending it in a round chamber which becomes the nest. It is astonishing that, given their poor diet, Kangal bitches are able to produce milk at all, but they generally succeed. They are often helped by other, usually related, bitches in the community who will come into milk despite having no pups of their own and act as welcome wet-nurses as the pups grow. Sadly, little human support is offered to the lactating bitch; her welfare is largely ignored and she is seen as simply a means to an end. The process of weaning starts at around three weeks, when the bitch begins to regurgitate her own meal to feed to the pups, who devour it ravenously. Small wonder, then, that by the time the pups are weaned the Kangal bitch is herself at quite a low ebb.

Kangal litters are often large, averaging six to ten pups. There is no way that a shepherd and his family could afford to raise such large numbers and the litters are culled to retain only the biggest and strongest specimens. Bitch puppies are kept only if there is thought to be a need for new breeding stock, although, in fact, females make excellent working shepherd dogs, being fast and alert. Promising puppies are fed well on a diet supplemented with offal, eggs and milk. They may be passed to friends or relatives in neighbouring villages as a valued gift or exchange.

The general strength, soundness and size of the adult dogs seen working in Anatolia must be attributable to this early rearing – and the process of selection – for by the time they are a year old they are on subsistence rations.

As the pup grows, its mother plays a major role in its character development. She will tease it to come forward and play-fight with her, often rolling it over and nipping its throat and then rolling over herself to let the pup imitate her. She will teach it to stalk and pounce, and not to take liberties with its elders – all part of the unique training of a good working dog. Later, the shepherd himself will take a hand in the learning process, encouraging the pup to worry a stuffed wolf-skin. It is at this point that he will single out the bravest of the litter for work; the less forthcoming will be discarded or stay as watchdogs around the village.

HISTORY

Quite how the modern population of large Mastiff-type dogs in Anatolia developed is a matter for conjecture and would make interesting archaeological research. One important fact to bear in mind, however, is the proximity of Asiatic Turkey to the ancient territories of Babylon, Assyria and Mesopotamia in neighbouring present-day Iraq. In fact, the Tigris and the Euphrates, rivers which cradled these ancient civilizations, both rise in Anatolia. It is fortunate indeed that so much material has been preserved from these civilizations, among which are sculptures depicting dogs that bear a striking resemblance to the Kangals of modern-day Turkey, accompanying the hunting-parties of the Assyrian King Ashurbanipal (668–627 BC).

A large, powerful breed of 'Indian Hound' is described in the writings of Herodotus (485–425 BC) as being kept by the Babylonians. It seems likely that there is some common ground between the Turkish dogs and those from adjacent countries of the Middle East, of which we have evidence.

Over the centuries Turkey has been occupied or invaded by various civilizations, each of which, must have introduced its own domestic animals into the melting-pot. In the eleventh century Turcoman tribes fleeing from Genghiz Khan swept into Anatolia from central Asia, bringing with them their sheep and, presumably, the means of guarding them. The last major influx was by the Seljuk Turks from Persia, who made their capital in Konya.

The earliest reliable account we have of shepherd dogs being bred selectively comes from the seventeenth-century writer and historian Evliya Çelebi. In his *Seyahatname*

(Book of Travels) he describes the ceremonial parades of the Janissaries, an elite Ottoman force, in which guarding-dogs including the *samsun* from the Black Sea coast – 'large dogs, like lions' – were displayed in full regalia by their keepers.

ESTABLISHMENT OF THE BREED OUTSIDE TURKEY

It is known that a few Turkish dogs were brought to the West before any attempt was made to recognize a breed officially; for example, a Mr Buckland is reported to have imported an impressive dog called Arslan into England in the early 1900s.

FOUNDATIONS IN GREAT BRITAIN

In 1961 Charmian Biernoff (later Steele) was introduced to the sheep-guarding dogs of Anatolia while a student of archaeology travelling in Turkey. She had already studied Assyrian and Babylonian sculpture and remarked on the similarities between the dogs they depicted and the distinctive working dogs around Konya. This kindled an interest that led, after some years of working in Turkey, to her return to England in 1965 with a pair of 'Anatolian (Karabash) Dogs' as they were later to become registered at the Kennel Club. This particular form of words was chosen deliberately in the knowledge that there was more than one breed of Anatolian shepherd dog and that others could follow. 'Karabash', meaning 'black head', was the popular name for these big fawn-coloured dogs, although Dr Steele acknowledged that 'In the Ankara Zoo, where good examples of the breed have been bred for many years it is known as the Kangal-Sivas shepherd's dog (as so many of the best examples from which the Zoo has been breeding have come from that area)' (*Our Dogs* February 23rd 1984).

Gazi of Bakirtolloköyü and his mate Sabahat of Hayirogluköyü produced Britain's first litter of Anatolians in 1967 under Dr

Gazi and Sabahat, Britain's first imports, photographed at Crufts in 1966.

Seacop Yosun.   *Photo: Garwood.*

Capar of Anadol.   *Photo: Garwood.*

Steele's Konya affix. Dogs from this original line formed the foundation of Mr and Mrs Broadhead's Seacop stock.

Of necessity the first Seacop litters were closely line-bred, but in 1973 Dr Withof-Keus imported two males, Capar and Haki, from Ankara Zoo as the basis for her Anadol breeding, having acquired an imported bitch, Korumak Tyana, from Mr and Mrs Aston, and Capar later moved to Seacop as an important outcross.

Mrs Betty Marshall, an established breeder of German Shepherd Dogs under the Marchael affix, acquired three siblings born in quarantine in 1973 from Turkish parents exported by an American breeder, Mr Burnap. The male, Fena, was used at stud at Anadol kennel, and progeny of the Marchael

dogs became foundation stock at Mr and Mrs Emmett's Kurtkir and Mr and Mrs Reed's Kamish kennels, both later to become prolific producers.

BEGINNINGS IN OTHER COUNTRIES
Kangal dogs have become established as working dogs in the USA, Australia and New Zealand, where they are able to function in much the same role as they have in their homeland. After some initial false starts in successfully bonding the dogs to their flocks, farmers have become experienced in the use of livestock guardians and have made significant reductions in losses of sheep and goats to coyotes, dingoes, feral dogs and rustlers. The Livestock Guard Dog Association and Oregon State University,

USA, have carried out extensive comparative trials and published the results of their research, using Turkish dogs and shepherd dogs from other parts of Europe.

At the same time, the dogs have found little difficulty in adjusting to a more domestic setting in other European countries where, given sufficient space and understanding, they are content to devote themselves to family and property. They have become particularly well-established in Germany as a result of Turkish guest-workers bringing their dogs with them and forming a network of owners. There have been significant exports of British-bred dogs, which have proved to be capable of functioning equally well in a farming and a domestic situation.

Regrettably the FCI and, since 1983, the Kennel Club in Britain do not differentiate between the Kangal (or Karabash) dog and other Turkish shepherd dogs, and all registrations are currently (1998) as Anatolian Shepherd Dog, to accommodate dogs of non-Kangal type. In Australia and the USA, however, official Kangal Dog registers have recently been established by the Australian National Kennel Council and the United Kennel Club respectively.

THE STATUS OF KANGAL DOGS IN TURKEY TODAY

In recent years Turkey has become aware of the need to protect not only certain native species of wildlife but its domestic animals, among them the Kangal dog.

With the explosion of interest in the breed during the 1980s, when a number of dogs were exported to American researchers and European breeders, the Kangal suddenly became a fashionable acquisition for affluent Turks, most of them city dwellers in the western towns. Government officials had the authority to commandeer dogs from the Sivas area for their own purposes. The Army decided to train the breed for work already being done by German Shepherd Dogs and Dobermanns, only to discover after several years and numerous failures that this breed, which instinctively works on its own initiative and has a quite different character from other 'sharper' breeds, was not a good candidate for obedience. Horror stories of whole lorryloads of Kangal dogs being shipped like livestock out of central Anatolia are, sadly, well-founded. Numbers declined alarmingly, exacerbated by the arrival of Parvovirus, which swept through the area.

Eventually, many dogs were turned out on to the streets or abandoned outside cities when their owners could no longer cope with a full-size, headstrong, often confused Kangal in a confined space. Today the dog is still a status-symbol, but the initial mania has subsided.

The export of Kangal dogs to non-Turkish nationals is now illegal. Government-controlled breeding centres have been

Entrance to the Kangal dog breeding centre at Kangal town, 1996.

Photo: Nippers.

A Kangal dog at Ankara Zoo.   Photo: Mellor.

established at Kangal town and Ulas, where every dog's breeding, development and health records are charted, whether the animal is kept at the centres or based in a village and used for work.

A number of universities have embarked on studies of the breed, notably Seljuk University in Konya, which has its own breeding programme and held an International Symposium on Turkish Shepherd Dogs in October 1996, and more recently the University of Uludag in Bursa, already well-known for its work on the rescue

and rehabilitation of bears that have been exploited for entertainment.

For more than twenty years Ankara Zoo has bred and exhibited 'Sivas-Kangal çoban köpegi', alongside other native and foreign breeds. Early importations into Britain came from this source.

ASSESSING THE BREED

THE BREED STANDARD
In Great Britain the Kangal dog can only be registered as an Anatolian Shepherd Dog and the following is the Interim Breed Standard published in 1986 by the Kennel Club.

GENERAL APPEARANCE
Large, upstanding, tall, powerfully built, with broad, heavy head and short dense coat. Must have size, stamina and speed.

CHARACTERISTICS
Active breed used originally as a guard dog for sheep; hard working; capable of enduring extremes of heat and cold.

TEMPERAMENT
Steady and bold without aggression, naturally independent, very intelligent. Proud and confident.

HEAD AND SKULL
Skull large, broad and flat between ears. Slight furrow between eyes and slight stop. Mature males have broader head than females. Foreface one-third of total head length. Slightly pendulous black lips. Square profile. Nose black.

Two Turkish breeds side by side in Anatolia: The Tazi, a hunting dog (left), and a Kangal.

Photo: Rose.

Mr & Mrs Hill's Telkari Efendi, top winning Anatolian in Britain 1997.

Photo: Carol Ann Johnson.

EYES
Rather small in proportion to size of skull, set well apart and deep, showing no haw. Golden to brown in colour. Eye rims black.

EARS
Medium-sized, triangular in shape, rounded at tip, carried flat to skull and pendant, higher when alert.

MOUTH
Teeth strong, with a perfect, regular and complete scissor bite, i.e. the upper teeth closely overlapping the lower teeth and set square to the jaws. Lips black.

NECK
Slightly arched, powerful, muscular, moderate in length, rather thick. Slight dewlap.

FOREQUARTERS
Shoulders well muscled and sloping. Forelegs set well apart, straight and well boned; of good length; strong pasterns, slightly sloping when viewed from side. Elbows close to sides.

BODY
Chest deep to point of elbow, ribs well sprung. Body powerful, well muscled, never fat. Level back. Body in proportion to leg length, slightly arched over loins, with good tuck-up.

HINDQUARTERS
Powerful, lighter than forequarters; moderate turn of stifle.

FEET
Strong feet with well arched toes. Nails short.

TAIL
Long, reaching at least to hock. Set on rather high. When relaxed carried low with slight curl, when alert carried high with end curled over back, especially by males.

GAIT/MOVEMENT
Relaxed even gait, with impression of latent power, very supple movement. Noticeable straight line of head, neck and body, giving impression of stalking in some dogs. Great drive when viewed from side.

COAT
Short, dense with thick undercoat. Flat, close-lying, neither fluffy nor wavy; slightly longer and thicker at neck, shoulders and tail; no feathering on ears or legs.

COLOUR
All colours acceptable but it is desirable that they should be whole colours, cream to fawn, with black mask and ears.

SIZE
Weight: Mature dogs 50-64 kg (110-141 lb); bitches 41-59 kg (90.5-130 lb). Dogs 74-81 cm (29-32 ins) at the shoulders; bitches 71-79 cm (28-31 ins).

FAULTS
Any departure from the foregoing points should be considered a fault and the seriousness of the fault should be in exact proportion to its degree.

NOTE: Male animals should have two apparently normal testicles fully descended into the scrotum.
Reproduced by kind permission of The Kennel Club.

In the USA and Australia a more specific Standard applies for the Kangal Dog, based upon one set down by Turhan Kangal (of the Kangal family from which the Turkish town takes its name) in 1984. The 1989 FCI Standard (No. 331) for the Anatolian Shepherd Dog, on the other hand, is much more general, having been drawn up to be suitable for non-Mastiff types of shepherd dog.

Anatolians are classified as a Rare Breed and a judge who has done his or her homework will know to look for the characteristics that make the breed special: its lion-like grace on the move, the aloof expression, the distinctive tail-carriage and colouring, and the practical attributes of the working dog, such as weatherproof coat, good muscle and substance, surefootedness and a steady temperament.

THE ANATOLIAN CHARACTER

The Kangal dog as a companion makes for a rewarding relationship, provided the nature of the breed is respected. These dogs are not fawning creatures, constantly looking for directions and clinging to your heels, but they are inquisitive and like to know where you are, and what you are doing. They are strong-minded, independent and can seem aloof; however they bond naturally to those who care for them.

Their unsuitability for obedience training does not mean that they are stupid; on the contrary, provided you talk to them as companions, they soon come to understand and will go along with reasonable requests. However, do not expect them, for instance, to retrieve more than once (if you throw it away twice you clearly do not want it back), or to stop in mid-flight if they are seeing a strange animal off the premises.

They are no respecters of boundaries and will use as wide a radius as they are allowed, so secure fences are essential. Unfamiliar visitors will be viewed with suspicion and are likely to be warned off unless welcomed by the owner, so the path to your front door needs to be secure. They will live happily with other domestic animals, including dogs, provided the Kangal is allowed to be top dog, so other dominant breeds are inadvisable. All this makes perfect sense given the mindset of the working Kangal in his traditional environment as described earlier in this chapter.

CHOOSING A PUPPY

A good-sized puppy will weigh nearly 2 lb (900 g) at birth and by the time he is ready to go to his new home at seven weeks he is likely to have reached 22 lb (10 kg). His colour, a surprisingly dark grey when he was born, will have started to clear to almost the adult fawn and is thick and dense with a distinctive velvety texture. At this stage even the most experienced breeder finds it hard to spot the future show winner, but there are a few points it is worthwhile bearing in mind when making your choice.

A good breeder will allow you to see the puppies' dam; if the sire is not from the same kennel, then ask to see good photographs and find out as much as you can about him from his owner and the owners of other pups he has sired. The more you know about the temperament and conformation of the parents, the better you can predict the likely character and type of their progeny. Watch the puppies together as they play, for clues as to dominant or shy, placid or vivacious natures, and be alert to any sign of aggression. If this is your first Kangal, choose a placid puppy, and possibly a bitch rather than a dog; in inexperienced hands a big, boisterous, adolescent male can be quite a trial.

Pups of this age are so loose-limbed, and have so much growing to do, that it is hard to predict how they will shape up as adults.

Litter feeding contentedly at four days old.

Photo: Hill.

Pay attention to the hindquarters and watch for any difficulties in getting up on to four paws. Cow hocks, which may occur in larger pups, are unlikely to straighten later. Feet may turn in slightly at this stage and will improve as the limbs grow and muscles develop with exercise, but turned-out feet might not.

Coat colour and texture are important. While a little white on paws and chest is acceptable, there should be no patches of white on the face or body; sometimes puppies are born with a slight white 'smudge' on the nose but this disappears within the first two to three months. A dark strip down the back and black on the tail are indicators of good pigmentation. A black mask and ears are breed characteristics, but a black muzzle and shaded ears are acceptable. There is a tendency for the mask to fade at around six months but intensify again in the mature dog.

Very occasionally a long coat may occur: it is a serious fault in this breed and a long-coated dog is not suitable for show or breeding. In a pup it is detectable by fluffy ears and tail and noticeably thicker, soft, wavy hair.

Kangal dogs are exceptionally long-lived for a large breed, and can reach the age of 12 to 14 years, so make your choice carefully, for this puppy is likely to be your companion for a very long time. Above all, once safely home, treasure your Kangal dog, for this rare breed is the pride of Turkey, and is a privilege to own.

Puppies ready to go.

Photo: Hosker.

14 *HEALTH CARE*

By Dick Lane FRAgS FRCVS

For the dog's comfort and for the owner's benefit of having an alert companion or guard, it is essential to maintain a dog in as good health as is possible. A dog that is undernourished or anaemic will tire easily and be unwilling to perform too many tasks. Similarly, the dog with aching hips, or a dull but constant pain from bad teeth, will become bad-tempered and quick to turn if it thinks that, by being touched, the pain will intensify. The veterinary surgeon will want to co-operate with you, as the owner of the Mastiff, in keeping the animal well for as long a natural life as possible, but the dog must be handled well when brought into the surgery to allow a full examination to be made.

Co-operate with your vet by attending for the annual booster vaccines and remember it is beneficial to allow the dog to be inspected for early signs of disease. Visits early on in life when there are no painful procedures, and when rewards can be offered by the veterinary staff for good behaviour, will make future visits all the easier. Simple tasks such as weighing the puppy in the surgery, or handling it to trim its nails at the first visits, will make the dog more trusting and easier to handle in the surgery when adult. With large breeds the collection of blood samples for disease screening may be impossible unless the dog is first muzzled or well sedated, as

the person withdrawing blood from the dog's forearm is placed in a very hazardous situation. Some vets prefer to collect samples of blood from the jugular vein at the lower side of the neck and this is especially useful when larger volumes of blood are needed for analysis.

Between visits, you should inspect your dog for any changes in coat condition, breath odour or for any unusual lumps or swellings. Daily brushing and grooming helps you to get to know the dog and pick up any early signs of disease. Improved diet and preventive vaccinations are contributing to a much longer life for all domestic animals. The dog's weight should be observed, and weighing at three-monthly intervals, if suitable scales can be found, helps to detect any gradual change in condition.

SELECTING VETERINARY CARE
The choice of a vet may be based on accessibility, especially if you like to walk your dog to the surgery. Dogs excited by car travel may be frustrated if, after a journey, they are deposited in a waiting room full of other dog's odours and no opportunities to work off their pent-up energy. If there is no practice nearby to which the dog can be walked, some people will make enquiries from other Mastiff owners they meet before deciding which veterinary practice will have

the greatest sympathy to their dog and their requirements for veterinary care. Treatment prices will vary and it is fairly easy to phone around and enquire the cost of a booster vaccine, or the cost of neutering, to judge the level of charges, especially if you are new to an area. Facilities in practices are not all the same and a practice or veterinary hospital with 24-hour nursing staff residing on the premises and equipment for emergency surgery will have to charge more than the smaller practice, which adequately provides for vaccination and other injections but requires you to go elsewhere for more complicated procedures.

PET INSURANCE

Pet insurance has proved a great incentive to veterinarians to provide additional equipment and provide veterinary experts with a specialist knowledge of your breed. Once it is known there is insurance cover, the vet is confident that payment will be made for all treatments given to the dog and is less likely to be cautious on embarking on expensive procedures. With large breeds, treatment costs are often higher because of the larger doses of drugs, which are based on body weight, unlike humans who have a standard dose regardless of their weight. Large breeds require more room if hospitalisation is needed; but although their appetites may be larger, this is often the least of the additional cost of treating the larger hospitalised dog. Just as the vet should be chosen to provide the type of health attention needed, the insurance companies' provisions should be compared to find the one with an annual premium that will deliver the most help in times of difficulty. The excess you have to pay on each claim may not be as important for a large dog compared with that for a cat or for a small breed of dog where charges for veterinary attention are relatively lower. Caution in asking for treatment for some

Photo: Sheila Atter.

disorders of an insured dog is necessary as inherited disorders are not covered by insurance, nor are booster vaccines, routine neutering and some chronic or continuing disease states. Many companies do not pay for visits to a dog in your home, nor pay in full for prescription diets that could be part of your dog's treatment.

GENERAL GROOMING AND HYGIENE

Mastiffs have relatively easy coats to maintain but they do require daily grooming, especially at times when they are moulting. The sooner a health problem is noticed, the quicker the vet can be asked for an opinion, and the better the chance of a full recovery from a progressive disease or a tumour.

The Mastiff puppy should be brushed and groomed from the earliest age so that such handling will be looked on as a pleasurable experience. Procedures will be easier to carry out if they are started early in life. If a dog is used to be handled, it will be far easier for a veterinary surgeon to make an examination, and a visit to the surgery becomes less stressful for the owner as well as the dog.

225

Photos: Anne-Marie Class.

Before you start to groom the dog, carry out a thorough physical examination to check for any abnormalities. Always start at the head end as your hands are cleaner for looking at the orifices on the head, before handling the dog's feet and the anal region.

EYES: Inspect the eyes first for matter or discharges in the corner. There should be no excessive watering and the white of the eye should be briefly observed to see that it is not red or discoloured. The surface of the eye should be clear and bright and the expression one of alertness. There are specific diseases that affect the eyes, so any abnormal signs

should be noted and reported to the vet if necessary.

EARS: A painful ear can be a very irritating complaint for your dog, so the prevention of ear problems is important. If there is a noticeable build-up of wax in the ear canal, this can be easily removed by first softening the wax with a ear-cleaning fluid and then wiping gently with cotton wool. The use of cotton wool buds in the ear is discouraged and all cleaning should be the most gentle possible. There is a range of ear cleaners suitable for the Mastiff and the vet will advise on one most appropriate for routine use.

If there is an excessive amount of wax in the canal, or if the ear is hot, reddened or swollen, this is an indication of infection or inflammation and veterinary attention should be sought quickly. Should an infection be left untreated, the dog will scratch the affected ear repeatedly, often introducing other infections which have been carried on its soiled hind toenails. Oozing, and the multiplication of harmful bacteria in the moist discharges, will make the ear much worse and treatment becomes more difficult. In some Mastiffs, ulcers will be seen in the base of the wide-open ear and any cold wind, or inadvertent touching of the ear, may make the dog cry out, having experienced a sharp pain.

MOUTH: Check your dog's gums each day for redness or inflammation. Gum diseases can develop as tartar builds up on the teeth and food particles get caught at the gum margin. The decaying food will produce breath odour if not removed, and mouth bacteria can produce even worse halitosis. The teeth and gum margins have pain receptors, so any tartar build-up can lead to a disease which puts the dog off its food and even causes bad temper. With some Mastiffs it may be almost impossible to examine the condition of the back molar teeth until the dog is given a general anaesthetic or a deep sedative.

Canine toothpastes are now available, which can be used to help prevent a build-up of tartar. If the dog's teeth are cleaned regularly, you will avoid a state of dental neglect so advanced that your Mastiff needs a general anaesthetic to have the teeth scaled and polished at the vet's. Start brushing a dog's teeth at about four months of age but avoid the areas where the permanent teeth are about to erupt. At first the puppy will want to play but, little by little, will become used to having all its teeth cleaned while

young and small, rather than you waiting until you have a fully-grown dog that objects to the procedure.

Puppies lose their milk teeth between four and six months and sore gums will be apparent at that age. Massaging the skin just below the eye will help when the molar teeth are about to erupt. While grooming the older dog, look for signs of abnormality such as mouth warts, excess saliva or white froth at the back of the mouth.

NOSE: Again, remove any discharges and look for cracking or fissuring. There is little point in worrying about a 'cold wet nose' as a health indicator.

SKIN AND COAT: Examine the whole of your dog's body when grooming. Telltale black dirt or white scurf may indicate a parasite infection. Patches of hair loss, redness of skin and abnormal lumps may first be found during grooming. Your Mastiff's coat will normally have a slight shine, and oil from the sebaceous glands will give it the water-proofing grease that gives that smooth feel as the hand is run over the hair.

NAILS AND FEET: Nails should be worn short, as over-long nails may splinter painfully, especially in cold weather when the nail is brittle. If the dog is regularly walked on hard surfaces such as concrete, paving stones or rocks, the nails will wear down naturally. Tarmac and grass does little to wear nails down at exercise times. If the nails are left to become too long they are difficult for the dog to wear down, the heel takes more of the weight of the leg and the nails may split, with painful consequences.

Clipping nails is a delicate task. If you cut the nails too short, into the quick, blood will flow and the dog will find it painful. The dog may then become very wary of anyone who tries to get near its feet with nail clippers in hand. Exercising on concrete may be safer for the beginner than attempting to cut across the nail with new, sharp clippers.

Make a habit of feeling the area between the toes where tufts of hair attract sticky substances. Clay soils can form little hard balls between the toes, and tar or chewing gum can be picked up on a walk with equally damaging effect. You will notice any cuts or pad injuries when handling the feet for grooming.

PERINEUM AND GENITAL AREA:
Check for swollen anal sacs or unexpected discharges. Segments of tapeworms might be seen near the rectum. The bitch's vulva should not discharge except when signs of her being on heat are present. The prepuce of the male dog should have no discharge and the penis should not protrude, except if the dog is unwisely excited during grooming or handling.

PREVENTIVE CARE

VACCINATIONS
The use of vaccines to prevent disease is well established for human as well as for animal health. The longer life-expectancy of the animal, and the comparative rarity of puppy disease and early death, is something that has become taken for granted in the last forty years. Yet many older dog breeders remember the very ill puppies that died of distemper fits

Photo: Anne-Marie Class.

Photo: Anne-Marie Class.

or were left twitching with chorea for the rest of their lives. The appearance of parvovirus in 1979 was an unpleasant shock to those who thought that veterinary treatment could deal with all puppy diarrhoeas. There were many deaths in puppies under twelve months old until the use of vaccines gave protection, Some died of sudden heart failure caused by the parvovirus damaging the heart muscle. Immunity would protect the puppy, either through its mother's milk, or by the early use of vaccines to stimulate the puppy's own body defences as it became old enough to respond to an injected vaccine .

The vet is the best person to advise on the type of vaccines to use and at what age to give them, since vets have a unique knowledge of the type of infection prevalent in a locality and when infection is likely to strike.

An example of this is in the Guide Dogs for the Blind Association's breeding programme where, for over 25 years, early vaccination was given to the six-week-old puppy. No isolation after this early vaccination was needed. The procedure was contrary to general advice given in the 60s and 70s when puppy disease was at an acceptably low figure. Later, when parvovirus infection was widespread in the early 80s, the mortality rate of GDBA puppies was much lower than among puppies of breeders that had kept their puppies in kennels until 12 weeks or older before selling them. The temperament of some breeds was also suspect, due to a longer enforced isolation after vaccination. Proper socialisation did not take place, as the new owners of such puppies were advised not to take them out until four months of age when a final parvo booster had to be given. This meant that there were no opportunities to mix with people and other dogs until an age when the older puppy had already developed a fear of being handled by strangers or was suspicious of other dogs met outside the home.

DISTEMPER: This is the classic virus disease, which has become very rare where vaccine is used on a regular basis. From time to time it is seen in the larger cities, where there is a stray or roaming dog population unprotected by vaccination. This may subsequently lead to infection of show or other kennel dogs, that do not have a high level of immunity.

The virus has an incubation period of seven to 21 days and infection is followed by a rise in temperature, loss of appetite, a cough and often diarrhoea. Discharges from the eyes and nose may be watery at first but often become thick mucoid with a green or creamy colour due to secondary infections. The teeth are affected when the puppy of under six months of age is infected by the virus; enamel defects shown as brown marks last for life and are known as 'distemper teeth'.

The 'hard pad' strain seen in the sixties is now considered to be nothing more than the hyperkeratosis of the nose and footpads that occurs after all distemper infections; the name is still in use when dog illness is written or talked about. In over half of all dogs affected with distemper, damage to the nervous system will show as fits, chorea (twitching of muscles) or posterior paralysis. Old dogs may develop encephalitis (ODE) due to latent distemper virus in the nervous tissue.

The vaccines in use today are all modified live vaccines and are highly effective in preventing disease. The age for a first injection will partly depend on the maker's instruction sheet and partly on a knowledge of the amount of protection passed by the mother to the young puppies. Maternally derived immunity (MDI) might block the vaccine in the young puppy, but the blood-sampling of bitches during their pregnancy was used as a method of estimating how soon the puppy would respond to vaccine. The use of a first vaccine at six weeks is

becoming more widespread; this allows for the all-important early socialisation period of the puppy's development.

PARVOVIRUS: This is probably the second most important virus disease and, like distemper, is largely preventable by the correct use of vaccination. The speed with which an infection could spread from kennel to kennel surprised many, but the disease is caused by a very tough virus that can be carried on footwear that has walked though virus-infected faeces. The virus may then persist for up to a year; it is untouched by many commonly-used kennel disinfectants. The sudden death of puppies caused by damage to the heart muscle, often just after sale, is no longer seen, but the gastro-enteritis form still occurs from time to time.

The sudden illness takes the form of repeated vomiting in the first 24 hours, followed by profuse watery diarrhoea, often with a characteristic sour smell and a red-brown colour. The cause of death was often from the severe dehydration that accompanied this loss of fluid. However, once it was understood that puppies should be treated with intravenous fluids similar to the treatment of human cholera victims, the death rate fell. Fluids by mouth are sufficient in less severe cases, provided they replace the essential electrolytes. The traditional mixture of a level teaspoonful of salt and a dessert-spoonful of glucose in two pints of water has saved many lives.

Vaccination of the young puppy is recommended, although the MDI may partially block the effectiveness of the vaccine, as is the case with distemper. A live vaccine at six weeks followed by a further dose at twelve weeks, will protect most puppies. The four-month booster is no longer in common use, but it is now more usual to see parvovirus in the recently weaned puppy or the five-month old puppy, where

Photo courtesy:
Jaime Pérez
Marhuenda.

immunity no longer protects that individual against infection.

HEPATITIS: This disease, produced by an adenovirus, is now quite rare but one form (CVA-2) is often associated with 'kennel cough' infection in dogs. After infection, the virus multiplies in the lymphatic system and then sets out to damage the lining of the blood vessels. It was for this reason that the cause of death was liver failure, so the name hepatitis was given, as, on post mortem, the liver was seen to be very swollen and engorged with blood. Other organs are also damaged and about 70 per cent of recovered dogs are found to have kidney damage. The eye damage known as 'blue eye' seen on recovery is not recognised in the Mastiff but was once quite common in certain other breeds. Vaccination at six and twelve weeks, using a reliable vaccine that contains the CAV-2 virus, is very effective as a prevention against this disease.

LEPTOSPIROSIS: Caused by bacteria, it differs from the previous group of viral infections as protection has to be provided by at least two doses of a killed vaccine, and a 12-monthly repeat dose of this vaccine is essential if the protection is to be maintained. It is for this disease that the annual 'booster' vaccine is most essential. The type of leptospirosis spread by rats is the most devastating to the dog and frequently results in jaundice, then death from kidney and liver failure, unless early treatment with antibiotics is available

The other serotype of leptospira that

damages the dog's kidney is less often seen since vaccination and annual boosters have been regularly used. Gun dogs and dogs that walk in the country where rats may have contaminated water courses are especially at risks. Mastiffs kept outdoors in kennels with yards have been known to die of jaundice, as rats cross the exercise yards and leave infected urine traces for the dog to sniff at or lick up.

KENNEL COUGH: As a troublesome infection that causes harsh coughing in dogs, originating from the trachea and bronchial tubes, kennel cough is one of the best known diseases. Traditionally dogs became infected in boarding kennels but it has recently been suggested it should be called 'infectious bronchitis', as any dog coming within droplet infection distance of another dog's coughing at a show, or in public exercise areas, may catch the illness. There are five known viral and bacterial agents that may all, or, perhaps, only two of them at a time, cause the disease known as kennel cough. Vaccination by nose drops of a Bordetella vaccine can be offered to give protection, and these drops are often given just a week before a dog goes into kennels. The normal booster injection given contains protection for three of the other known causes.

The diseases develops within four to seven days of infection, so it may not be seen until after a dog has just left the kennels. The deep harsh cough is often described as 'as if a bone or something was stuck in the throat'. The dog coughs repeatedly. Even with treatment coughs last for 14 days, but in some dogs the cough lasts as long as six weeks. Infection may then persist in the trachea. A dog who is a 'carrier' may get subsequent bouts of coughing if stressed. This explains why some non-coughing dogs put into board may cause an outbreak of kennel cough. Once it was a summer-time disease, but kennel cough outbreaks now occur at any time of the year,

often after a holiday period when more dogs than usual are boarded.

RABIES: The virus disease is almost unknown to most UK veterinarians due to a successful quarantine policy that has kept the island free of rabies in dogs and in wild life such as foxes. However, the existing quarantine policy cannot be maintained as the six-month period of isolation does not have a strong scientific basis. The Swedish government's switch to a compulsory vaccination and identification policy for all has provided a basis for modification of the UK laws on importing dogs. In countries such as the Philippines, where very recently rabies was widespread and causing human deaths, it was found that at least 75% of a dog population had to be compulsorily vaccinated, including the rounding up of all strays, to delay the spread of this disease. The virus disease must always be rigorously controlled in animals because of the devastating effect of one human becoming infected with rabies. Rabies control also involves vaccinating foxes and this will be provided once the disease enters the UK. Inactivated rabies vaccine is available in the UK; it has been used for many years in dogs intended for export. Elsewhere in the world, both live attenuated vaccines and inactivated vaccines are used on an annual basis.

BOOSTERS: Thanks to the development of effective canine vaccines by the pharma-ceutical industry, most of the diseases described above are now uncommon in Europe and North America. The need for an annual booster is essential to keep up a high level of immunity where killed vaccines are used, and with live virus vaccines it probably does no harm to inject repeat doses every year. There has been a suggestion that thrombocytopenia (a decrease in the number of platelets in circulating blood) occurs after

The 'Beorcan' family

repeated vaccine administration, but this does not seem to be a problem in the breed and should not be used as an excuse to discourage the once-a-year visit to the vets. It is easy to become complacent about the absence of infectious disease in Mastiffs and it is false economy to overlook the need for revaccination.

PARASITES

INTERNAL PARASITES
ROUNDWORMS: The most common worm in puppies and dogs up to a year of age are *Toxocara* and *Toxascaris*. Puppies with roundworms will start to pass worm eggs into the environment as early as three weeks and most eggs are released when puppies are about seven weeks of age. This is the most dangerous time for the exercise areas to be

contaminated with eggs, and for any young children who play with the puppies to get the slightly sticky worm eggs on their hands. Then they may lick their fingers and consequently catch *Zoonotic Toxocariasis*.

Adult dogs also pass roundworms, which in severe infestations have been seen emerging from the rectum of the nursing bitch that develops diarrhoea. Worms may also appear in the vomit, if the worm moves forward from the intestine into the stomach by accident.

Control of worms depends on frequent dosing of young puppies – from as early as two weeks of age and repeated every two to three weeks until they are three months old. To prevent puppies carrying worms, the pregnant bitch can be wormed from the 42nd day of pregnancy with a safe licensed wormer such as fenbendazole. The wormer

233

can be given daily to the bitch until the second day after all the puppies have been born. Routine worming of adults twice a year, with a combined tablet for roundworms and tapeworms, is a good preventive measure. If there are young children in a household, even more frequent worm dosing may be advisable to reduce the risk of roundworm larvae migrating to the child and possible subsequent eye damage.

TAPEWORMS: They are not known to kill dogs but the appearance of a wriggling segment coming through the rectum, or moving on the tail hair is enough to deter all but the most unsqueamish dog lover. Responsible, regular worming of dogs is needed, to avoid harm that dog worms can do to other creatures. The biggest threat is from the *Echinococcus* worm that a dog obtains if feeding from raw sheep offals. The worm is only six millimetres long but several thousand could live in one dog. If a human should swallow a segment of this worm it may move to the person's liver or lungs, in the same way as it would in the sheep. A major illness of the person would be the unpleasant result, another example of a zoonotic infection.

The most frequently found tapeworm is *Dipylidium caninum*. It is not a long tapeworm compared with the old-fashioned *Taenia* worms, but when segments break off they can be recognised, as they resemble grains of rice attached to the hairs of a dog's tail. The tapeworm has become more common in dogs and cats since the number of fleas has increased; the intermediate host of this worm is the flea or the louse. When dogs groom themselves they attempt to swallow any crawling insect on the skin's surface and, in this way, may become infested with tapeworms even though worming twice a year is carried out. Flea control is just as important as worming in preventing tapeworm infection. Three-monthly dosing with tablets

is a good idea – less frequently if the dog is known to be away from sources of reinfection. The other tapeworms of the *Taenia* species come from dogs eating raw rabbits (*T. serialis* or *pisiformis*) or from sheep, cattle or pig offals (*T. ovis, hydatigena* or *multiceps*).

HOOKWORMS: These are less frequently found as a cause of trouble in the UK but are prevalent in other parts of the world. The hookworm does damage to the intestine by using its teeth on the lining. *Uncinaria* may be the cause of poor condition and thinness. Diarrhoea is seen as permanently soft, discoloured faeces that can respond dramatically to worming. The other hookworm, *Ancylostoma*, may be found as the reason for anaemia and weakness. Exercising dogs over grass used by wild foxes for excretion and scent marking allows the dog to reinfect itself with hookworm eggs.

OTHER INTERNAL PARASITES: *Giardia* is a parasite that occurs in dogs in kennels. It should be investigated in dogs with diarrhoea that have come through quarantine. It is a protozoan organism that likes to live in stagnant surface water: it is of especial interest because a similar strain is a cause of dysentery in humans, especially where water-borne infection is blamed for the illness. It may be necessary routinely to treat all dogs in kennels with a drug such as fenbendazole to prevent a continuing problem. Whipworms are found in the large intestine and may be identified when faeces samples are examined after mucoid dysentery affects a dog. Treatment is effective using a reliable anthelminthic. Heartworms are almost unknown in most of the UK but are a great problem in other countries. Bladder worms are only detected when urine samples are examined: they are similar to whipworms and fortunately are rare. Any obscure illness in a dog should require the

examination of fresh faeces samples by a veterinary laboratory.

ECTOPARASITES
External parasites may cause intense irritation and skin diseases from scratching and rubbing. In recent years the cat flea has become by far the most common ectoparasite of the Mastiff but more traditional sarcoptic mange, demodectic mange, lice and ringworm skin infections do appear from time to time. Demodectic mange may have a hereditary basis associated with low immunity, as it is seen more frequently in certain strains and litters.

FLEAS: The flea that hops may never be found in the Mastiff's coat but its presence may be detected by the flea dirt or excreta containing dried blood. Grooming your dog over white paper or a light table top may reveal black bits: if moistened, the dark red colour is noticed, as they are dried blood spots. Once the flea dirt is found, a closer inspection of the dog may show fleas running though the coat at skin level. At one time the fleas preferred to live in the hair down the spine towards the tail root but now they are found in the shorter hairs of the abdomen or the neck. This may relate to the fact that cat fleas are the most commonly found variety in dogs. Such fleas prefer a softer hair structure for their 'living space'. All fleas are temporary visitors who like to feed from the dog by biting to suck blood, but in their development and egg-laying stages they may

Photo: Anne-Marie Class.

live freely off the dog, thereby escaping some of the parasitic dressing put on their host's coat. Re-infestation then becomes possible and many flea treatments appear to be ineffective unless the flea in the environment is eliminated at the same time.

There is a wide range of antiparasitic sprays, washes and baths available and the Mastiff owner may well be confused as to how and when to apply these. There is the further problem that some dogs seem able to carry a few fleas on them with very little discomfort, while others show intense irritation and bite pieces out of themselves in an attempt to catch the single flea. A cat in the household, or the cat crossing the garden, may drop flea eggs, and in a warm

place these eggs can hatch out and develop into more fleas waiting to jump onto the dog.

Flea eggs and immature larvae may lie dormant for months waiting to complete their development and become ready to bite. Adult fleas too can wait for months off an animal until able to find a host to feed from, so treating the dog is only tackling part of the problem; the kennels or the house have to be treated as well. Vacuum cleaning, and having a place that is easy-to-clean as sleeping quarters for the dog, help enormously in dealing with a flea infestation once an environmental spray has been applied. The choice of aerosol spray, medicated bath, tablet by mouth or agent that stops larval development is a wide one, and experience will show which method is most suitable for each dog affected.

LICE: These may be found in the dog's coat occasionally – especially in a dog leading an outdoor life, more than the average pet dog. Lice spend their whole life on the dog and fairly close contact between dogs is necessary to spread the parasites. Large numbers of lice cause intense irritation with hair loss. Biting lice can produce anaemia when they are present in large enough numbers to remove blood continuously, at a rate similar to a bleeding ulcer. Liquid treatments applied as a total bath soak are best. Lice eggs can be transmitted from dog to dog on grooming implements. The lice and their eggs are visible to the naked eye and should be spotted during the normal grooming routine.

MANGE MITES: These mites cannot be seen during grooming. If they are suspected, scrapings from the skin surface are sent for examination under a microscope. The two forms of mange, *Sarcoptes* and *Demodex*, can be distinguished in this way, but bare skin patches of low-grade mange infection may at first seem similar when a dog is examined. A new blood test for *Sarcoptes* recently became available and this helps to distinguish why a dog may scratch a lot but not appear to have mange. There are a number of differences in the two forms of mange that need not be enumerated here but the one simple distinction is that Sarcoptic mange is very itchy and spreads from dog to dog, while Demodectic mange in the older dog usually remains as a scaly, hairless patch and, although an obvious blemish, does not cause a lot of itching. Antiparasitic baths with pyrethroids or amitraz, and topical applications of organophosphorous washes, will have to be repeated, but usually are effective. The antibiotic Ivomectin in the

Photo: Sheila Atter.

food has also been used to treat Sarcoptic mange, but great care is needed as fatalities have been recorded when this product is used in dogs.

TICKS: Ticks are large enough not to be missed and can be expected in those dogs walked where sheep, and other livestock, leave tick eggs about. Applications of pyrethroid or other 'spot' liquids on the neck and rump will keep ticks off a dog for a month. Baths are also effective. Ticks may be removed by first soaking them in vegetable oil, then gently coaxing and lifting the tick's head away from the dog's skin.

CHEYLETIELLA: These cause surface irritation of dogs and intense itching in humans living with the dogs who happen to get bitten. The so-called 'moving dandruff' show up as white flecks on a dark dog's skin but may be more difficult to see on a light-coloured dog. Antiparasitic shampoos will kill the surface feeding mite but carrier dogs in kennels may show very few symptoms at all.

MALASEZZIA: This is a yeast-like surface organism that appears in dogs with low resistance to infection. If there is a patchy coat and dull hair appearance in a Mastiff, the owner may suspect the presence of these yeasts in unusually large numbers. The organisms which occur in greatest numbers in moist areas and places such as between the toes and under the tail are used for sample taking. Once identified, baths and general hygiene, with improved nutrition, help the dog to overcome this problem. The yeast will also be found in the ear canal and can multiply to cause a type of discharging otitis. Malasezzia may be shown to be present under the microscope on a stained smear, often in large numbers. Baths with a preparation of Miconazole are effective and the baths should be repeated as often as the veterinary surgeon directs.

RINGWORM: Ringworm is found in dogs as a fungal infection of the hair. The signs of a 'ring' are not always present, and some dogs show quite a violent itchy skin response once infected. Cattle ringworm can be transmitted to country or city dogs exposed to livestock. Ringworm spores can remain in the environment and old woodwork for a long time. Diagnosis by skin tests is slow but reliable, as the 'Woods' lamp, which uses ultra-violet light, does not identify all types of ringworm. Treatment with antifungal washes, or the antibiotic griseofulvin, may be used to eliminate the mycotic infection.

ACCIDENTS AND FIRST AID
The few simple procedures described here are not meant to suggest that there are no other things that can be done as 'first aid' but, in most cases, the sooner the patient gets to the veterinary surgery, the better the chance of a full recovery. For this reason, splinting broken bones is now out of favour, and more pain may be caused in trying to tie on a splint than if the dog is quickly transported to a place where any shock and pain can be treated professionally. X-rays will better show the nature of a fracture and what is the best method for treatment.

TRAFFIC ACCIDENTS: Mastiffs, being solidly-constructed dogs, seldom go underneath vehicles; so they tend to get severe chest injuries if hit in front, or pelvic limb injuries if struck on the side. Fractures of the long bones of the leg are another common result of injury with a fast-moving car. Any dog hit by a car will be distressed and because of fright and pain will tend to bite, even when its familiar owners attempt to help. After an accident, first assess the injuries by noting any gaping holes and where blood is lost. Do this before touching the dog's head. Some frightened dogs may try to run away at that point, so a lead or scarf round the neck will help to steady the dog and a tape muzzle may have to be used before a dog is lifted into a vehicle for transport to the surgery.

A pressure bandage applied to a bleeding area is the best way of staunching blood flow, but improvisation with whatever cloth is to hand is acceptable in a life-saving situation. The dog may be breathing rapidly or gasping with 'air hunger' signs. In this case the mouth and nostrils should be wiped free of dried blood or saliva to help unblock the airway. If you suspect a spinal injury, slide a board under the dog before lifting it up. Otherwise a blanket is the best way of allowing two or more persons to pick up an injured dog without aggravating the injuries.

Photo: Anne-Marie Class.

CHOKING AND VOMITING: Try to find out the cause of any sudden attack. Grass awns may enter the throat and airways in the summer months, and at any time of year a dog that has been playing ball or stick retrieval games may get an obstruction at the back of the throat. Even a fine bamboo cane may become wedged across the upper molar teeth. Bones are the most common cause of foreign bodies in the mouth. Poisonous substances may cause retching and vomiting; and thirsty dogs have been known to drink from toilet bowls and unsuspectingly drink bleach and other cleaning substances.

Having initially looked for a foreign body, your first aid measures should be to provide as good an air supply as possible. If there is any blistering or soreness of the lips or tongue, use honey or salad oil to coat the inflamed surfaces. A vomiting dog should be prevented from drinking water and then regurgitating it as fast as it is swallowed. Ice cubes in a dish left to melt may be a way of helping the dog, as it will drink the iced water more slowly.

COLLAPSE AND UNCONSCIOUSNESS: As in the road accident, assess the dog before touching to determine the cause of the incident, so that appropriate first aid can be given. The dog running in a field on a warm day may have had a circulatory collapse; the dog convulsing may be throwing an epileptic fit. And the elderly dog found in the morning semi-conscious after voiding urine and faeces may have had a 'stroke' or vestibular disease. Acute enteritis, as with a virus or Clostridia infections, will also cause dogs to appear collapsed. Each condition in turn will need different treatment but, as a general rule, pull the tongue forward to ensure there is an airway to the lungs, keep

the animal cool and avoid unnecessary noise and commotion. Look for any drugs or poisons that a dog may have swallowed, gently feel the left side of the abdomen for gas distending the abdomen, see if the whole abdomen feels gas-filled, look at the pupils of the eyes and their response to a bright light. The veterinary surgeon will be better able to deal with the situation if a timetable of events, and any contributing factors, can be given to him in a concise manner.

WASP STINGS: These occur more often in the late summer. Usually the foot swells rapidly or, if the dog has caught a wasp in its mouth, the side of the face swells up and the eye may become partly shut. Vinegar is a traditional remedy to apply to the stung area. If an antihistamine tablet is available, this can be given to the dog immediately to stop further swelling. Other biting flies cause swellings on the body and may be the cause of the 'hot spots' or acute moist eczemas that Mastiffs can suffer with. Calamine lotions cool the skin but the dog should be discouraged from attacking its own skin

Photo courtesy: Betty Baxter.

Photo: Berthous.

because, if licked, the calamine causes vomiting.

SHOCK: This occurs to a greater or lesser extent with nearly all accidents. Keep the patient warm, wrapping a blanket coat or wool garment around the body of the dog. Unless you have reasons to think an anaesthetic will be given, or other contra-indications exist such as throat damage, offer fluids by mouth in small quantities. Oral rehydration solutions can be obtained from the vet and a packet should be kept in every emergency first aid kit. As an alternative, a solution of half a teaspoon of salt and half a teaspoon of bicarbonate of soda in a litre of water may be given, a few dessert-spoonfuls at a time. There are certain conditions, such as acute pancreatitis collapse, where nothing must be given by mouth.

SKIN DISEASES

Fleas are probably still the most common problem but there are many other causes of skin disorders. Flea bites may not be obvious, especially in a dense-coated breed. Once a dog becomes sensitised to the proteins injected by the flea when it first bites, any subsequent contact with flea saliva may bring on an itchy rash, even though no live fleas are found on the dog. The various other causes of parasitic skin disease have already been outlined in the section on external parasites.

OTHER PRURITIC SKIN CONDITIONS: Anal sac irritation will cause

a dog to nibble at the hair around the tail base, or it may cause licking and nibbling anywhere around the hindquarters. The glands may be so impacted that they cannot be emptied out during the dog's normal straining to pass faeces. An infected lining of one or both sacs may be the cause of irritation, and this can often be detected by a fruity odour to the sac's contents or, at its worst, a smell like rotten meat. Bacterial dermatoses result from multiplication of skin bacteria such as *Staph. intermedius*. Red blotches and ring-like marks around a central pustule are most clearly seen when the hairless areas of the abdomen are inspected. Skin swabs may be used to recognise the bacteria present, and this information can be used then to choose the most appropriate antibiotic for the infection causing the irritation.

HAIR LOSS AND ALOPECIA: Mastiffs'

coats are normally shed twice a year, but sometimes the growth of new hair is delayed and the coat appears thin, lifeless and, if groomed excessively, bare patches develop. Investigations into the possibility of thyroid disease may be needed when there is a failure of hair to grow. Other hormonal skin disease may cause symmetrical hair loss in the flanks of a bitch, or bare tail head areas (stud tail) in some dogs. Feminisation of the older male dog will have hair loss as one of the signs of a Sertoli cell tumour. Veterinary advice should be sought.

DIGESTIVE SYSTEM DISORDERS

SICKNESS & DIARRHOEA: Occasional sickness is not a cause for concern in the younger dog. The dog is adapted to feeding from a wide range of different foods, and part of a protection against food poisoning is the ability to reject unsuitable foods by returning them from the stomach by reflex vomiting. If there is a yellow coloration to the vomit, it means that the bile from the liver that normally passes into the small intestine after leaving the bile duct, has, for some reason, been passed forward to enter the stomach. The bitter bile acids will cause reflex vomiting as soon as they reach the stomach wall, and will be vomited up, together with any food left in the stomach.

Bacterial infections such as those of *Salmonella* and *Campylobacter* can only be detected by the culture of faeces. *Helicobacter* are another stomach bacteria that are of recent comparative interest but Helicobacteriosis is not known as a cause of disease in dogs. *Clostridia*, which are spore-forming resistant bacteria, have been known to cause fatal toxic enteritis. The importance of strains of *E. coli* among the causes of diarrhoea in dogs is an interesting development; renewed interest in this organism, that was at one time thought to be harmless, is accompanied by recent human deaths from the 0157 strain found in cooked and raw meat. Certain viruses are also known to cause gastro-enteritis.

Repeated sickness, starting off with

recognisable food followed by slime, or food followed by mucus alone, is a more serious sign. It may be associated with obstructions due to a foreign body, or to infection such as pyometra or hepatitis. Some outbreaks of diarrhoea will start with food being vomited, as this will stimulate the intestine. As soon as food enters the small intestine the stomach empties itself reflexly by vomiting any food remaining within the stomach. Sometimes a reversal of normal flow of food will cause the appearance of a faecal vomit.

Diarrhoea is the passage of frequent loose or unformed faeces: it is associated with infections and irritation of the intestine. The rapid transit of food taken in by mouth means that water cannot be absorbed by the large intestine, and soft or runny product

results from the incomplete digestion and water reabsorption. When blood is present it may appear as streaks from the large intestine. If blackish and foul-smelling, it means that the blood has come from the small intestine and has been subjected to some of the digestive fluids. The condition is then known as dysentery.

Chronic diarrhoea is a problem where the looseness of faeces lasts more than 48 hours. It may be associated with malabsorption, where the lining of the intestine is incapable of absorbing digested food. There are other diseases such as food intolerances, bacterial overgrowth, lymphoid and other tumours that may cause maldigestion, where there is some failure of the digestive juices to break down the food. Other causes are exocrine

Photo: Anne-Marie Class.

pancreatic insufficiency (EPI), inflammatory bowel diseases, or any disturbance in gastric or liver function. Investigations by the vet will include blood tests and faecal laboratory examinations. These may be followed by X-rays or endoscope examinations.

The treatment of sickness and diarrhoea involves, firstly, withholding solid food for 24 hours and giving small quantities of replacement fluids as soon as the dog stops vomiting (proprietary electrolyte fluids are probably best); then introducing a highly digestible food with low fat is best, in small quantities – about one third of the normal amount fed on the second day of the illness. The amount should be increased slowly until, by the fourth day, a full ration of food is given again. In the recovery period fats should be avoided, as well as milk and dairy products, because of the dog's inability to digest lactose.

GASTRIC DILATION: This disease is better known as bloat, and 'torsion' can be a problem in any of the larger breeds. It is especially associated with feeding regimes where a highly digestible food can be swallowed rapidly and, if this is followed by the drinking of large quantities of water, the situation contributes to the development of the bloat. Feeding immediately after strenuous exercise has been blamed too. When a dog is fed in the late afternoon or evening, there is the greater risk of the dog lying down, so that abdominal movement associated with walking or jumping up does not allow for eructation, or the dispersal of gas from the stomach.

Greedy feeders that swallow air as they gulp down their food are considered at greatest risk, but it does seem associated with the deep-chested dogs that have loosely suspended stomachs. An enlarged spleen, as is found in some Mastiffs, may contribute to the gastric dysfunction.

Where the bloated stomach rotates as a 'torsion' or volvulus, the gastric dilation and volvulus (GDV) condition means an acute emergency. The dog needs to be rushed to the veterinary surgery for treatment of shock and for the deflation of the stomach. Affected dogs look uncomfortable, become depressed and look at their flanks with expressions of disbelief. At first, the left side just behind the ribs is the only side to bulge; percussion with the finger tips will produce a drum-like resonance over the left rib-cage edge and over the distended abdomen behind. Within a few hours both sides of the abdomen appear distended behind the rib cage, the dog becomes more uncomfortable and lies down a lot as the pain increases. The gas-filled stomach presses on the diaphragm restricting the breathing, the colour of the tongue becomes more purplish, and breaths are more frequent and quite shallow. Sometime at this stage, the weight of the enlarging spleen attached to the greater curvature of the gas-filled stomach makes the stomach twist in a clockwise direction. The signs of discomfort become more noticeable as the stomach's exit to the oesophagus is pinched off by a 180-degree rotation. If a stomach tube is passed through the mouth down the oesophagus at this stage the tube can be pressed down no further than just beyond the entrance level of the oesophagus into the abdomen. No gas will pass back up the tube, even though the stomach is still tight-filled with gas.

Emergency treatment at the veterinary surgery will usually mean setting up an intravenous drip to deal with the shock. Decompression of the stomach will be attempted, possibly first by passing the stomach tube as described above or, more successfully, by inserting a wide-bore (18G needle) canula at the point behind the left rib arch that shows the most distension by the gas. The finger should then be kept on the needle hub protruding through the skin,

Bullmastiffs owned in Switzerland by Catherine Grimm.

partially to hold it in place as the size of the stomach reduces, and partially to vent the gas out slowly or in pulses. This ensures that the blood in the veins can start to flow towards the heart again, once the abdomen size returns to normal.

Frequently a laparotomy will be necessary to empty the stomach or to provide a means of fixing the stomach to the abdominal wall so that an adhesion will make it less likely that the gas distension will again appear. A number of operation techniques are used; some involve suturing the stomach wall to a rib while others rely on a tube to vent gas from the stomach, and the aim is to have a permanent adhesion to prevent rotation of

245

Photo: Sheila Atter.

the stomach at a later date. Some vets believe that feeding a complete canned food diet to the dog is the best preventive available.

CONSTIPATION: This disorder usually occurs either through the dog eating too many bones whose chalky residue clogs up the rectum or, in older male dogs, it may be associated with enlargement of the prostate gland. Occasionally a tumour inside the rectum will cause straining and apparent constipation. Treatment with oily lubricants and enemas should be followed by high-fibre diets. Soluble fibre, as found in oatmeal, is thought to add to the moist faecal bulk and thus retain water from the large intestine lumen, so that the faeces are not bone-hard and painful to pass. Allow exercise or place the dog in the garden 30 minutes after feeding, as this will stimulate the reflexes for normal defecation.

BREEDING AND REPRODUCTION
There are no specific problems in the Mastiff breeds and both mating and whelping should proceed with the minimum of trouble. See Breeding A Litter, Chapter 16.

The condition in the bitch of vaginal hypertrophy and prolapse has been reported by some breeders. Known as vaginal hyperplasia it may be caused by excessive oestrogen production by the ovaries or from ingesting oestrogen-like substances in the drinking water or food. Some moulds are known to produce toxins that mimic the action of the oestrogens produced naturally that cause the signs of 'heat' in breeding-age bitches. Affected bitches may require a surgical operation to remove some of the swollen tissue, but a careful check should be made on foods given, and the water supplies should also be monitored if this becomes a kennel problem.

Photo: Sheila Atter.

THE OLDER MASTIFF

GERIATRIC CARE: The Mastiff breeds have a shorter life span than some of the lighter-built, relatively smaller breeds; six to 10 years of age was considered a good age for a dog, but a number may be able live to 12 years provided they avoid arthritis and injuries. Some of the oldest dogs are the leanest dogs, so dietary control makes it possible for your dog to live longer. After about seven years of age it may be of advantage to divide the daily ration into two small feeds to help absorption and digestion; any tendency to overweight must be checked, and regular weighing helps to control the dietary intake. The older dog will use up less energy in exercise and, if housed for most of the day, fewer calories will be burned up to keep the dog warm. Some reduction in calorie intake is desirable and there are special diets prepared for the older dog that are higher in fibre and lower in energy than the diet for the younger dog,

Keep a careful watch on the condition of the mouth, as breath odour is one of the first signs of dental disease or of decayed food trapped between the gums, and 'ledges' of tartar that may have built up on the teeth. Mastiffs may have cracked teeth from chewing bones, or iron bars, earlier in their life and only in old age does the tooth root become infected and an abscess develop. The back upper molar teeth are often affected and an abscess will show as a swelling immediately below the eye if a carnassial (cutting) tooth has infected roots. Chewing as a form of jaw exercise is a method of keeping the teeth healthy, but when there is a build-up of plaque on the tooth surface,

Photo: Diane Pearce.

cleaning the teeth using an ultrasonic scaler followed by a machine polisher is the better way of keeping a healthy mouth.

Monitor the length of your dog's nails, since less exercise and possible arthritis sometimes lead the older dog to put less weight on the affected leg and nail overgrowth occurs. Careful trimming to avoid cutting into the 'quick' or live part of the nail will help many older Mastiffs. The elbows, too, should be inspected for calluses on their outer side, as dogs that are stiff do

Photo: Anne-Marie Class.

not move as often as they might to relieve their body weight on the surface they sleep on. The skin over the outside of the elbow has little padding from fat or muscle and bone lies just underneath, so leathery skin or a callus can easily occur. In extreme cases the callus develops cracks and fissures and a bacterial infection is set up so that the surface becomes pink and oozing.

URINARY INCONTINENCE: This is one of the problems found in many older dogs. Leakage from the bladder, resulting in damp patches in the bedding overnight, may be remedied by taking up the water bowl after seven o'clock to prevent evening drinking. Also effective is the use of one of the

sympathomimetic group of drugs to promote bladder storage. A urine sample should be examined; sometimes a mild cystistis bacteria will be found in the urine. Treatment with an appropriate antibiotic will reduce bladder sensitivity and storage will be better. If large quantities of urine are being voided day and night, then investigation of the dog's urine-concentrating powers and blood biochemistry tests are necessary, to look for major disease. Diabetes insipidus or mellitus, Cushing's disease, liver disease and nephrosis may all be first reported as the dog being 'incontinent' when left indoors for more than a few hours. Blood tests are necessary to distinguish many of these conditions of the older Mastiff.

15 BREED ASSOCIATED DISEASES

By Dick Lane FRAgS FRCVS

As the Mastiff breeds originated as working dogs, a sound dog was obviously essential in order to fulfil its duties. Fitness involved good eyesight, rapid movement and plenty of lung and heart capacity for active work. Natural selection in breeds produced for fitness at work eliminated many of the diseases which occur in breeds produced only for their appearance.

INHERITED EYE CONDITIONS

EYELID DISORDERS

The most commonly found eye disorder in Mastiffs is entropion. The condition of entropion can be an inherited defect of the eyelid structure. It is seen in some Mastiff breeds as an inturning of the eyelids; there may be excessive tear formation and the overflow of tears is seen on the faces of light-coloured dogs. When entropion does appear, it is often the result of a genetic tendency, although an injury to the eye, such as a dog fight, may cause a similar eye problem. Once diagnosed, the severe cases will need surgery to evert the eyelid edge. This is a relatively simple operation and good results are expected. Occasionally it is necessary to operate a second time if more rolling-in takes place subsequent to the first operation.

Ectropion is the opposite condition to entropion as it is a looseness of the eyelids, with undue exposure of the pink lining of the lid known as the haw. It may develop after a facial injury. Ectropion can be a hereditary disease in some breeds with loose skin on the head, but in the larger breeds ectropion is often the result of some injury.

EYE COLOURS

Greenish or light blue eyes are discouraged in the Mastiff breeds, except in the Neapolitan, where eye colour is related to coat colour. Generally, light eyes indicate a relative lack of melanin in the iris that surrounds the lens. Eyes should be dark brown by eight weeks of age, or sometimes have a deep blue colour that will later turn brown. It is not known whether eye colour in any way affects the dog's ability to see. Lack of melanin pigmentation in the muzzle can be a problem in show dogs and the early lack of pigment deposit in the iris may be a future indicator of coloration or lack of pigment elsewhere in the body.

CHERRY EYE

This condition, seen as a pink mass in the corner of the eye closest to the nose, is a prolapse of the nictitans gland of the third eyelid. The third eyelid is not seen normally but it is an important structure for the health of the eye as it carries lymphoid tissue and some tear-forming gland tissue on its inner surface. Swelling of the lymph tissue may cause the whole gland to bulge and become prominent. The nictitans gland has been called the tonsil of the eye because it has a protective function, but it may become enlarged and a cause of discomfort to the dog. Treatment with eye drops may be sufficient, but sometimes surgical measures have to be used to remove most of the bulge.

RETINAL ATROPHY

Retinal atrophy is now well-known as a cause of poor vision and blindness. The Mastiff breeds have a good record, so the infrequency of such retinal disease is quite notable.

Progressive retinal degeneration (PRD), known in many countries as PRA or progressive retinal atrophy, is a disease of the retina at the back of the eyeball and in the early stages can only be recognised by the use of an ophthalmoscope.

PERSISTENT PUPILLARY MEMBRANE (PPM)

This condition has been recognised in some Bullmastiff puppies but is not known to have a specific genetic basis. During the last three weeks of the puppy's development before birth, the blood supply to the back of the developing lens of the eye withers away so that, at ten days after birth, when the puppy opens its eyes for the first time, the lens is clear enough for the light to pass through to reach the retina. In the Basenji breed it has been proved that there is a hereditary basis for the blood vessels failing to wither away in time, so that there is a persisting membrane appearing like a spider's web on the lens of the eye. There are various causes of such a condition but only a few Bullmastiffs have been found affected as puppies. The Kennel Club eye improvement scheme for PPM will help to reduce its frequency.

CATARACT

Any opaqueness in the lens of the eye is known as a cataract. It is often confused with the bluish tinge seen in the ageing dog's eye or with a scar or other opaque area on the surface of the eye – a corneal opacity. Examination by the vet using an ophthalmoscope is necessary to confirm and classify the type of cataract. The Mastiff is rarely affected with cataract unless there has been some injury to the eye that causes the lens to become opaque. The hereditary cataract seen in many breeds of dog has not been recognised in any Mastiff breed.

BONE AND JOINT DISEASES

HIP DYSPLASIA (HD)

The disorder of Hip Dysplasia was a major consideration in the breeding of dogs and the problem is still widespread in many breeds of dog. Any breed can be considered to have a problem where more than 5% of the population are showing recognisable signs of hip dysplasia. A sudden pain or discomfort in the young dog may be associated with a rupture of the round ligament of the hip, causing subluxation of the joint with a short period of pain when the head of the thigh bone (femur) partially comes out of the hip joint. Fractures of the edges of the acetabulum may also cause some of this pain. This possibility of pain being suffered becomes a problem later in life if osteoarthritis develops in and around the hips and it could then be a long-term problem, with reduced activity and the tendency to put on more weight.

Hip Dysplasia is not entirely an hereditary disease and environmental factors such as feeding, exercise and, even, the position the young dog is made to sit in, all may be responsible for up to 60% of the occurrence of the hip dysplasia changes as seen on X-ray. The disease has only a moderate hereditability of 30 to 45%.

CONTROL: Hip X-rays are examined of dogs over 12 months of age and a 'score' is allocated based on nine features of each hip joint. Anyone considering breeding should find out the scores for the intended parents; there would usually seem little justification for attempting to breed from any stock that has an above average score. It must be remembered that low scores on hips do not always improve when the puppies are examined; some of the matings of 0/0 hip score dogs in other breeds have produced litters of puppies with a hip score little better than the breed average. This policy of only using low hip score parents may be modified by breeding from higher scoring bitches that have other characteristics that could be of especial value to the breeder in a programme to seek a particular type of dog.

1. Guidelines for Hip Improvement
i) Score all stock. This necessitates having X-rays of all young breeding stock.
ii) As far as practicable, breed only from stock with a hip score better than the breed mean score average. Preferably breed from those well below the breed mean score.
iii) Follow recommendations about feeding and exercise to avoid undue injury and stress to the growing hip joint.

2. Regularly review all inherited diseases in the dog group, e.g. in a kennels, or enquire about the litter mates or parents. Hips should not be the only criterion for selecting, as elbows, eyes and temperament are all important. Expect to get evasive replies when asking others about their dogs' hip scores!

Some breeders resist reporting hip scores or may even refuse to have dogs examined. There are the fears of the general anaesthesia that will be necessary in order to position correctly a dog for the 'extended' hip view needed to make a hip score. In the UK the rules for protecting humans against radiation injury prevent the use of people to help hold down a dog so that an X-ray picture can be taken. Some persons consider that this extended position is an unnatural strain on the hip joint, as it attempts to force the head of the femur out of the cup of the pelvic bone, known as the acetabulum.

An alternative system is used in the USA to assess joint laxity as well as for measuring the shape of the hip joint bones. X-rays are taken in a 'distracted' view. To obtain this view, a mild compressive force is applied to both hips to show if the femoral heads are well-seated in the acetabulum. A second view of the hips is obtained by using a device to place between the hind legs so that the femoral heads are displaced laterally. The amount of femoral head displacement measured gives the distraction index (DI). A DI of 0 indicates a well-fitting hip, while a DI of 1 is the worst possible with complete luxation. Hip scores of below 0.3 in this measurement rarely develop osteoarthritis in old age.

ELBOW DYSPLASIA
A disease with a hereditary basis seen in many large and giant breeds of dogs; elbow dysplasia is also known as OD or OCD. Mastiffs may suffer from elbow osteochondrosis, as can many of the larger breeds. X-ray views of each elbow are taken to assess the joints. Three radiographs are taken of each elbow and a score awarded according to the presence of typical dysplasia or secondary osteoarthritis. Each elbow is scored 0 to 3, and the overall score is the highest of the two elbows (the scores are not summed as in the Hip Dysplasia Scheme). The threshold level not to breed is a score of 2.

The elbows may be held slightly outwards so the front toes seem to turn in; when the dog walks a slightly rotary or 'circumambulatory gait' may be noticed by the experienced eye. The condition of an ununited anconeal process, which may be detected in breeds such as the German Shepherd Dog on X-ray at or just after six months, is less common. Rapid bone growth is considered a factor in delaying the mineralisation of the cartilage at the growing joint ends of the long bones. Restricting exercise and not feeding a puppy to full appetite demand may help to reduce the incidence of osteochondrosis. Supplements should not be given as most dog foods are balanced and contain sufficient Vitamin D. Calcium supplements are now very much frowned upon as they upset the calcium/phosphorus ratio of the diet, so bone formation cannot proceed normally.

CRUCIATE LIGAMENT RUPTURE

The stifle or 'knee' joint is not robustly constructed, but as long as Mastiffs are kept reasonably lean and fit, there is not a great risk of this injury. Once a dog becomes overweight, the stifle which depends on a number of ligaments and cartilages to hold it together and give free movement, may become at risk. The stifle is used in jumping and for forward propulsion; overweight dogs that are asked to perform tasks, even as simple as jumping out of four-wheel drive vehicle or station wagon rear door, may land heavily and damage the ligaments. Bursts of activity such as free-range ball-chasing in an unfit dog may produce a similar result.

The cruciate ligaments are those crossing the centre of the stifle joint, and there are two other collateral ligaments that support the sides of the joint. The knee cap, or patella, also has ligaments that run at the front of the joint and these, too, can fail to support the stifle joint, throwing a greater strain on the two ligaments at the centre. It is usually the front ligament in the centre of the stifle joint – the anterior cruciate ligament – that takes the greatest strain when the dog jumps or turns awkwardly and this may tear or, at the worst, completely break in half.

The tearing of the ligament happens because a weakness has been developing in the fibres so, after partial tearing and stretching, the ligament ruptures. The result is a very lame dog; often the stifle joint is so unstable that the two bone ends that form the joint can be slid over each other; this instability is used in the 'draw forward' test. Cruciate rupture can be recognised as one that usually happens suddenly during extreme exercise. It does not improve with enforced rest, unlike many other injuries. Heavy dogs will usually require a surgical operation to repair the torn ligament. There are a number of techniques employed but most require a ligament implant inserted through or around the joint. Provided the operation is done before arthritis changes develop in the joint surface, the results are very good as the joint is stabilised again.

PANOSTEITIS

This may be found as one cause of sudden lameness in the younger dog or bitch, most often in a fore leg but, sometimes, the lameness will alternate from front to back legs. The lameness is quite severe and it might suggest that a bone has been broken but, if an X-ray is taken, it will show no damage to the bone structure at all. It is believed that this is an auto-immune condition, as it does not appear until six months of age and only infrequently does it cause lameness in the middle-aged or elderly dog.

Treatment involves resting the dog for a few days then giving controlled exercise until the dog eventually walks soundly again. Non-steroidal anti-inflammatory tablets can be given, and severely lame dogs may benefit from corticosteroid injections.

OSTEOARTHRITIS

Usually seen affecting the older dog, this condition limits joint movement which starts as an erosive joint disease due to a loss of the cartilage on the joint surface. As the disease progresses, additional bone may be laid down round the edge of the joint, possibly as a result of inflammation and an attempt to support the joint. The disease develops slowly, leading to lameness, pain, the grating feeling known as crepitus and then joint instability. The joint feels thickened from the outside and there is limited movement when the joint is bent to stretch it or flex it. If a joint is not moving, then the muscles around it weaken or atrophy so that the leg becomes wasted. X-rays should be taken to assess the degree of any new bone building up around the joint. A management plan for the dog can be drawn up. Pain control is the first priority in treatment. Osteoarthritis is thought to be aggravated by the dog being overweight, so dietary control is the second important way of helping a dog with joint pain or swelling. Although not considered a hereditary disease, osteoarthritis is often the result of hip dysplasia and osteochondrosis, both of which have a genetic basis.

CORKSCREW TAIL
The congenital condition of a small stumpy tail may appear in newborn puppies and is a recessive condition now rarely seen. As the puppy grows, the tail may press down on to the perineum and, in extreme cases, may be associated with difficulty in passing faeces. If corrective surgery of the young puppies to elevate or straighten the tail is attempted, the procedure must be reported to the national Kennel Club. Fortunately this defect is now very infrequent in the Mastiff breeds.

SKIN DISORDERS WITH A POSSIBLE INHERITED BASIS

The Mastiff breeds are fairly resistant to skin disease and most skin problems in the breed are probably the result of skin parasite infections; there is no known hereditary basis

for such infections. The nature of the short coat and loose skin may encourage the growth of Malasezzia, especially in the moister skin folds of the body. Parasitic diseases such as Demodectic mange may have some hereditary basis; these are described in the chapter on Health.

DIGESTIVE SYSTEM DISORDERS

BLOAT
The sudden accumulation of gas in the stomach will cause distress and, if left untreated, eventual death. (See also Chapter 14.) Gastric Dilation and torsion of the stomach (GDV) can be a problem in any of the larger breeds. It is especially associated with the giant breeds and Setters. The feeding routine should be such as to avoid hungry dogs swallowing food rapidly then being left un-exercised and unobserved. The Guide Dogs for the Blind Association kennels' routine was to feed in the morning, before the two work periods during the daytime, so that gas could not accumulate in the stomach when the dog was left unattended and unexercised. Any dog with a tendency to bloat will be seen in the daytime at the earliest stage of discomfort; often a special tablet can be given at this stage to stop bubbles of gas being held in the stomach. Dogs known to 'bloat' can be made to eat more slowly by supervising them, and feeding them on their own, when there is no competition from other dogs stealing their food. Canned dog food seems less likely to cause bloat than some of the complete or semi-moist diets containing small particles of food.

DIARRHOEA FROM BACTERIAL OVERGROWTH
The condition, now known as SIBO (small intestine bacterial overgrowth), is a disorder that may be the cause of persisting diarrhoea, increased appetite and weight loss. To explain

it simply, it is a disorder where too many bacteria are living in the small intestine for the dog's health; these bacteria take some of the best nutrients out of the eaten food that passes from the stomach to the small intestine. Diagnosis has to be confirmed by blood tests; then a month-long course of antibiotics together with a modified low fat diet is usually sufficient to clear the disorder entirely.

COPROPHAGIA

This is a habit acquired by dogs kept in kennels, since dogs which are adequately supervised at a time when defecation is about to occur will have little opportunity to explore the smells, or the taste, of recently voided faeces. The flavouring agents and palatable residues that are found in faeces after prepared foods have been digested, apparently to a dog's satisfaction, must be blamed for another dog's subsequent nose investigation, then taste exploration, before ingestion of the faeces. Treatment of such an eating disorder, which is associated with boredom, should be attempted; deterrents such as garlic, paprika and even fresh pineapple have been used to curb a dog's desire to eat faeces. Blood tests for SIBO (as above) should be taken. The habit may not be so revolting as at first thought, since rabbits use the method of eating faeces taken from their own rectums as a way of further digesting cellulose for food, and many free-range animals will eat faeces from herbivores left on the ground, as a way of obtaining extra Vitamin B.

EXOCRINE PANCREATIC INSUFFICIENCY (EPI)

This is uncommon in Mastiff breeds, and in all breeds there now seems to be less of the illness than was found 20 years ago. This may be due to more accurate diagnostic tests being used and the fact that, once identified, litters from the same blood lines have not been bred from again. The disease may not show up until middle age as a chronic diarrhoea with weight loss due to a failure in the digestive enzymes in the small intestine. The EPI blood test is used to confirm a diagnosis. The response to treatment using low-fat diets, supplements of digestive enzymes in dried pancreatic extract, combined with drugs to lower stomach acidity, is good. Unfortunately, long-term treatment adds to the expense of medication.

CIRCULATORY AND HEART DISEASE

HEART DISEASE

There are no proven hereditary heart diseases in the Mastiff breeds but all heavier breeds of dog may be subject to cardiac disorders that can lead to earlier than normal ages for deaths. The various congenital heart defects that occur in dogs can be managed medically or, in some cases, by advanced surgery. The most common congenital defects in all breeds of dogs today are aortic stenosis (AS), patent ductus arteriosus (PDA), pulmonic stenosis (PD), mitral dysplasia (MD), ventricular septal defect (VSD), tricuspid valve dysplasia (TD), and the rare Tetralogy of Fallot (ToF). Myocardial degeneration is the disease of the heart muscle that leads to congestive heart failure. Any severe heart condition such as heart valve disease can eventually produce heart muscle damage leading to heart failure. The driving force of the cardiac pump becomes weakened and failure of the right side of the heart leads to distended veins, swelling of the abdomen due to fluid (ascites) and muscle weakness of the hind legs due to poor blood circulation. If the left side of the heart fails first, then there is rapid breathing and breathlessness after moderate exercise, all due to oedema fluid in the lungs. Coughing is not so common a sign of lung congestion due to heart failure as in some other breeds

TUMOURS AND GROWTHS

All the larger breeds of dogs seem more subject to bone tumours, but Mastiffs are no more affected than others. In the giant breeds of dogs that weigh more than 35kg, individual animals are 60 times more likely to develop bone tumours than in breeds weighing less than 10kg. Rapid early growth and stress on weight-bearing legs may explain some of this tumour problem.

There was a specific problem of lymphoid tumours in some strains of Bullmastiffs. The most common first sign is an enlargement of a lymph gland somewhere on the body surface. One of the sites is a swelling under the throat where the lower jaw joins the upper neck and a lump may first be noticed when patting or grooming the dog. Involvement of other organs such as spleen, liver or bone marrow may be indications of advanced disease. Swelling of the lymph node in the chest – the one known as the mediastinal, may cause coughing or shortness of breath.

In one group of 59 dogs studied it was reported that nine developed lymphoma over a three-year period and there seemed to be a family susceptibility. It is also known that the dogs weighing less than 15 Kg are the ones more responsive to treatment and they will live longer than the larger dogs who may be given identical treatment. The earlier the condition is diagnosed, often with the help of blood tests and X-rays of internal organs, the better the chance of successful treatment.

The Mastiff breeds are probably no worse affected with tumours than many other larger breeds, so the situation should not put off the intending purchaser. As all dogs now live longer, tumours are more likely to develop, but in breeds such as the Mastiffs the effects of cancer may seem more devastating than, say, in smaller breeds or breeds with rough coats, where the changes are less obvious.

16 BREEDING A LITTER

By Douglas Oliff

In many countries indigenous dog types have been propagated for hundreds of years. By judicious outcrosses to the other breeds, the present-day so-called "pure" breeds have been evolved. A certain degree of canine snobbery exists towards some breeds of comparatively modern introduction when compared with those breeds which, in name at least, suggest great antiquity. The basic type of some breeds has not been drastically altered over the past hundred years, but in the majority of breeds there are now differences in size, type and temperament. Such changes were probably made to improve the working qualities of a breed, or in the hope of breeding out hereditary weaknesses.

Until the advent of the railway system, travelling between different areas was extremely limited, with the result that in many breeds there were strong regional differences.

In our present age of computerisation, rapid transport, easier dog feeding methods, and an increased knowledge of the science of heredity, it should be possible, in theory, to outpace the Victorian and Edwardian breeders to whom such aids were unavailable, but I query whether these aids to better breeding are seriously considered by the majority of breeders today. Fortunately, or unfortunately, animal breeding is not a

precise science. So much depends on knowing the background of the animals concerned, and on possessing the ability to look dispassionately, and critically, at your own stock. The other essential is the breeder's flexibility in order to alter course when the breeding plans go consistently wrong, or the attempts to eliminate a fault fail to stop it persisting for generation after generation.

Successful animal breeding calls for years of dedication, and deep knowledge of the strengths and weaknesses of the bloodlines within which you are operating. Today, we have "dog breeders", a band of enthusiasts who spend time, and often a considerable amount of money, in attempting to improve the overall quality of their chosen breed. Such breeders often have the courage and foresight to use an outcross for a specific purpose for improvement of their stock, even when such an outcross line is owned by their "dearest enemy".

Unfortunately, we also have so-called "breeders" for whom the term "puppy producers" would be the more correct appellation, as the production of a saleable commodity is their main aim. If the group were small, the chances of damage to the breeds would be negligible, but the danger lies in puppies registered by unknown "breeders" from unknown stock, and carrying no affix. There is always a possibility that a few quality puppies could result from these hit and miss alliances, but of what value will such animals be to the breed's future?

As a young man I was fortunate in having some good dyed-in-the-wool dog mentors who were steeped in animal breeding lore. One of them was the late Mrs Doris Mullin, who owned a famous pre-war Bullmastiff kennels with the prefix Mulorna. Her advice to me, over forty years ago, was " Breed in such a manner that, when you choose to leave the breed, you can truthfully say that you have left it in a better state than you found it." Wise words.

GENETIC IMPORTANCE
Gregor Mendel, an Austrian monk (1822-1884) was probably the earliest geneticist. His initial studies were carried out on pea plants. He began by crossing a tall pea plant with a short pea plant which, at that stage, he thought should produce all medium-sized pea plants. But this was not so. He then inbred and interbred the plants for some years and discovered that there was a ratio of plant heights occurring from this interbreeding. He postulated that there was a hereditary combination of genes from the parent cells. His conclusions where published in 1866 but his theories were ignored.

We have already defined the gene as being the unit of heredity, but where does it occur?

Body tissue consists of millions of cells which are in a perpetual state of being broken down, and of being replaced. Each cell has a nucleus, a complete spherical protoplasmic body containing thread-like structures called chromosomes. Arranged along the chromosomes are the genes which determine and transmit hereditary characteristics. The number of chromosomes per cell is constant for each species. Whilst the number of chromosomes per cell is constant, the hereditary effect of genes is not. Some genes

are dominant, some are recessive. We now know what the gene is, where in the cell it is located, and that the gene will dictate not only physical and mental characteristics, but also susceptibility to disease and, probably, longevity.

Let me give an example of the dominant and recessive effects by using the coat colour of Mastiffs, Bullmastiffs and, I believe, Great Danes. In these breeds the brindle colour is dominant; fawns and reds are recessive. When a brindle is mated to a red or fawn, several colour variations are possible within the litter which results. Theoretically, as brindle is dominant, all the progeny should be brindles, but this is not always the case. Very few brindles are completely dominant genetically, although appearing to be brindle physically. Many brindles, due to past ancestry of reds or fawns, carry the recessive plain colours. This can, and often does, result in the litter consisting of some brindles and some plain colours, or it can, occasionally, have no brindles, despite the parent colour.

It is emphasised that the brindle, though dominant, can carry the recessive plain colour, but the plain colour cannot carry brindle – in fact, it will breed as if no brindle was in the background. In the breeds under consideration it is genetically impossible to produce a brindle unless at least one of the parent stock is of that colour.

I know breeders – who should know better – who will quite categorically state that, as the plain coloured bitch has a lot of brindles in her background, she should produce a high proportion of that colour if mated to a brindle. As you can now see, such a statement is nonsense. But it is often repeated.

As proof that genetics work, a few years ago I had a dark brindle Mastiff stud dog who, even when mated to a fawn, never produced anything but brindles. He was obviously carrying no recessive colour genes.

If any breeder wishes to find out whether the brindle stud dog, or brindle brood bitch, is carrying the recessive plain colour, mate it to a plain colour. If all the puppies are brindle, then the animal is free from the recessive. If only one of the puppies is plain-coloured, then the animal is not free from the recessive.

Always remember that you cannot eliminate a recessive completely, but you can reduce its incidence by attempting always to breed to the proven dominant characteristic.

To breed from two animals, both of which are showing physical evidence of an undesirable recessive influence, will intensify its prevalence in a bloodline. If, in a previous litter, undesirable recessive characteristics occur, care should be taken to reduce its incidence by breeding into a bloodline in which the characteristic rarely, if ever, occurs. It is fortunate that in many breed standards the dominant is called for.

Having skimmed the surface of genetics, we will apply this knowledge to the other considerations of breeding a litter.

CRITICAL BREEDING

Do not believe that by producing a litter your bitch will be spared, in later life, some of the reproductive tract diseases, such as pyometra (pus in the uterus). Bitches which have been bred from are as prone to such conditions as maiden bitches.

Consider the accommodation and resources which will be needed for the bitch and her litter. Are you prepared to hand-rear the litter if the bitch fails to produce milk? This will be a twenty-four-hours-a-day job for at least three weeks. In most instances the bitch will not experience these difficulties, but have you the accommodation to house a big breed litter for at least eight weeks – and even longer if ready sales are not forthcoming? Again, it is a major consideration in time and costs. On the positive side, there is great satisfaction and a sense of achievement

should a litter be produced with every indication that it is of a quality considerably better than the parent stock.

BREEDING METHODS

There are three standard methods of livestock breeding – outcrossing, line-breeding and inbreeding. Unfortunately, the only guidance which is readily available to anyone comparatively new to any breed is the animal's pedigree. If the listed ancestors are known, even if only from photographs, such knowledge can be of help, but you must realise that some animals of great show quality, and frequent use at stud, could have been genetically incapable of passing on those very qualities which led to their own show triumphs. If the pedigree is carefully studied, and the animal bred by a person of experience, the pedigree should indicate a breeding pattern. So often, over the years, enthusiastic newcomers will delight in informing me that their dog's pedigree has "twenty or more Champions in it". From a serious breeding point of view, such a pedigree would reflect badly on the animal concerned, and suggest that, despite the multiplicity of Champion names, the animal has been so haphazardly bred that only a supreme optimist could expect much uniformity in the progeny which would be produced.

However, if told that the same Champion occurred twenty times, the pedigree would indicate some serious thought having gone into the breeding, and the chances of uniformity of progeny would be greatly enhanced.

LINE-BREEDING

This is a method used by many successful animal breeders, and not just dog breeders. It is the mating of two animals, both of which carry a mutual ancestor, or ancestors, plus some outcrosses. So often the dog-breeding fraternity pay a great deal of attention to the pedigree and qualities of the sire, but scant attention to the same qualities in the dam. In reading a pedigree, the bitch is of equal importance; in fact I sometimes feel that the bitch seems to be of greater dominance. Line breeding will help you with consistency where the ancestors are known; but, if they are unknown, there is always the possibility that you may be perpetuating a consistent fault.

INBREEDING

This is the ultimate breeding method, whereby animals of close relationships – father to daughter, brother to sister – are mated together. Some breeders find the method distasteful. Others consider it unnatural. Others claim that it will produce deformities and mental instability. But is the method really "unnatural"?

Inbreeding cannot produce any new fault or characteristic. What it can, and certainly will do, is to expose any faults or characteristics which are carried in the parent stock but disguised by outcrossing. Where inbreeding scores, if applied to animals which are typical and sound, and where the breeder is prepared to cull, is the stability of the resultant stock and their ability to reproduce themselves with greater consistency due, of course, to the greater genetic similarity of the parents. Never discount the value of the method, nor dismiss it as a method which will produce abnormalities as well as a lack of vitality.

Inbreeding cannot weaken stock unless that stock is carrying a genetically transmitted weakness. The only phenomenon which I have found from inbreeding is the tendency, after a few generations, to lose size. This has not occurred in every case, nor with every form of livestock, but I feel that it should be mentioned as a possible disadvantage.

The proof that inbreeding will stabilise type can be illustrated by the inbreeding methods used by the owners of the famous USA Tailwynde kennels of Bullmastiffs, owned by Mr and Mrs Pfenninger. The kennels are now disbanded but the type produced in the kennels is still seen, and is easily recognisable in many parts of the world.

SELECTION OF BREEDING STOCK

Most prospective breeders will own a bitch, or bitches, and will carefully select the stud dog which they feel will suit the bitch and bring about the strengthening of the points in which she fails.

No bitch of any of the breeds featured in this book should be bred from under the age of two years. The skeletal frame of these large dogs is slow to consolidate and calcify. The physical strain of puppy production and subsequent feeding can, for an immature bitch, be detrimental to her future health and well-being.

The bitch normally comes 'in season' or 'on heat' at six-monthly intervals after the age of approximately a year or eighteen months.

Before the present-day blood tests were perfected, breeders used to consider that the bitch had ovulated and was therefore ready for mating about the twelfth day after bleeding from the vulva was first noticed. Nowadays, a blood test to measure the progesterone level of the blood of the bitch will pin-point ovulation very precisely. If an outside stud dog is to be used, the owner should be advised of the result of the progesterone test.

STUD TERMS

This may be an opportune time to point out that the stud fee is payable for the act of mating. Most owners have an agreement that, should the bitch miss conception, a free service will be given next time. Provided that the stud dog is proven to be capable of siring puppies, the bitch owner has no grounds for claiming a refund of the fee, or part of the fee, should the bitch not conceive.

THE MATING

I am presuming that most readers will be conversant with the mechanics of dog mating, but a few helpful observations may not come amiss.

All too often the bitch owner travels to the stud dog owner without allowing sufficient time to keep the appointment and so both owner and bitch arrive late, and in a state of agitation. The bitch is taken out of the car and, within minutes, is expected to stand for a mating by a dog which has never been previously seen, and in an environment with which the bitch is completely unacquainted. When she then violently rejects the stud dog's advances, patience on the part of the owners tends to flag. This is sensed by the animals, and what should be a straightforward natural act becomes fraught with difficulty.

On arrival at the premises the bitch should be put on her lead, and allowed to empty her bladder, or bowel if she thinks it necessary. She should then be introduced outside the stud dog's pen, and their reactions noted. If neither shows aggression, both animals on their leads should be allowed to get acquainted with one another. Sexual foreplay is important as a stimulant. When it is apparent that both are ready, the bitch owner should hold his animal securely by the collar as the dog mounts. The handling of the stud dog should be left entirely to the owner. A few stud dogs get aggressive if they feel that a stranger is going to handle them, and a young stud, who may not be overconfident, can be put off from his intended job if handled.

One point about the stud dog. Nature seems to have decreed that, once the male in the mating is securely tied to the bitch, he should dismount and turn so that the heads are facing in opposite directions. It was probably a natural instinct for the male to be able to defend himself from the attack of rival males at a time when he is most vulnerable. While completely against forced matings, I do think that every mating, especially in these breeds, should be controlled. I do not allow a stud dog to dismount and turn when tied. They are trained to stand alongside the bitch, facing in the same direction, enabling both stud dog owner, and the owner of the bitch to have efficient control over the procedure. There are instances where a stud dog has been permanently damaged in an uncontrolled mating. Nature may give good instincts, but nature is also extremely wasteful.

CARE OF THE PREGNANT BITCH

As soon as her season is due, it is a wise precaution to worm the bitch. Provided that she is in good condition, and well nourished, there is no need to alter her diet or exercise for the first five weeks of pregnancy. In these days of ultrasound scans, pregnancy can be determined at about four-and-a-half weeks. At five weeks after mating you can usually notice body changes suggesting that a litter is in the offing, but I have had experience of bitches not looking pregnant even at seven weeks, yet whelping four or so puppies of good size.

If her diet is balanced, and contains the necessary vitamins and minerals within that balance, there is no need to add supplements to the diet for the first five weeks. It may be necessary slightly to increase her food intake but it would be detrimental to allow her to put on an excessive amount of body fat. As her pregnancy progresses, it may be beneficial for the breeder to spread the food intake so that, although the amount of food may be the same, it is spread over a greater number of meals. If you are a regular client of a local veterinary surgeon, it is a wise policy to inform him of the bitch's pregnancy and the estimated date of whelping, as his professional services may be required.

The pregnant bitch should be acquainted with her whelping box well in advance, especially if she is to whelp in a room to which she is not accustomed. For several days before whelping, the expectant bitch will spend time scratching and preparing her whelping box, and is often in a mild state of agitation, especially if it is her first litter.

WHELPING

Once labour is imminent, the bitch shows an increased state of discomfort, with much panting, and an inability to settle. When labour commences and the bitch starts to strain, the first puppy should be born within half-an-hour of the commencement of straining. If no puppy is produced within one hour, professional advice should be sought from your vet. Whelpings are usually straightforward but it is essential that the owner remains with the bitch to supervise proceedings and obtain help if required.

A prolonged whelping, especially if the litter is a large one, can be a very debilitating experience for the bitch both mentally and physically. Some bitches commence whelping, strain for a short while, then develop uterine inertia and just give up. This can happen at any stage of the whelping process, and in such cases there is often a need for a veterinary surgeon to remove the puppies by Caesarean section, or to inject the bitch to induce uterine contractions. All too often, the owners develop a state of panic at whelpings and become over-anxious, but it is far better to request a professional opinion earlier rather than later.

In these early stages it is essential that the puppies are kept clean, warm and dry and that the bitch is allowed to rest and mother her litter, but a very careful check should be made to ensure that she has sufficient milk. The 'first milk' or colostrum contains the antibodies from the bitch, and it is important that the newly-born pups take this for the sake of their own immunity.

Provided that the bitch and pups are well, that the bitch is eating and drinking normally and leaving her whelping box for the necessary gentle exercise, both bitch and litter benefit from not being interfered with unnecessarily. Occasionally you have to deal with awkward bitches who will unwittingly lie on or step on a puppy, but such misfits of Nature are comparatively rare.

CAESAREAN AFTERCARE

Mention should be made about puppies born by Caesarean section. Because of the anaesthetic it is not uncommon for the bitch to be slow in producing milk, and not infrequently to seem half-afraid of the puppies, even, on occasion, to the extent of being aggressive towards them.

The act of sucking stimulates milk production, so it is essential that the bitch is restrained to enable the puppies to suck, but great care needs to be shown to ensure that at this very vulnerable age, each puppy receives nutrition, if not from the bitch then by artificial feeding. Cows' milk is not an ideal food for young puppies, but goats' milk is nearly ideal, due to the smaller fat globules which are homogenised – naturally dispersed throughout the milk. As an enthusiastic beekeeper for a major part of my life, I am an advocate of the use of honey both medicinally and in nutrition and, in fact, will go so far as to say that I could not contemplate rearing any puppy without the use of honey.

A LIFE-SAVING MILK FORMULA

The rearing/weaning/invalid mixture is as follows:
To one pint milk, preferably goats' milk which is available in many supermarkets now, add one dessertspoonful of honey and the yolk of one egg. Beat together and warm to blood heat. If you use a 'set' honey rather

than a liquid one, care must be taken to ensure that it is dissolved. Prepare freshly for each meal and keep warm in a thermos flask as the puppies are being fed.

Unless the litter is extremely large, supplementary feeding during the early stages should not be necessary unless the bitch obviously has a failing milk supply. Hungry puppies usually cry a great deal and look dry and dehydrated. When this happens, a prompt feeding regime must be immediately instituted, as they soon become weak and then die.

HAND-REARING AND WEANING
There will come an occasion when the litter may have to be hand-reared from birth, a process which calls for endless patience and dedication. The mixture outlined above can be used and feeding will have to be every two hours through the day, and through the night, until the litter is old enough to start lapping food.

As the newly-born puppies need the stimulus of the mother's licking of the anus and genitals to produce evacuation of the bowel and bladder, the owner will have to pay attention to this necessity by gently wiping those parts with a piece of cotton wool on which a little olive oil has been spread. This should be performed after the feeds. Obviously the orphan litter must be kept warm. An infra-red bulb over their nest is probably the most reliable form of supplying such heat. Care must be taken to ensure that the puppies can move away from the centre point of the heat should they so wish.

If the litter has to be hand-reared due to the dam being either unwell with post-whelping complications, or because she has failed to produce milk, a great deal of care and dedication is needed if the litter is to live.

For the first week each puppy should take approximately a tablespoonful of the

milk/egg yolk/honey mixture per feed. This must be fed every two hours round the clock, and the quantity gradually increased to two tablespoonfuls at the end of the first week. Puppies which are cold, or hungry, are often noisy and have a narrow and dehydrated look. In these early days they have little resistance and, unless carefully nurtured, they will die.

Having got them through their first week, and if they appear to be taking their food easily, cut back on the number of feeds to once every three hours, but increase the amount of intake to three tablespoonfuls per meal.

At about three weeks of age, introduce a little pulped, finely chopped raw beef, and attempt to get the litter lapping the milk mix. At four weeks they should be lapping well, so introduce some proprietary puppy meal well soaked in the milk mixture. Two meat meals and two milk/cereal meals should be fed daily.

At six weeks it is not too much to feed five small meals spread over the day. Puppies at this age would need half-a-pound of meat and three milk/soaked puppy food meals. All puppies should be wormed at five weeks and should be ready for their new homes at eight weeks.

The basic routine of puppy feeding and rearing given above is based on the requirements of a litter of Bullmastiffs; obviously some of the larger or heavier breeds will need proportionately more.

The most successful puppy rearers are those who stick rigidly to the feeding regime, and introduce any changes of diet very gradually. When quite young and being fed by their dam, care should be taken to ensure that the pups' nails are lightly clipped. The nails tend to grow fairly rapidly and they develop into sharp little hooks which can lacerate the bitch when she is feeding her litter and cause soreness of the teats.

THE NURSING BITCH

While you are devoting much time to the litter, do not forget that the nursing bitch needs extra attention. Her fluid intake increases because of her milk production, and she too needs a nutritious diet to maintain healthy vigour. After about three-and-a-half weeks even the most devoted of mothers should be allowed some freedom from her ever-demanding family and she will appreciate some light exercise.

As the bitch begins to relinquish her maternal duties, she will probably need to be built up for a few weeks, then gradually returned to her pre-whelping diet.

Old-time breeders when assessing and advising on rearing puppies used to say that "half the pedigree goes in at the mouth". As a breeder you aim at quality, but an equal level of responsibility rests with the puppy owner's observation and ability to cut back slightly if the puppy is too heavy, or increase the food if it is becoming too thin. I am firmly of the opinion that the true rearing foods are meat, milk, egg yolk, honey and a good-quality mixed micronised grain feed. To overdose with various additives and supplements is, in my opinion, a mistake and can often prove to be a costly one.

WEIGHT INCREASES

Very few breeders maintain accurate records of the weight increase in puppies from the time of birth to the age of one year. Mrs D. Williamson, who has kept accurate records, has kindly supplied the following table which may be of help to less experienced Bullmastiff breeders.

These weights can be compared with those of a Mastiff. Ch. Beaufort was considered to be the ideal weight and type for the breed in 1910. His weight when fully grown was recorded as 165 lbs, and height at shoulder was twenty-nine-and-a-half inches. Orlando, when mature, was 29 inches at the shoulder

and weighed 172 lbs. The bitches, The Lady Gladys and The Lady Isabel, who were both highly thought of at the time, were 26 inches at the shoulder and 27 inches respectively.

ORLANDO		THE LADY ISABEL	
Months	Weight in lbs	Months	Weight in lbs
1	10-13	1	9 1/4
2	23 1/2	2	7 1/2
3	43	3	40
4	69	4	58
5	88	5	70
6	110	6	92
7	124	7	97 1/2
8	140	8	110
9	148	9	114
10	154	10	120
11	160	11	118 1/2
12	170	12	120

When adult The Lady Isabel weighed in at 135 lbs.

REST AND EXERCISE

Breeders should impress upon their clients when selling any puppy of this group that a very high level of nourishment is required because of the rapid growth rate, but excessive weight at an early age can, and does, produce ligament and joint problems in later life. The client should also be advised not to allow strenuous exercise in the young puppy. There should be exercising times and enforced resting times if the animal is to grow up soundly. This should not be misconstrued as a suggestion that the puppy should be treated as an invalid, but over-exercise should be avoided.